Praise for *Naked Conversations*

"*Naked Conversations* is like the unofficial sequel to *The Cluetrain Manifesto*. Whereas *Cluetrain* predicted the power of blogging, *Conversations* illustrates how powerful blogging can be. Scoble and Israel have created the ultimate guide to business blogging because they, themselves, are the ultimate business bloggers."
Chris Pirillo
Chris Pirillo Show, Lockergnome.com
http://chris.pirillo.com

"Robert Scoble and Shel Israel have pieced together the best collection of anecdotes that capture the essence of the blogosphere—its culture. That's why *Naked Conversations* will outlast others. It's written by two experts who, through blogging, live inside the zoo, not just visiting it."
Steve Rubel
Vice President, CooperKatz
http://www.micropersuasion.com

"*Naked Conversations* isn't just another book about the theoretical possibilities of blogging and social media. It's a remarkably well-researched and well-written book about the people who are out there setting the precedents for social media. And it's an explanation of the basics and the resources that'll let businesses join the blogosphere."
B. L. Ochman
What's Next Blog
http://www.whatsnextblog.com

"A brilliant and lucid meditation on exactly why and how the world of business is changing, and what we mere mortals can actually do about it."
Hugh MacLeod
http://www.gapingvoid.com

"Not sure how to grok business blogging? *Naked Conversations* will definitely give a feel for why, how, and where blogging will benefit your company. If it can change the external perception of Microsoft, just think about what this can do for you."
Jeff Clavier
Software Only
http://blog.softtechvc.com/

Naked
Conversations

Naked Conversations

How Blogs Are Changing the Way Businesses Talk with Customers

Robert Scoble and Shel Israel

John Wiley & Sons, Inc.

Published by John Wiley & Sons, Inc., Hoboken, New Jersey

Published simultaneously in Canada

For general information on our other products and services or for technical support, please contact our Customer Care Department within the United States at (800) 762-2974, outside the United States at (317) 572-3993 or fax (317) 572-4002.

Wiley also publishes its books in a variety of electronic formats. Some content that appears in print may not be available in electronic books. For more information about Wiley products, visit our web site at www.wiley.com.

Library of Congress Cataloging-in-Publication Data:

Scoble, Robert, 1965–
    Naked conversations : how blogs are changing the way businesses talk with customers / Robert Scoble and Shel Israel.
        p. cm.
    Includes index.
    ISBN-13: 978-0-471-74719-2 (cloth)
    ISBN-10: 0-471-74719-X (cloth)
    1. Weblogs. 2. Business communication. 3. Internet—Social aspects. I. Israel, Shel, 1944– II. Title.
    TK5105.8884.S3 2006
    659.2—dc22
                                            2005027678

Printed in the United States of America

10 9 8 7 6 5 4 3 2 1

To our wives, Paula Israel and Maryam Scoble. We could not have done it without you and we wouldn't have wanted to.

Contents

Scoble and Israel

I've had my Best Year in 20 Years!

Why? On July 27, 2004, I began to Blog. I've had a ball.
My "constituency" has had a ball.

MY LIFE HAS CHANGED . . . THANKS TO . . . BLOGGING.

I'M HAVING THE **"CONVERSATION"**-OF-MY-LIFE . . .
WITH MY . . . "COMMUNITY" . . . WORLDWIDE.

Robert Scoble, single-handedly at first, has given the EVIL EMPIRE
(Microsoft, who else?) a "Human Face" . . . thanks to his Blog.

"Business Blogging" is incredibly important . . . or at least it can be
if you follow some **"simple rules"** . . . Openness & Honesty & Cool
(not exactly business's Big Three).

*This Foreword (I've written over 50 "Forewords"!) is . . .
PERSONAL.*

Biz Blogging . . . **WORKS.** It is of . . . **MONUMENTAL
IMPORTANCE.**

(Or can be.)

These guys know.

Listen.
Please.

(If you don't you're a Damn Fool.)

tom peters ("The Blogging Guru")

Naked
Conversations

Introduction: Of Bloggers and Blacksmiths

"It began with conversations. Then we got into broadcast media. Now we are going back to conversations. It's a full circle."

—*Terry Catchpole,* The Catchpole Corporation

If you came here expecting to see a couple of middle-aged white guys talking in the nude, you've come to the wrong book. This one's about a revolution that is transforming the way businesses and customers communicate with each other. It's about stripping out all the crap that gets in the way of understanding and trust between them. Mostly, it's about blogging, the most powerful tool so far in this revolution.

Naked Conversations is no objective examination, although we have worked hard to make it fair and accurate. We are blogging champions. We believe that blogging is not just wise for businesses wishing to be closer with their customers, but essential. We envision a day in the near future when companies that *don't* blog will be held suspect to some degree, with people wondering whether those companies have something to hide or whether the owners are worried about what the people who work for them have to say.

We're not kidding when we say there's a revolution going on. From where you sit, your business might seem the same today as it was yesterday. Your PR folk may be shoveling out words, your direct marketing campaigns may be garnering responses exceeding 2 percent from people who never asked to be reached—but the stuff, as you probably already know, is getting more expensive and less effective all the time. And between yesterday and today, another blog will start at a rate of nearly one per second, according to the *New York Times,* Pew Research, and other sources. Some are indeed the work of teenage diarists and the politically obsessed, but to an increasing degree, new bloggers are talking business.

Perhaps these business conversations are about your market, customers, or products. Chances are highly likely that if people aren't talking about your company in blogs today, they will be soon. You would be wise to join these conversations, if only to thank those who sing your praises or to correct possible factual errors. If you ignore the *blogosphere*—the term used to describe the global network of blog postings—you won't know what people are saying about you. You can't learn from them, and they won't come to see you as a sincere human who cares about your business and its reputation.

Naked Conversations is about how and why you should join the conversation. It also tells you how to "blog smart" to succeed—not from the perspective of what tools to use, but from the sense of what strategies to put in place and why. *Naked Conversations* tells you why employers should encourage middle and upper management team members to blog from their hearts, talking about the parts of the business they know best. We explain why it's good business to protect these employees from status quo guardians who would prefer to control and centralize messages.

If you choose to join the conversation, your company will be the better for it, and your customers will be happier. You will develop better products and services by enjoying their collective wisdom, and you will save a ton of money by dumping expensive marketing tactics that not only don't work, but annoy the people they target.

We cannot promise that blogging will make you taller, thinner, or more sexually robust. Like you, we've grown jaded by too many such claims already. What we *can* do is introduce you to a great many business people who blog—and blog successfully. Much of this book simply lets successful bloggers tell you their stories. We use their words as often as we can so you can hear their testimonies and judge for yourself. Occasionally, we disagree with what they have to tell you, and we respectfully tell you our own views. We published early drafts of *Naked Conversations* on our own blog, and we've included a few comments from people who visited and disagreed with us. We owe these blog visitors a good deal. They were the source of many of the stories we tell here. They were our fact-checkers and sounding boards. In short, they helped us make this a better book.

We hope that some of these stories will apply to you and your business, wherever and whatever that may be. We spoke with bloggers who operate in Fortune 10 boardrooms as well as alone in home offices. We report on Japanese dentists and sports team owners, t-shirt makers, and a tailor who makes some of the world's most expensive suits. Feel free, if you are reading this in a bookstore, to thumb through these chapters to see whether any of these consultants, technologists, entrepreneurs, artisans, restaurateurs, lawyers, developers, startup jockeys, and public company executives have something to say about blogging that you might find useful. If you are online, you might want to read the complete interviews at http://nakedconversations .com; we provide longer versions of most interviews, and you can see exactly what these people had to say.

Make no mistake: *Naked Conversations* champions blogging, but this book looks at its dark side as well. We examine the risks and restraints such as time consumption, legal concerns, negative comments, conflicts with PR, getting fired, giving away competitive information, and so on. We also tell why every one of these bloggers—more than 100 of them—has found blogging worth-while despite their business diversities.

Naked Conversations also puts blogging into "Big Picture" perspective. On one hand, a blog may simply be a tool, but on the other that tool is one of the most powerful components to emerge so far in a communications revolution that has been going on for quite some time and is now reaching its tipping point. The revolution is about the way businesses communicate, not just with customers but with their entire constituencies—partners, vendors, employ-ees, prospects, investors, and the media.

There have been many conversational technologies to emerge before, such as e-mail, SMS, instant messaging, chatrooms, even the telephone. All these tools use technology to enable people to talk to each other in a direct, informal fash-ion. Bloggers don't caution each other about forward-looking statements and re-use of intellectual property or that their eyes may bleed if they take a headache remedy. They don't promise each other that whiter shirts make better marriages or killing weeds connotes superior testosterone among suburban males.

Bloggers just talk to each other. They make grammatical errors. They bop from one topic to another and back again. They interrupt each other to ask questions, make suggestions, challenge arguments. These conversations build trust. One blog pioneer, Dave Winer, calls it "come-as-you-are conversations" and says he enjoys seeing an occasional typo because it reveals authenticity, showing you are reading the unfiltered work of a real person.

Conversely, bloggers, like a great many other people, are generally suspicious of the smooth-and-refined language of official spokespeople. They use terms like "suits" to imply a suspicion that there is no human inside. Spokespeople use a strange language that we call "corpspeak," an oxymoronic hybrid of cautious legalese seasoned with marketing hyperbole. Corpspeakers talk to people when they want to speak, not when people want to listen. They use ads, press releases, direct marketing, and web sites to reach their targets. It's like the Cold War. People buy or develop mental filters and technology such as TiVo and spam filters to avoid these marketing messages. Then the marketers develop technology to bypass the filters. But when customers want to speak to *them*, those same marketers install technology and bureaucracy such as voice processing, web site FAQs, or uninformed and under-populated remote customer support teams to dim customers' voices and avoid human contact.

Most people take a negative view of marketing. One communications executive at a large corporation admitted to us that he no longer reads the press releases from his own communications department. "They're just a bunch of crap," he told us and then added, "But we have some really cool bloggers." We found this anticorporate sentiment pervasive in large companies, small businesses, and home offices. This sentiment is key to why blogging happened and why it matters.

Naked Conversations is about businesses and their constituencies just talking with each other on an equal plane. This is not really new. It's what the butcher, baker, and candlestick maker practiced before their businesses either became chains, franchises, and superstores or were exterminated by them. But the philosophy ignited in 2000, when a book called *The Cluetrain Manifesto* touched a nerve in its argument that markets are conversations—particularly among unemployed developers who were about to build blogging's essential tools and among marketing people who were wondering why so much had soured.

Philosophically, *Naked Conversations* can't add much to what was presented in *Cluetrain*. Nor do we see a need. We think universal truths, as one of *Cluetrain's* authors says, are pretty much self-evident. David Weinberger, one of *Cluetrain*'s authors, uses the e-mail address self@evident.com. We find this particularly apt.

But in the six years since that book was published, a great deal has happened. Blogging has begun to saturate businesses on three continents. When we began this project less than a year ago, much of the business community dismissed blogging as a passing fad. Now many managers and executives are acknowledging it with trepidation. This is progress, or so it seems to us. Author-philosopher Arthur Schopenhauer once observed, "All truth passes through three stages: First, it is ridiculed; second, it is violently opposed; third, it is accepted as being self-evident." Blogging has passed the denial and most of the anger phase. Now, businesses see blogging's huge potential and have begun to adapt it to business needs.

Owners and executives we talked with told us they felt the stress that comes from realizing that change is necessary and the systems in place are not performing to expectation. A decade ago, some felt the same kind of stress as the Web exploded around them. Ten years from today, something new will probably come along. By then, blogging will be as old-hat as the web site has become today. We may even look back to marvel at how quaint it was back in 2006.

But we doubt that blogging's conversational capabilities will ever be seen as antiquated. It's the first technology to enable a simple conversation to go instantly global. It's the first to decentralize corporate communications, wresting it from those who historically controlled it, and it eliminates many of the geographic barriers that have restricted relationships between people sharing similar interests.

We're not quite certain what to name this revolution. In writing *Naked Conversations*, we heard this phenomenon referred to as conversational marketing, open-source marketing, two-way marketing, even corner grocery marketing. We think they all fit, and maybe it's indicative of this new marketing that a single name has not emerged. No one has seen fit to brand it, yet so many people understand and care about what it is about.

As in every revolution, there will be casualties. In this case, we think many will be the incumbent proponents of one-way, command-and-control broadcast marketing who argue that things are just fine the way they are. Perhaps they should each go home and ask their family members how they feel about TV ads, junk mail, and banners. We predict their demise without glee. We do not argue that marketing in itself will or should perish—only the broadcast aspect of it, the part of it that says "We talk. You listen."

We think those who do not adapt may soon face the same fate as the black-smith of the last century. When he first laid eyes on the automobile, he must have chuckled at the pathetic mechanical oddity. Perhaps he raised a mighty arm and banged his hammer against his anvil with a bemused expression on his face, oblivious to the fact that most of those in his profession would soon be unemployed.

Our passionate advice is that the time to join the conversation is *now*. The barriers to entry are minuscule, the benefits great, and *blogging just happens to be fun*.

Enjoy *Naked Conversations*. Come to our blogsite[1] and tell us what you think. We're always up for a good conversation.

---

[1] http://nakedconversations.com

What's Happening

"*Nothing great has been and nothing great can be accomplished without passion.*"

—G. W. F. Hegel

1 Souls of the Borg

"[Corporations] cannot commit treason, nor be outlawed, nor excommunicate[d], for they have no souls."

—*Sir Edward Coke (1552–1634)*

We live in a time when most people don't trust big companies. Headlines gush with tales of malfeasance, abuse, and old-fashioned plunder, but that's just part of the problem. There's a general perception that large companies are run by slick lawyers and book-fixing accountants who oversee armies of obedient, drone-like employees. Companies are perceived as monoliths without souls. In short, we see no humanity.

For a very long time, Microsoft has been among the first companies you think of when this picture is drawn. Often perceived as predatory and heartless, Microsoft has a reputation for ruthlessly rolling over competitors, wrestling in courtrooms against government prosecutors, and exposing its customers to security flaws and frustrating glitches. To see how people express their views on Microsoft, check it out with any search engine. When we conducted a Google search, "Evil Empire + Microsoft" brought up 471,000 responses. The words "Microsoft sucks" delivered a whopping 669,000 responses, and "Microsoft + Borg" generated more than a quarter-million returns.

In reality, Microsoft is not a monolith, but rather an organization composed of more than 56,000 individuals, most having little or no idea what sins were committed in the past, or by whom. A great many of these employees weren't there at the time the controversies occurred, and if they were, they served too far down the ladder to be in on the secrets. And well-documented Microsoft product flaws may be amplified by the fact that just about everyone uses some Microsoft products. Still, the company unquestionably has been hurt by these dents in its reputation. Some talented people simply refuse to work there, and many of those who do work there admit that they have sometimes been demoralized by all the negativity.

In recent years, Microsoft has made serious efforts to improve its public image. Walter Mossberg, author of the influential *Wall Street Journal* Personal Technology column, observes:

> *Since the end of the anti-trust trial, Microsoft has been on a massive charm offensive. It has methodically settled lawsuit after lawsuit with rivals and governments. It has reached out to all sorts of constituencies. [Chairman] Bill Gates himself has become calmer, less publicly combative, since leaving the CEO post. His charitable foundation has taken off in a very public way. And the company has allowed numerous employees to show a human face by blogging. All of this has improved their image.*

Our informal research bears this out as well. Wherever we've looked, we've found a recent diminution of animosity toward the company. Examining those Google results closely shows that recent negative articles and postings are on a downcurve. Publications are covering Microsoft from a more neutral standpoint, and respected magazines such as *Fortune* and *The Economist* have recently sung tunes of at least faint praise. In addition, product launches such as MSN Spaces (Microsoft's free blogging service) have been received with less general skepticism in the technical community.

Even the oft-demonized Gates seems to be enjoying slightly friendlier receptions. In late September 2004, the chairman addressed a half-dozen Silicon Valley venues and seemed more comfortable than during past visits. Media observers expressed surprise and even disappointment that most audience questions were polite. The few audience challenges addressed security flaws and Linux server issues rather than the usual ethical diatribes. Another anecdotal piece is that the five-year-old "Evil Empire Blog" shut down in January 2005. Its author maintained it was because mainstream media were covering the issue so well. Others noted the blog's readership was in decline.

Even Mitch Kapor, chairman of the Open Source Application Foundation (OSAF) and long outspoken in his distaste for Microsoft, seems to have mellowed. Speaking at a May 2004 conference, he told an interviewer, "Singing songs about the Evil Empire may still be fun, but they're merely tunes for aging hippies." Other long-time nemeses, such as Apple CEO Steve Jobs, Sun Microsystems co-founder Scott McNealy, and Oracle CEO Larry Ellison, for varying business and legal reasons, have collectively sat down and shut up.

In addition to such anecdotal evidence, Microsoft has hard evidence: surveys showing that customers are viewing the company in more trusting terms, according to a survey Microsoft conducted of visitors to its Channel 9 blog.

Press observers see a change in what they hear from readers as well. *PC Magazine* editor-in-chief Michael J. Miller told us, "I think many people, particularly in Silicon Valley, have softened their views towards Microsoft. There are probably a lot of reasons for this, including Microsoft's larger presence in the Valley, more outreach to the industry, and the post-Internet bust economy."

But a growing number of Microsoft-watchers and people at mid-level desks inside Microsoft think there's another factor—blogging. And the people actually doing it are downright certain that they are making a difference.

People, Not Borg

XML team program manager Joshua Allen acknowledged there were many factors involved in the apparent shift in perception, but he felt that "Blogging unquestionably has had the most impact." Allen was Microsoft's first blogger. His current blog, Better Living Through Software,[1] began in 2000, at about the time the accusations and assaults against Microsoft were at an apex. Governments wanted to dismember the company, and an "Anything But Microsoft" movement was gaining momentum. He recalled a lot of internal angst at the time: "We were afraid to get out there and just talk with people. We were worried about getting the company in trouble with bad publicity." Allen didn't ask for permission from his superiors or Legal or PR. He just started posting to his blog because "I wanted to say that I am a Microsoft person and you can talk with me."

---

[1] http://www.netcrucible.com/blog/default.aspx

"I knew better than to do something stupid in public and I thought I would make a good test case," he recalled. Allen thought that if he started blogging, fellow employees might follow and "we'd show that we were real people, not the Borg." He thought the company's culture would be conducive to blogging. Like other Microsoft bloggers we interviewed, he cited CEO Steve Ballmer as consistently encouraging Microsoft employees to talk with customers whenever and wherever possible.

In less than a month, his boss received the first internal e-mail demanding Allen be fired. Such e-mails would continue regularly.

In time, a few associates close to Allen started blogging as well, then a few more. When the number reached about 15, Legal started worrying and muttering about risk. The bloggers, according to Allen, began walking on eggshells. "Everyone was worried someone would do something stupid and the whole thing would fall down. The legal people kept worrying and contemplating guidelines."

As of March 2005, there were more than 1,500 active bloggers at Microsoft. "Legal is still worrying," shrugged Allen, but "we haven't had anyone do something so incredibly stupid that it required a blogging policy and none has ever been issued."

While the legal folk fretted about risk, some customers waxed enthusiastic, many not even realizing they were visiting something called a blog. The customers were more interested in the two-way conversation that was taking place than in how it was happening. They were happy that a real person inside Microsoft was talking with them and was listening and responding.

The conversations begat more conversations. People like Dave Winer, father of blogging technology; Doc Searls, co-author of blogging's bible *The Cluetrain Manifesto*; and Tim O'Reilly, founder and CEO of O'Reilly Media, all started pointing to Allen's blog. The fact that a Microsoft guy was blogging was sufficiently newsworthy for Winer to point his readers to Allen five times in 2000. Allen recalled he got traffic just from people curious to see what the Evil Empire was up to. "Other bloggers would link, saying, 'This is what the Borg is thinking,'" Allen said.

But Winer, long-considered one of Microsoft's harshest critics, repeatedly asked why *more* people at Microsoft didn't blog. Each time he asked, a few more people would start blogging. Allen felt that as numbers rose, it revealed a company of diverse individuals that was "more like herding cats than the

Borg. People could see for themselves that there were camps and trends within the company."

Looking back, Allen said, "I think Microsoft has experienced a vast softening of its image. People, including journalists, have a lot more information about Microsoft now." Perhaps more significant, he thinks, has been the impact on employee morale and the company's ability to attract new talent.

But management remains far from unanimous on the benefits and liabilities of employee blogging, and it may turn out that the lack of a blogging policy may prolong ambivalence. While some senior executives advocate actions that would get bloggers to sit down and shut up, other executives protect the backs of the bloggers and encourage them. Although Chairman Bill Gates may have issued no internal dictums, he is on the record as seeing the value and inevitability of business blogging. In September 2005 he thanked co-author Scoble for blogging and his work on Channel 9. "You are letting people have a sense of the people here. You're building a connection. People feel more a part of this. Maybe they'll tell us how we can better improve our products," Gates said during an exclusive interview.

Tony Perkins, CEO and publisher of *AlwaysOn, the blogazine of innovation*, reported in the hard copy version of *AlwaysOn* on comments Gates made at dinner in the chairman's Lake Washington home in Seattle. According to Perkins, Gates commented that "Blogging makes it very easy to communicate. It gets away from drawbacks of e-mail and the drawbacks of a web site. Eventually, most businesses will use blogs to communicate with customers, suppliers, and employees, because it's two-way and more satisfying."

Perkins added, "Gates knows that the referral power of the blogosphere is also exploding, and marketing and PR executives must embrace this reality or risk losing control of their messages." Both Gates's comment to Perkins and Scoble seem to indicate that Gates is not contemplating a blogging shutdown or questioning its strategic value.

Allen politely implies a narrow view in the company's anti-blogging constituency: "Personally, I think [Microsoft's blogging opponents] are well-intentioned, but they worry too much and they underestimate the power of word of mouth."

What does Microsoft's experience have to teach other businesses? According to Allen, "Your whole company won't collapse if you do this and your customers will love you."

Gates in the Way

Lenn Pryor joined Microsoft impressed with the company's technology accomplishments. When he came on board in 1998, as a tech evangelist he hadn't realized the full scope of the company's worldwide unpopularity.

"The first thing I learned when I visited customers was that people were not always happy to see you," he said. "What got in the way of my relationships was the fact that I worked for Microsoft. The two people who represented the company—Bill Gates and Steve Ballmer—got in my way." He felt he had been painted into the corner by being associated with "two of the wealthiest people on the planet."

Pryor would have this recurring experience. He'd go out to dinner with a customer. They'd be having a pleasant enough time; then the customer would become quiet and pensive for a while, then blurt out: "You know, Lenn, I'm really surprised that you're such a nice guy. I didn't expect you to be." Pryor would ask, "Well, why not?" And the customer would say, "Because you're Microsoft and Microsoft is fundamentally evil. You just don't seem evil, so you're either really good at concealing it or I've read you guys wrong."

These experiences bothered Pryor. Because he represented Microsoft, customers seemed certain he could not be trusted. He stewed over this dilemma for years.

A brief interlude in Microsoft hating occurred for one week every two years in the form of Microsoft's Professional Developer's Conference (PDC). Around 6,000 developers would mingle with 2,000 Microsoft people. They'd see previews of new technology, share ideas, eat pizza, drink, joke, show each other family photos, and generally bond. "We were actually everyone's friend. We became human in our customers' eyes and they became human in ours. All the misconceptions went away," recalled Pryor.

But when the event ended, so did the magic. Pryor knew that unless he thought of some way to sustain the good feelings, they would dissipate: "We'd be Microsoft again, the evil guys." It had been a long week. He had an emotional hangover and drove home with a cold. A few days later, he was taking a long shower to shake off a Nyquil-induced haze. That's when the epiphany hit him.

At PDC, there had been a human connection. Microsoft employees saw and heard the customers as more than just statistics, and customers saw Microsoft representatives as real people. If Pryor could somehow bring this humanizing factor into everyday life, Microsoft's customer relationships might forever change. What Microsoft needed, Pryor realized, was some form of open channel that would humanize Microsoft, a daunting challenge if ever there was one. Maybe, Pryor thought, he could create a form of reality TV inside Microsoft that he could distribute to people using the Internet. He'd bring a camera inside Microsoft to show the developers and tech gurus exactly as they are, when and where they work. He would keep the footage raw, with no editing, no marketing polish, and certainly no slick commentator in a suit with a suntan.

This idea had been kicking around Microsoft for a while. Now, it would become Channel 9, the quirky, impromptu video blog—and the only official company blog. The name is derived from the United Airlines (UA) open audio channel, on which passengers can listen to pilots during take-offs, flights, and landings. Pryor knew it well, because *that* Channel 9 had helped cure him of his fear of flying: "I had this terrible relationship with United Airlines and its product. I was scared to death of their product even though I had to use it for business and no one was doing anything about making me feel better about them or their product. Sound familiar?" Pryor asked, smiling impishly at his own metaphor. Pryor said he cured his fear of flying by learning about the life of a pilot: "The more I could understand him, the more I could feel that his best interests were my best interests. I don't think there's any better way to describe how people feel about Microsoft than how people feel who are afraid to fly."

Microsoft, Pryor and the Channel 9 team decided, should build its own Channel 9. His idea was to "just share our lives with people and then they'll see we're human and they'll trust us." He envisioned that Channel 9 would redefine evangelism. Historically, evangelists have extolled the virtues of their company products by spreading the word about features and benefits. Pryor wanted to shift the focus from products to relationships.

Pryor and co-worker Jeff Sandquist presented this idea to their boss, Vic Gundotra, general manager for Platform Evangelism, who thought the idea of having some guy walking around with a video camera filming people in hallways and cubicles and having them talk about their jobs and their lives sounded a bit crazy. But he liked the idea and told them to go for it. They agreed the project should start low-key, certainly without marketing hoopla. They also knew there would be people at Microsoft who would oppose it. Gundotra would provide the air cover and his significant support.

Pryor would have to re-jigger his team. There was this guy, Robert Scoble, a relatively new hire who hadn't quite found his place at Microsoft yet. Pryor had known Scoble previously. Winer had been Scoble's mentor and boss at Winer's UserLand a couple of years earlier. A prolific, passionate, and perhaps fanatical blogger, Scoble was posting up to 50 times a night on his personal Scobleizer[2] site.

Before going to Redmond, Scoble had been NEC's evangelist for the tablet PC. In that role, he had attended a developer's conference where he publicly advised Ballmer to "give Microsoft a more human face." (Ballmer rewarded the idea with an autographed dollar.) When NEC first shipped its acclaimed tablet PC, Scoble made certain two people in Redmond each got one of the first units to ship. One was Gates. The other was Gundotra, who would eventually hire him.

Scoble wasn't your typical Microsoft kind of guy, certainly not one you'd expect to find in the front office. Said Pryor, "Robert lets his flaws hang out on his sleeve. He's curious like a child and it's hard not to like and trust him." Scoble had already started his "Scobleizer," which was often critical of Microsoft, but Pryor noticed that while most Microsoft critics tried to climb up and get in your face, "Robert always came across in a way that made me want to listen. He'd say, 'You guys did something wrong. Let me tell you why it hurt me and why it hurts you and why I think you can do better.' Robert tells you a lot about himself. He puts himself on the line. He delivers criticism from his heart."

In fact, Pryor had first discussed the concept of bringing a video camera inside Microsoft the previous March, when Gundotra was recruiting Scoble away from NEC and into Microsoft. Gundotra had invited Scoble to a Sonics basketball game where Michael Jordan would make his last uniformed Seattle appearance. Turns out that Gundotra couldn't make the game, so at the last minute he asked Pryor to stand in for him. After Jordan's courtside introduction, the two never again glanced at the playing floor. Instead, they spent three hours brainstorming and germinating the video concept. Neither recalls who won the game, but both left feeling certain that, if the idea ever became a reality, Scoble would be the right guy to put behind the camera.

Scoble joined Microsoft shortly after that, but the video idea remained dormant until Pryor's shower stall revelation. Scoble became a Microsoft evangelist, and blogged at home every night. Six months passed before Pryor had his shower epiphany that the Microsoft video blog would emulate Channel 9. When he and Sandquist pitched Gundotra, Gundotra told them to make Scoble the interviewer.

---

[2] http://www.scobleizer.com

The team, which also consisted of two developers, Bryn Waibel and Charles Torre, and program manager Sandquist, envisioned a hybrid, real-time format, rich in communication and very two-way, with the audience's voice being as relevant as the video itself. Channel 9 would encourage real conversation, not just drive-by stuff, where people hurled inflammatory comments and moved on. "In my mind," Pryor recalled, "Microsoft could *start* the conversation, but it wouldn't work if Microsoft *controlled* the conversation."

Channel 9 began as a standard text blog. Pryor recalled, "I wanted everyone to have a face on the site, to eliminate anonymity. The video came soon after, with Scoble's voice being heard asking people about their jobs and projects. The viewers never saw Scoble, but they would hear him mutter an occasional 'Oh crap,' as he inadvertently walked into a wall he didn't see because he was looking through the lens. A Forum section allowed developers to debate issues of all sorts. A collaborative system called a wiki was added to let people inside and outside Microsoft work together on software. "We showed who we are and where we work. We said: 'Come look inside and see and hear our people, hear our thoughts and passions.'" And people did—approximately 2.5 million of them in the first six months.

When asked about the risk involved in a project as visible and open as Channel 9, Gundotra said the project was about increasing transparency, which "is not high risk unless you have something to hide." He thought Channel 9 would accurately portray "a bunch of optimistic geeks who think we can change the world for the better through the power of software. I didn't *agree* to do Channel 9—I was driving the creation, funding, and hiring of the team."

Said Pryor, "We used Channel 9 as a way to respond to customers. If people wanted to know something, we put up a video about it. If there was a new product coming out, we put up a video. We started responding to issues in real time. This was not a documentary. This was a new approach—an interactive video of real people talking about their work with customers."

Channel 9 has been generally recognized as among the most innovative forms of blogging or, for that matter, corporate communications. It was the first corporate video blog. It was the first to put the words and faces of customers on the front page, thus creating a form of "equal time" for those who either praise or admonish Microsoft. It was also the first to use wikis to allow a product team to collaborate with customers to improve products and upgrades. It uses RSS, the technology that enables syndication, on every page and was the first full corporate site to do so.

It's open to speculation how Channel 9 will evolve. The Channel 9 conversation strayed one time from its usual technocentric bastion into politics. While some were concerned that Microsoft had lost control of the conversation, Pryor was elated. The conversational shift indicated that Channel 9 was no longer about Microsoft: "It's about the community. Maybe the future of this site is to turn the Channel 9 keys back to the community."

Although Pryor's background is in marketing, he eschews data mining and sees no value in surveys. But he does admit the company has data that shows Channel 9 has shifted perceptions of Microsoft from the negative to positive in less than six months. "There's no doubt we've moved the needle," he said, adding with apparent pride, "and we did it without so much as a press release."

Pryor expresses faith in the anecdotal evidence that perceptions of Microsoft have moved from a net negative to a net positive. He noted that blog polling site Technorati[3] reported nearly 1,300 other blogs linking to Channel 9 and that PubSub[4] rated Channel 9 in March 2005 at 5,877th of more than 8.5 million sites tracked at that time.

But Where's the ROI?

Pryor admitted that management support for blogging is "far from unanimous." On one hand, there's Scoble and a steadily increasing number of blogging employees, building what they call a "trust network" while simultaneously generating a steady flow of favorable media coverage. On the other, there are people whose job it is to reduce risk and control corporate message. Finally, there are those who believe in nothing that does not have a business model showing a return on investment (ROI) as a direct result of an effort.

But a great number of the people inside think the risk is paying off. They feel it in their everyday lives. "Today, Microsoft is building relationships, while six months ago we were losing them," Pryor stated flatly.

Still, he conceded that someday Scoble or another prominent blogger could stomp on the wrong foot and get himself fired: "If Robert goes, it will suck, but it's not about one guy anymore. You can't put the genie back in the bottle again. Once you establish that this is how you're going to communicate with customers, you cannot go back to the way it was."

---

[3] http://www.technorati.com
[4] http://www.pubsub.com

Pryor, who has since left the company, noted that bloggers have to respect the established turf. For example, bloggers almost never break hard news at Microsoft, nor do they launch products, although sometimes they've posted within minutes after an official announcement. But most day-to-day blogging focuses on supplementing information for customers. "Our job is not to be the place for the *New York Times* to find scoops." Still, he maintains, blogging gets good ink and lots of it, so it has to be good for attracting and retaining customers.

But the question that lingered in most people's minds: What about Gates and Ballmer? Gates gave tacit endorsement to blogging in his interviews with Scoble and Perkins in *AlwaysOn*. But then Ballmer's position became clear on July 7, 2005, during another exclusive interview with Scoble on Channel 9, when Scoble asked his CEO why he allowed blogging to happen at Microsoft.

"In the world of developers I don't think it would have mattered if I wanted to allow blogging to happen or not," Ballmer replied. "But I think it's been a great way for us to communicate to our customers—and for our customers, more importantly, to communicate with us. We trust our people to represent our company. That's what they are paid to do. If they didn't want to be here, they wouldn't be here. So in a sense you don't run any more risk letting someone express themselves on a blog than you do letting them go out and see a customer on their own. It just touches more people. Hey, if people need to be trained, we can do that, but I find that blogging is just a great way to have customer communications."

Sounds pretty definitive to us.

Diversity and Fan Clubs

Microsoft bloggers and their styles, topics, and frequency of postings are highly diverse. The number of visitors to a Microsoft blogger's site ranges from fewer than 10 per day to more than 10,000. Yet each links into the blogosphere, where each will be heard by those interested in the topic covered.

While Scoble may be Microsoft's best-known blogger, others have their admirers. Betsy Aoki, a community program manager, has a blog that has inspired a fan club.[5] When she investigated, she discovered it had only one member—Phil Weber, who wrote about Aoki with great admiration bordering on reverence. When they eventually met, Aoki thought it was an awkward

---

[5] http://www.philweber.com/2004/07/08.htm

encounter and that Weber would go away disappointed. But he didn't and he continues to be the leader of her fan club, which has since tripled to three members. We found abundant anecdotes like this in the business section of the blogosphere and find them indicative of how blogging puts a human face on companies.

Aoki's job is to keep the company's employee blogs running and to help employees blog effectively. "People come to me in varying states of blog readiness. They recognize blogging's power and the importance of the admonition 'blog smart.'" If there is a Microsoft blogging policy, it would be those two words: "Blog Smart." Employees sense that the longer they can keep an open blogging policy, the more unlikely it will be shut down. They argue that by blogging, they have an important competitive advantage over companies that don't allow it, such as Apple Computer.

Said Aoki, "Customer complaints go straight to my inbox. They get responses. I exchange tons of e-mail, so customers [see that] they have an impact. You also see you have an impact yourself. You blog and someone comments. It makes your work at Microsoft much more ground level." She said her blog "is where I get to hear from other people and [this] lets me feel real about my job."

Aoki shared the view that businesses of all sizes and in all fields will have little choice but to blog moving forward: "First there were phone books, then web sites and [businesses] know that if they don't have [one], it works to their disadvantage. Blogs are just the next logical step."

Mike Torres is a lead program manager for MSN Spaces, Microsoft's highly consumerized blog authoring toolset, which garnered 10 million downloads before it was a half-year old. He said he used search services such as Technorati, Feedster, and PubSub to quickly find and respond to any comments for or against MSN Spaces. "It stops the rants," he said. "A lot of times when you do that, there's a 'Sorry—I didn't know you were listening' reply. One guy posted, 'Big retraction: I was wrong.' What happens is that if they know you're in the conversation, people get respectful. They may still criticize you, but they don't lie."

MSN Spaces has grassroots supporters. Torres said readers become self-appointed service advocates, posting tutorials and defenses for Spaces. Torres caused a minor stir early on when he posted "5 Things I Dislike about MSN Spaces"[6] to his personal blog: "Here was a member of the team ranting in

---

[6] http://spaces.msn.com/members/mike/Blog/cns!1pG4qKNdtRA5Nl-UhvZI_1rQ!940.entry

public about how the product could be better. It showed that we don't just ship and walk away."

Blogging for Recruits

Almost every Microsoft blogger we interviewed pointed to blogging's advantages as a recruiting tool. There are two HR blogs giving advice on applying to Microsoft and demystifying the process. For Channel 9 Scoble toted his camera around to show applicants what a typical recruiting day looked like. He even interviewed the shuttle bus driver.

Kim Cameron, in charge of Microsoft's identity strategy, sees blogging as improving cooperation inside the global organization, where one hand has at times been known to be oblivious to the other's activities. He said, "Blogging creates discussions with people from other teams who are building complementary or potentially competing technologies."

Blogging seems to be accelerating the rate of change at Microsoft. It was a game of inches gained slowly back in 1999 when Allen became the first Microsoft blogger. Today, the rate of new bloggers at the company and the number of posts increase daily. The bloggers are swimming up the corporate stream. Steven Sinofsky,[7] the vice president who oversees Office, started a blog, making him by title, the senior ranking blogger. The longer blogging is allowed to continue, the safer it seems in contrast to the lonely days that surrounded Allen when he first started. And, as Aoki observed, "now the more cautious people are stepping up."

So, ultimately, what does all this mean to Redmond? Do we mean to imply that employee-bloggers have persuaded the world to love Microsoft? Don't be silly. That day is still far off. And there is that nagging security issue. Observes the *Wall Street Journal*'s influential Mossberg:

> *Just as things were looking up for the company, a serious crisis hit the Windows world—the seemingly unstoppable plague of viruses, spyware and other security threats. Tens of millions of Microsoft customers, especially consumers and small businesses without IT staffs, have been hammered by the security mess, which has cost time, money and, too often, lost data and*

---

[7] http://blogs.msdn.com/techtalk

productivity. Many are furious at Redmond for failing to pro-
tect them, for allowing its software to be so easily compro-
mised. The company is responding with security initiatives and
may eventually win back the trust of consumers. But, until
then, I believe the security crisis has undone much of the good
Microsoft did in improving its image—at least in the main-
stream community, where most people don't read technology-
oriented blogs or attend technology conferences or post their
feelings on web pages that Google can search.

This security issue, and a wildfire started by an open-source, free Internet browser named Firefox and most recently a hailstorm of innovative announcements from Google, which has emerged as its most threatening competitor, means the once-unstoppable software giant still has speed bumps in its road ahead, some of them significant. But the people we spoke with, who were generally at the middle of the company, are convinced that Microsoft has moved the needle toward humanizing a company so recently likened to the Borg. As Gundotra said, blogging has "allowed people to see who we really are. People know us through the lens of our employees."

Our point is this: If blogging can do all this for Microsoft, think of what it can do for your company.

2 Everything Never Changes

"Ideas and products and messages and behaviors spread just like viruses do."

—*Malcolm Gladwell,* The Tipping Point

In October 2001, Israel had the inspirational experience of sharing drinks with futurist-philosopher John Naisbitt,[1] author of *Megatrends*, a best-selling business book of the '80s. Thirty days earlier, two hijacked planes had crashed into the World Trade Center. Israel told Naisbitt he felt everything had changed. Naisbitt studied Israel, as if he were examining a slower-than-average student. "Everything never changes," he said. "Something has changed and it impacts everything else. Your life is the same. People go to the same jobs, in the same places. They go home to the same families and watch the same TV programs. Everything never changes. Something has changed and that something will impact a great deal. But life as we know it will continue."

He was right. Only something, not everything, has changed. And it's only when we look back at an incident—good or bad—that we can fully understand the effect and how the world adjusted. Blogging is, of course, a minuscule issue compared with 9/11. But it is another example of how one thing's changing impacts a great deal more. We think that blogging and conversational

---

[1] http://westpoint.k12.ms.us/FSWeb/myweb/John%20Naisbitt.htm

marketing are about to change the world most significantly. But we won't be able to prove our claim until we look back at it several years from now to see how business conversations have changed.

We don't want to overstate blogging's case, like makers of detergents boasting of miracle ingredients. The birth of the blog was a little-noted incident. A brilliant, curmudgeonly technology pioneer—Dave Winer—was fiddling with a project and organized a series of entries in a new way. He looked at it, thought "Wow, that's cool," and circled back to expand on it later. He added a variation on an emerging technology and created a syndication feature that would eventually emerge into Really Simple Syndication (RSS). Other people—such as Ben and Mena Trott, who founded Six Apart, Inc., and Evan Williams, who co-founded Blogger—would make blogging tools easier so a great number of people could use them. The number of users has just been going through the roof ever since. Before anyone knew it, one of Malcolm Gladwell's tipping points had occurred. Something has happened, and a great many things—if not everything—have begun to adjust.

Let's take another quick look at Microsoft. Has everything changed at Microsoft because about 2.6 percent of its employees now blog? In most aspects, Microsoft remains pretty much the same as it was before Joshua Allen made his first post. But we think something has changed, and the impact is spreading. Perhaps we were right in our Introduction to call the changes revolutionary. Perhaps not. We shall see.

But if we were to have met you in 1994 and told you that some young developers at Netscape were finishing up a "browser" that would let you read Internet pages and get to these pages by just clicking on a link, and it would change world information sharing, you might have just stared at us blankly before returning to your regularly scheduled program. Your life was just fine without the World Wide Web. What possible change could it mean to you? We would speculate that revolutionary change usually just creeps in on you. We doubt that the first stagecoach driver who watched a locomotive speed past him realized that this would doom his chosen vocation. Or the monks with quills realized the full implications of the Gutenberg press. No one even noted the name of the guy who developed the wheel. He or she probably just invented it out of necessity.

We believe the chain of small incidents that caused blogging has revolutionary implications to businesses, in marketing, customer support, internal communications, investor relations, product development, and even R&D. We think Lenn Pryor is right. The genie is out of the bottle, and there is no going back.

Businesses of all sizes will be wise to pay heed. Revolutions may be hard to predict, but ignoring them often has unfortunate consequences. For businesses, deciding what to pay attention to is often a tough call. False revolutionary claims have become a daily occurrence, and most turn out to be fads or just duds. In the early '90s, multimedia CD-ROMs were hyped as the next big thing, but by the time a business infrastructure could be built to support them, the category had been rendered obsolete by Internet delivery systems. Many retail stores had stripped out shelves and retooled to accommodate hundreds of disks, and then they had to change back.

Revolutions usually start off small, making few claims. The social kind are usually fomented off in the hills, far from the urban centers where incumbent powers hold firm, dismissing the feeble attempts of a few ragtags with rifles. A good number of businesses have been dismissive of the blogging. They contend blogging is either a passing fad or irrelevant to serious businesses.

But in business, numbers speak. They indicate blogging is no fad, and its relevance to business cannot logically continue to be denied.

Speed of Adoption

According to David L. Sifry, founder and CEO of Technorati (a Google-like service that tracks blogging topics, links, and trends), the number of blogs has been doubling about every five months since 2003. Today there are about 20 million bloggers worldwide, and by the time you read this, the number will be higher still.

While as many as one-third of all blogs started may be abandoned within a year, the overall growth of blogging is among the fastest of any technology in history. According to Pew, one-fourth of all Web users in the United States read blogs, and that number is increasing at the rate of 60 percent annually.

How many of these blogs are business related? It is impossible to say. As Anil Dash, vice president at Six Apart, Inc., the world's largest supplier of blog authoring tools for business, told us, "No one kept track of numbers when this all started. No one knew how big it would become, or how fast it would become big."

Adoption is accelerating globally as well. Technorati says growth is even faster in Asia and the Middle East than it is in North America. In 2004, Sifry reported that after English, Farsi language blogs showed the fastest growth, and in July 2005, China was estimated to have 1.25 million blogs, although others challenge the number. There are bloggers in every country where Internet technology is common. Some bloggers post dozens of times a day and their blogs are read by tens of thousands of people; others post only occasionally and are content to share thoughts and experiences exclusively with inner circles.

Pew estimates that as many as half of all blogs are private, either shared by a few friends or family members or located behind corporate firewalls, password protected, or both. IBM has more than 3,000 internal blogs. Private blogs are growing in popularity in corporations where they are used as a "clean intranet" for collaboration.

What Is a Blog and Who Cares?

A blog is really quite simple. It's nothing more than a personal web site with content displayed in reverse-chronological order. New posts are placed at the top of the page instead of the bottom, making it easy to see what has changed. In most cases, site visitors can identify the author and can leave comments for others to see. Blogs are loosely joined to each other through hyperlinks. Find one blog, and you can probably spend hours clicking links from blog to blog to blog—many of which talk about ideas and theories and rants on other blogs. This linking means that any blogger who has something to say is part of a global network called the *blogosphere*. Whether you have three regular visitors and only one link on your blog or 10,000 daily visitors and thousands of links, each posting from every blogger had a potentially huge circulation of 20 million in July 2005, a reach of almost 12 times the circulation in the millions. We played with all the numbers being bandied about. They don't jibe with each other, but one thing is certain. They are huge.

This blogosphere has a power that some formerly formidable people have unwisely underestimated. Trent Lott, the former Senate majority leader, lost that title after bloggers persisted in taking issue with comments that revealed Lott's fondness for segregationist days. Dan Rather made unsubstantiated allegations about President George W. Bush's military record, and CBS staunchly backed him until the bloggers relentlessly took issue with contentions that seemed highly unlikely. Companies have also made the painful mistake of underestimating the power of individual bloggers who had "low ratings." Two lock manufacturers, whom we will discuss later, ignored blogged revelations on how to open their locks, and one electronic game maker is paying off a $15 million lawsuit that began with blog-posted complaints on working conditions.

The most important aspect of the blog is that it is conversational. While nothing beats face-to-face meetings, the realities of global business and relationships make it impossible to have such meetings with every customer, prospect, or potential investor. Phones, faxes, e-mails, SMS, and IM all extend the conversation, as do online forums, bulletin boards, and chatrooms. But none of them lets one person converse with many people in multiple locations from any point where he or she has a computer and Internet access—not until blogging. In the coming chapters, we'll introduce you to scores of people who are using blogs in remarkable ways for their businesses. Collectively, they give compelling evidence that a communications revolution is underway, moving from a controlled one-way model into a decentralized interactive one.

Businesses need to join the conversations because they build trust. Most companies know the value in that. Blogs also humanize companies, or at least the people who work inside of them. Your blog lets your potential customers see who the person on the other side of the desk is before they engage you in potential business. It accomplishes much of what the photo, diploma, or trophy in your office or cubicle does for visitors. It lets people know you just a little bit. The more you talk with someone, the better you understand who he or she is, and you are most prone to conduct transactions with people you know well enough to trust. Traditional broadcast marketing efforts cannot accomplish either. Real people are simply more authentic than actors pretending to be real people. A stammering product manager has infinitely more credibility these days than a polished official company spokesperson.

Because blogs are also the lowest-cost communications channel, you can reach thousands, perhaps millions of people for an investment of a few cents and some personal time. Blogs are infinitely more efficient than any other corporate communications medium.

If you don't blog, but you are reading *Naked Conversations*, you should also go to Technorati and PubSub so you can start reading blogs on your market and maybe even your company. Watch closely, and you'll see a worldwide conversation happening. Often this conversation is about products or companies. It's what someone we interview in the next chapter called "word of mouth on steroids."

Blogging's Six Pillars

We hope someone writes a book on the history of the blogosphere. Interesting people and amazing coincidences dominate the story. This is not the focus of *Naked Conversations*, which instead attempts to tell businesspeople why they should blog.

There are six key differences between blogging and any other communications channel. You can find any one of them elsewhere, but not all. These are the Six Pillars of Blogging:

1. **Publishable.** Anyone can publish a blog. You can do it cheaply and post often. Each posting is instantly available worldwide.
2. **Findable.** Through search engines, people will find blogs by subject, by author, or both. The more you post, the more findable you become.
3. **Social.** The blogosphere is one big conversation. Interesting topical conversations move from site to site, linking to each other. Through blogs, people with shared interests build friendships unrestricted by geographic borders.
4. **Viral.** Information often spreads faster through blogs than via a news service. No form of viral marketing matches the speed and efficiency of a blog.
5. **Syndicatable.** By clicking on an icon, you can get free "home delivery" of RSS-enabled blogs. RSS lets you know when a blog you subscribe to is updated, saving you search time. This process is considerably more efficient than the last-generation method of visiting one page of one web site at a time looking for changes.
6. **Linkable.** Because each blog can link to all others, every blogger has access to millions of other bloggers.

You can find each of these elements elsewhere. None is, in itself, all that remarkable. But in final assembly, they are the benefits of the most powerful two-way Internet communications tool so far developed.

Google's Ascendancy

Perhaps the most compelling strategic business argument for blogging is its interrelationship with Google and the other modern search engines.

When Google was born in 1998, the world paid little notice to yet another free search engine service. Times change. By 2003, Google was arguably the most influential of all online companies and had the most influence on the ranking of virtually all other companies. A high rank on a Google page has become more valuable than an army of PR operatives pumping out press releases. Some would argue that a high Google rank has more value than, say, a *BusinessWeek* cover story. Even if you prefer the *BusinessWeek* cover, a high Google page ranking is likely to get it for you faster than a PR effort or a full-page ad.

Blogging turns out to be the best way to secure a high Google ranking. Google spiders out onto the network in search of change. Blogs get updated all the time, while most web sites do not, so blogs get more search engine attention.

Every time you post, Google notices and that boosts your ratings. Google also pays attention to links—other sites that connect to you. Bloggers who find what you write interesting will post on their own sites and link back to you. Those links also boost your "Google juice"—in fact, nothing will boost your search engine standing better. Neither a press release nor a full-page ad in the *New York Times* will boost your search engine rankings as much as a regularly updated blog. If you want a high Google ranking, our advice is to blog and post often. Some businesspeople claim this is an unfair advantage for bloggers. Others speculate that Google will someday change its algorithms because advertisers don't like blogging's Google juice advantage. We have our doubts that search engines would or could easily make such changes to their core technology. For now, it is clear that the shortest, cheapest, fastest, and easiest route to a prominent Google ranking is to blog often.

As far as blogging is concerned, the sea change has already happened. The point has tipped. The genie is indeed out of the bottle, but history indicates some companies will persist in ignoring it.

It takes a while before revolutionary technologies prove themselves to be such. Revolutions are often declared only after we look back on them, not when we look forward, as we are doing in this book. As we write, many businesspeople are still scratching their heads wondering what the big deal is about blogging. The remaining chapters should supply the answers.

3 Word of Mouth on Steroids

"Now, the Web is enabling the market to converse again, as people tell one another the truth about products and companies and their own desires."

—The Cluetrain Manifesto

Our friends influence us more than any advertising or marketing campaign could ever dream of doing. They directly impact what we watch, read, and wear; where we live; and where we travel. A good sales professional will tell you that he or she is in the relationships business and that the most important customers require direct contact. A marketing professional will point out, however, that conversations are limited by range. In this era of superstores, chains, franchises, and global corporations, businesses need to reach mass audiences, and you just can't sit down and chat with everyone.

Or can you?

For the past 50 years or so, marketing departments have viewed conversational marketing as too limited in scope, relegating it to the back seat while letting broadcast marketing drive. But the car has started to backfire. Broadcast marketing may produce customers, but it must shoot wide to hit just a few.

To be economically advantageous, a TV ad or direct mail campaign needs to generate response in a mere 2 percent of the total audience. It doesn't matter whether 98 percent of the viewers don't like the ads, nor does it matter that so many other companies are shooting at the same people. It matters only if you are part of that 98 percent, as co-author Israel learned firsthand.

For a brief, unfortunate time in the mid-90s, he consulted MCI, which at the time was running a massive television-telemarketing campaign called "Friends and Family." Israel had nothing directly to do with the program, but was disturbed that it involved calling millions of people at home during dinner hours. After a few months, Israel took a risk and told an MCI executive to consider dumping the program. "People really hate the intrusion," Israel counseled.

"We don't care who hates it," the executive retorted coldly. "We are getting a response of at least 2 percent in all metro areas and as high as 5 percent in pockets. To hell with the other 98 percent."

To our way of thinking, this is at the essence of what's wrong with broadcast marketing. All too often the senders could care less what the overwhelming majority of the receivers feel about their ads and marketing messages.

Author-speaker Seth Godin,[1] whose books include *Free Prize Inside!*, *Purple Cow*, and, most recently, *All Marketers Are Liars*, describes such tactics as "Interruption Marketing"—unanticipated, impersonal, and irrelevant ads repeatedly hurled at involuntary audiences.

Slowly and steadily over time, Interruption Marketing has managed to annoy a great many people who have become resistant to it. They've installed mental and technology filters to avoid exposure to marketing noise. Their senses have become deaf and blind to marketing intrusions. They use anti-spam software and TiVo to block out as much advertising as they can. They use broadcast marketing time to run to the refrigerator, make quick calls, or check e-mail.

Consequently, this traditional marketing has become less effective at about the same rate that it has become more expensive. The National Advertising Council estimates that the top six TV networks alone in 2005 will receive more than $9 billion in advertising, even as their market share and total viewer audiences erode further.

Big advertisers wasting money don't bother us so much as the disregard and apparent disrespect for the people who have to see, hear, and read what they spew out in ads that shout at you or pop up and squiggle, or spam that has corrupted the e-mail channel.

---

[1] http://www.sethgodin.com

For a long while, people have had little or no recourse to avoid this stuff. But technology keeps delivering communications options away from broadcast and back to the conversation.

And this new technology has allowed conversational marketing to climb out of the back seat to which it has been relegated and to drive safely at high speed and at extremely low cost. Some companies are aggregating scores of millions of users while spending close to zero on traditional marketing programs.

How can this be possible? By listening to customers and engaging them. These customers become company champions. They encourage others to use the products and services. They defend companies from unfair or inaccurate attacks. They tell the companies they care about how to build better products and services.

As author-speaker Ben McConnell, a partner in Church of the Customer and co-author of *Creating Customer Evangelists: How Loyal Customers Become a Volunteer Sales Force,* told us, "There is simply nothing more powerful than customer evangelists. Blogging enables companies to convert customers into word-championing evangelists, a powerful mechanism for true believers to spread the word about what you do and why other people should believe in what you are doing."

Blogging is customer evangelism's most powerful tool so far, but word-of-mouth evangelism is nothing new and predates the butcher, baker, and candlestick maker by centuries. But the Internet came in and with the advent of conversational tools such as e-mail, IM, SMS, chat, and forums, conversational marketing started to gain scale, the grandness of which was proven by five innovative Israelis a decade before the blog exploded on the scene.

25 Million Customers Virtually Free

In December 1996, Arik Vardi sat with three close friends from high school, telling his dad, Yossi, a veteran Israeli investor in technology startups, about the "buddy system" he and his three friends had invented to chat with other friends online. They had originally told 40 kids and within two months 65,000 additional people had downloaded the software, all hearing about it by word-of-mouth conversations. They called it "ICQ" (for "I Seek You"). With a small investment from Yossi, they thought the project might have some potential. Yossi gave them encouragement and $10,000.

"I didn't tell them, but I was totally blown away. I told my wife this is the biggest thing I'd ever seen. I told her it's going to change the world and these kids don't even know it yet," Yossi said. He was right. Two years later, AOL purchased Mirabilis—the company formed with Vardi's $10,000—for $287 million. By the end of 1998, the service, now also called AOL Instant Messenger, had experienced 25 million downloads, less than 26 months after it started.

The total marketing expenditure, amortized over time, was near zero. ICQ's founders had printed a brochure but never used it. They sponsored a tech conference speaker, but only because Yossi liked the guy. They never hired or contracted a marketing employee, never launched a PR program, never even sent out a press release. Instead, they used a series of creative, low-cost tactics to ignite enthusiastic conversations. For example, whenever a new IM software version was ready, they'd contact 1,000 randomly selected users, giving them each the same "secret password," and urging each to reveal it only to their two best friends. As the company anticipated, users ignored the two-friend limit and spread the word far and wide. By giving users a sense they were insiders, the company sparked frenetic evangelical zeal.

Another successful touch was inserting a slightly sexual "Uh-AH" sound, played whenever a user received an instant message. A teenager would be talking on the phone, and as a new message came in, the grunt-sigh would be audible. It sparked further conversations, which spawned more downloads.

ICQ also pioneered the tactic of using other web sites as a distribution channel. The company offered ICQ "communications panels" to webmasters, and visitors downloaded ICQ so that they could chat with the webmasters and, of course, with other ICQ users. This quickly resulted in yet another 100,000 new downloads.

AOL won't reveal customer numbers, but several observers estimate total customers for ICQ and AOL Instant Messenger in mid-2005 to be about 400 million with tens of thousands of daily downloads. The overall business IM market grew by 130 percent worldwide from 2002 to 2003 and was expected to grow a further 85 percent from 2003 to 2004, according to Ferris Research. By 2007, the overall business IM market will increase to 182 million users, representing a compound annual growth rate of 79 percent.[2] Still spending next to nothing on marketing, the IM service is supported now by high-margin contextual advertising—unobtrusive Google-like ads whose subjects coincide with the page's content.

---

[2] http://www.pcworld.idg.com.au/index.php/id;368803475;fp;16;fpid;0

While AOL also declined to discuss margins, downloads, or any other numbers, we would assume 50,000 downloads daily as a conservative guess. What would that cost with a traditional marketing campaign like direct mail (DM)? DM experts claim efficiency when they spend 80 cents per mail piece, and they're still happy with a 2 percent response. On that math, they need to send out 2.5 million pieces a day to match AOL's current pace. The company would have to spend about $2 million daily. Free versus $2 million a day? You choose.

Until blogging came along, instant messaging as created by ICQ was considered the last great killer application. Although its current owner, TimeWarner, enjoys huge profits by inserting inoffensive contextual advertising, it still offers the product free, which of course helps the adoption rate.

But there was something else going on during ICQ's meteoric ascent, something that Yossi Vardi marveled at during his tenure. End users sent love letters to the service—not the people, but the service. Vardi called this phenomenon "tool lust." In his view, people develop emotional attachments to things that empower new, faster, easier, better, or cheaper activity. He sees blogging's magic as the next incarnation of tool lust. "What ICQ did for one-to-one conversations, blogging does for one-to-many. Blogging's a tool that lets you stay in touch with the whole world," he observed. "That invokes passion."

Talk Is Cheap

Even back in 1996, users could talk to each other by voice over the Internet via ICQ. However, because users were still on dial-up, connection was slow and rarely used. International dial-up conversations could also be expensive. That was probably a good thing for Skype (rhymes with *Ripe*), today's most popular Internet telephone service. Downloads of its free core service reached 25 million just 19 months after starting up, breaking ICQ's benchmark record. But Skype used instant messaging and blogs to market, neither of which existed for ICQ in 1996.

Like ICQ, Skype primarily used word of mouth to invigorate adoption, although the company made a few minor investments in traditional marketing programs such as conference sponsorships. Skype, like other companies, emulated ICQ tactics such as distinctive sounds and tell-a-friend programs to convert its user base to a global unpaid salesforce. Skype's low-cost marketing strategy has been lethal against other Internet telephone players, such as

Vonage, which advertises on TV. According to Reuters,[3] Vonage was acquiring its one millionth customer in May 2005, when Skype was crossing the 30-million-user mark.

But Skype has bigger plans. In its next phase as part of eBay, which acquired it in October 2005, it intends to unseat formidable traditional phone carrier incumbents by adding low-priced paid services, such as inbound and outbound calling to and from conventional phones. In that arena, the upstart Skype faces a steep climb against larger and more entrenched companies with far more money, customers, and brand recognition, not to mention friends in regulatory agencies. Skype believes it has two competitive advantages, however. First, most customers love the service. Few people seem to express love for Verizon, SBC, or WorldCom. Second, people have tool lust—they want the latest, coolest thing.

Because Skype uses the efficiency of word-of-mouth marketing, instead of big advertising and marketing campaigns, it goes into the new fray with a huge price-performance advantage in acquiring new customers. With its gaunt marketing budget, Skype is acquiring each new customer for fractions of a penny. In contrast, analysts estimate that a new customer costs a wireless telephone carrier about $125.

This incredible ratio may flatten over time. Skype recently announced it will begin brand recognition advertising and promotional campaigns. How big an investment this will become, and whether it is a wise strategy, remains to be seen. Skype estimates that about one in five free users will use the paid additional services. Its costs are so low, the company maintains, that it will use this advantage to build a next-generation dynasty.

Blazing Foxes

Skype's interim record of 25 million users in 19 months was short-lived. Firefox, an Internet browser considered simpler and more secure than Microsoft's Internet Explorer (IE), reached 25 million downloads in 99 days after launching exclusively from a blog that it also used as a central distribution conduit. By its sixth month, Firefox had passed the 50 million mark, and the rate of adoption was still rising.

The Firefox story is worthy of a book in itself. Its development team was never paid to work full time on the project as it bounced around through four

---

[3] http://www.vonage.com/corporate/index.php?lid=footer_corporate

parent organizations. Firefox emerged as a lightning rod for anti-Microsoft sentiment and open-source technology—software built to allow tinkering by end users and third parties. The combination created a worldwide grassroots army of supporters-in-waiting.

Blake Ross, now 20, was still in high school when he joined the Firefox development team. He started to blog as an outlet for his frustrations with the turnstile ownership tenures of Netscape, AOL, and TimeWarner. Eventually named SpreadFirefox,[4] the blog became a hub for a series of no-cost marketing activities and would become one of 2005's most popular blogsites. Each week on the site, Ross announced a new "community marketing campaign." For example, one week he'd proclaim an effort to attract college students. All he had to do was announce the campaign; the readers would do the rest, resulting in thousands, and eventually millions, of new downloads. "Most campaigns were wildly successful," recalled Ross, now attending Stanford University and co-launching a new startup. "SpreadFirefox ignited a groundswell of support that erupted organically."

Firefox reached the 25 million mark six times faster than ICQ. Then it shattered its own record by aggregating another 25 million downloads in half the time, using nothing but word of mouth enhanced by Internet technologies. It was also helped by the fact that so many more people came online over the 10 years between launches. Additionally, it had the advantage of seeing what worked for the ICQ pioneers. For example, early on, Firefox offered download buttons to other blog and web sites, so people could get the new browser software from those sites as well. Within a few months, more web sites were linking to the Firefox page via these buttons than were linking to the Microsoft IE site. If you go to Google today and type "Internet Browser," Firefox comes up before IE.

Firefox users were so evangelical that they took up a collection to post the first ad for the product—a two-pager in the Sunday edition of *The New York Times*. According to Joe Hewitt, another founding member of the Firefox team, the ad produced "a nice little blip" but was insignificant compared to the solid, steadily rising number of downloads that SpreadFirefox.com was generating. By April 2005, the blog was the fountainhead for a word-of-mouth system generating well over 200,000 daily downloads. With each Firefox download, you also get a free blog. "Our members use these blogs to invent, discuss, coordinate, and execute enormous marketing campaigns," said Ross.

---

[4] http://www.spreadfirefox.com

Thus, Firefox has built a word-of-mouth network across web and blog sites, amplifying any marketing efforts and extending the reach to global and back again. What would this have cost with an ad campaign? Would it have been as effective in inspiring troops of user-enthusiasts to spread the word with surprising zeal and effectiveness?

The Firefox press coverage has also been astounding. If you laid all the clips and cover stories end to end, they might extend from Firefox's Silicon Valley home to the doorstep of Microsoft's Redmond headquarters. The Firefox team is convinced that word of mouth has done more to accomplish this than the solitary press release they put out when Firefox came out of beta.

Firefox exemplifies what the blogging denizens call "the passion chamber," a recurring theme in conversational marketing. People start something new, motivated more by sharing with friends than by the promise of revenue. Friends try it, like it, and pass it on. According to Ross, "Firefox was born because it had to be born, because this product took residence in our minds and gnawed at us during work, at dinner, and on the weekends." Hewitt added that there was no thought of unseating incumbents or the resulting blazing fame. "We just wanted to build a good browser that we could use ourselves and share with our friends."

Word of mouth is most viral when the words credibly relay such passion. Viral also seems to work best when it is home-brewed, rather than part of a marketing push. Jackie Huba, co-author with McConnell of *Creating Customer Evangelists*, is wary of "organizations that set out to do something viral or generate buzz. They often end up coming across as cheesy." She warned, "Two-way marketing is essential to evangelism. Word-of-mouth tactics may backfire if they are one-directional."

Passion, Not Echo

There is another danger in the passion chamber, however. It may actually be an "echo chamber," as was evidenced in the abrupt rise and fall of the Howard Dean presidential campaign. His ascendancy was ignited by word of mouth, followed by passionate ubiquitous blogging. The effort raised millions of dollars and generated media speculation of a victory that never even came close. Dean's passionate supporters never managed to cross the traditional chasm between early enthusiasts and mainstream voters who generally had not yet turned to blogs for information and conversation. While they thought blogging was amplifying their voices, they were in fact merely talking to each other.

Even though Firefox took the tech community by storm—grabbing more than 10 percent of the total browser market in less than its first six months—IE still holds 87.28 percent, according to OneStat,[5] a web-analytics company. WebSideStory,[6] another analytics firm, observed shortly after that, however, the rate may be starting to taper off. BoingBoing,[7] one of the five most popular blogsites, estimated that 38.7 percent of its site visitors use Firefox, a four point margin over Explorer. The discrepancy in the statistics among sources reveals sharply that the blog enthusiast population does not represent the general market—and in casual observation, may actually mislead.

It is essential that bloggers know the difference between words that spread like Firefox or bounce back at you like Howard Dean's.

Continuing to spread the message is a key element of the Firefox strategy to have technologists seed the mainstream. "I don't get excited when I hear a developer is using Firefox," said Hewitt. "I get excited when I hear he went home and installed it in his mom's computer." Firefox is counting on third-party developers to help it bridge into the mainstream. Firefox team members estimated that 20 percent of the world's web developers adopted Firefox in its first 100 days. The Firefox team is hoping that these developers will produce all sorts of add-on products, making Firefox irresistible to more and more nontechnical end users as it prepares for Microsoft's next browser increasing market competition.

Other startups are beginning to more broadly emulate tactics invented by ICQ and refined by Firefox. On a quick search, in February 2005, we found SpreadOpera.com, SpreadNetscape.com, SpreadIE.com, SpreadSeamonkey.com, SpreadMozilla.com, SpreadOpenSource.com, SpreadOpenOffice.org, SpreadLinux.com, SpreadFreeBSD.com, SpreadMambo.com, and SpreadUbuntu.com. By July, about half of them had gone and another three or four Spread_____ sites had started. It apparently takes more than a catchy keyword to catapult you from oblivion to the top tier, but there are larger lessons to learn here. Companies need to offer something so unique, valuable, or compelling that people will want to tell others about it. While "tell-a-friend" campaigns might gain some traction with rewards and incentives, they aren't the prime motivators. What turbo-charges word of mouth is loyalty to people you trust—not companies whose brands

---

[5] http://www.onestat.com

[6] http://www.websidestory.com

[7] http://www.boingboing.net/stats/#browsers

you recognize. People come across something new, and they want to tell their colleagues about it. They like to be first and have influence. But none of this matters unless the product or service is really *remarkable*.

Remarkable or Invisible?

"The new reality of the marketplace is that consumers have a choice," said Godin. "They can ignore you. They can ignore your ads, your letters, your web banners, and your salespeople. As a result, you and every other marketer faces a choice: You can make something worth talking about or you can become invisible. There are now millions of blogs and each one is edited by a real person. If you create something remarkable, something worth remarking about, then they may choose to remark about it. And if they do, the word spreads."

Godin calls these remarkable products and services "Purple Cows," in reference to his book of the same name. Purple cows are remarkable. Brown cows are not. One is the center of attention; the other is boring. He bases Purple Cows on two fundamentals:

- **Ideas that spread win.** Because it's so difficult for a marketer to make direct contact with the people who can actually purchase something from them, he or she must rely on people telling people. The single best way to accomplish word-of-mouth publicity is not with a clever web site or tell-a-friend software or cash rewards. The best way to do this is to make something worth talking about. Marketing is now about product development, not product hype.
- **Remarkability is in the eye of the consumer.** If the marketplace doesn't think your product is remarkable, then it's not. It doesn't matter how hard you worked on it or how important it is to you.

"Not only are bloggers suckers for the remarkable, so are the people who read blogs," said Godin. "This is the most curious segment of the population, the people who are seeking out the new and the useful. This is the audience that doesn't need to be interrupted because they are already listening. They are alert, on the lookout for the next big thing. No need to yell. If you've invested the time and the energy and the guts to make something remarkable, this audience can't wait to hear about it."

From Free to Billions

There is a common attribute of our three company success stories—each markets freeware. While each company is at a different point in the process to monetization, all three began by providing goods or services that were free to the end users who evangelized them. Google is another example of reaching huge success with a service free to customers. But free is not an essential component. eBay and Amazon executed strategies that involved charging customers. What all these companies had in common was an ability to leverage the efficiencies of Internet-enabled word-of-mouth tools to amplify their offers of remarkable goods and services.

Not every company can execute a free now monetize later strategy. Many companies successfully try limited time or quantity free-trial offers, but starting free and then asking for money later has been a short route to the cemetery for a great many companies. In Chapter 13, "Blogging in a Crisis," we look at how Six Apart made a U-turn from that direction by effectively blogging.

Google, eBay, and Amazon are now global, branded successful companies. But each could not have happened without Internet efficiencies. Yes, a big factor was shedding needs for brick-and-mortar sales facilities But each also was quick to understand and take advantage of the incredible power of web-based word-of-mouth marketing. Despite the fact that each is a public company with values in the billions of dollars, each keeps word of mouth at the center of its marketing strategies. Amazon CEO Jeff Bezos recently declared his company will eschew TV advertising because Amazon considers it ineffectual compared with word-of-mouth campaigns. Amazon also has found an inoffensive way to financially reward bloggers for sending business its way: Bloggers can join the affiliate program and split profits on any book sales their sites generate.

Google began at the apex of buzz marketing in 1998. When startups were spending tens of millions on marketing and advertising, Google spent very little. At a time when home sites were starting to use gimmicks that popped up, made noises, and wiggled, Google introduced a uniquely sparse home page containing fewer than 30 words. People gave it a try. When they did, they discovered remarkable search capabilities compared with incumbent offerings of the time. While other search engines of the era dumped haystacks on user desktops, Google, more often than not, delivered the golden needles people were looking for. They continue to use almost all word-of-mouth tactics. In

2004, for example, the company introduced Gmail, an e-mail program with gargantuan Internet-based storage capability, and it used ICQ-type tactics to jumpstart it. Google allowed selected applicants a few beta copies and created a pseudo-scarcity by asking each to invite just a few friends. These select invitations somehow became sufficiently in demand to be auctioned off on eBay.

Apple Computer certainly utilizes traditional advertising, and many observers say it is one of the few computer companies to ever produce remarkable ads. But its iPod, a portable music-listening device, was sufficiently exciting and different to get the blogosphere to sing its praises in choir-level harmony. Apple also had the vision to create design details that provoked conversations—for example, white headphones. The color added no real user benefit except that it provoked conversation. On a recent jet flight, two strangers sat side by side listening to music on their respective devices. One asked the other about the white headphones. This simple question started a conversation. Other people in the row joined in. People asked to listen on the headphones to see whether they sounded any better. Portable audio devices are rapidly becoming a commodity, but touches like the white headphones keep people talking and build the perception of remarkability.

Apple also spends advertising dollars in nontraditional ways that generate word of mouth. If all you knew about computers was what you saw in movies and television, you'd be convinced that Apple Macintosh held about 97 percent computer market share instead of less than 3 percent. Apple has achieved this visibility because of its aggressive product placement program with the entertainment industry.

The "Awesome-Sucks" Factor

If anyone knows how to spend big bucks for promotion, it's Hollywood. Promoters have been known to invest up to $200 million in support of big budget movie premiers. Nowadays, however, small clusters of teenagers, armed with cell phones, are disrupting—and even destroying—these expensive efforts. Small groups get into the first daytime showings of a new movie and, after the first few minutes, they start transmitting SMS messages to a few friends outside the theaters. These messages are brief and to the point, such as "awesome" or "sucks." Friends receive the messages on their phones and start blogging about the movie. Before credits roll, these bands of youthful influencers, loyal to their peers and out of Hollywood's control, enormously impact the movie's fate before the first Saturday night showing.

Why do people go through such efforts to help others, most of whom they've never met? Why do people lend headphones to strangers on planes or tell their life stories to cab drivers? Yossi Vardi told us the world's second favorite entertainment is story telling, but the top is conversations. Even if we don't have TiVo, we let a phone call interrupt our program watching or we lay down our books. It seems collaborating is human nature, and at least one research experiment would indicate the reason is that collaboration turns us on.

Dr. Gregory S. Berns, an Emory University professor of psychiatry and behavioral sciences, uses functional MRI and other computer-based technologies to study how the human brain responds to various stimuli. In short, his team wires the brain to see how the brain is wired. A few years back, Berns studied the interaction of biology and altruism. He used a functional MRI to scan the brains of 36 women playing the behaviorist's game "Prisoner's Dilemma," in which participants are rewarded according to the choices they make. Berns found these women displayed cooperative behavior even when they knew they would receive greater rewards for not cooperating. The technology revealed that the striatum, a primitive brain sector, grew active during collaboration. In fact, it secreted five times the normal level of dopamine, the chemical that activates during such stimulating activities as sex and gambling. In short, humans are wired to collaborate. Altruism turns people on even more than making money.

That makes blogging the sex god of the Information Age. While word of mouth has always been the most credible way to expand awareness and adoption, blogging fits into all this as the most powerful word-of-mouth delivery mechanism to date. As Yossi Vardi told us, "Blogging is word of mouth on steroids."

To give us historic perspective, Vardi observed the three strongest brands to come out of his native country, Israel, are the Bible, Christianity, and ICQ. Each depended on passionate people spreading the word. To reach their current levels of recognition and strength, the Bible (including the Old Testament) took 2,700 years; Christianity did it in 2000; and ICQ reached global acceptance in less than 10. Vardi pointed out that ICQ claimed no greater relevance. It just came into being at a time when the tools had further evolved.

Our point: Blogging is faster and more effective than walking from village to village and knocking on doors.

Blogging's Key Advantages

Blogging is one huge word-of-mouth engine. Instead of being relegated to the back seat, it now is efficient, powerful, and fast enough to drive the whole car. Actually, two cars would probably be more accurate, because it drives in two directions—outbound and inbound.

Blogging lets you listen to what people are saying about your product, company, or category and gives them the opportunity to respond. The result is that your business becomes connected to a new kind of smarter, more efficient word-of-mouth network. Blogging lets you:

- **Find and join the conversation.** Nearly in real time, people can extract comments relevant to their business through search engines such as Technorati, Feedster, or PubSub, each of which tracks millions of blogsites similar to the way Google tracks billions of web sites. These search engines are faster and usually deliver results in hours or even minutes, letting you see what people are saying—pro or con—about your market, product, and company. People are talking about these things already, so it would be wise for you to participate, even if you do not maintain your own blog.

  As Microsoft's Mike Torres told us, "People are much more respectful when they know you're listening." Imagine you are a car enthusiast and you see a cool new Corvette at the Detroit Auto Show. You post a blog about it and perhaps post a photo or two about it. Within a few hours, Bob Lutz, GM vice chairman and a blogger, sees your post, passes it around to the Corvette team, and then links onto their blogs and perhaps places a comment on yours. Imagine the kind of brand loyalty created when a big company notices your blog and links to it. There are also catch-all blogs that watch entire industry categories—in this case, Autoblog.[8] They see it, post, and link to yours. Thousands of car enthusiasts drive directly to your site.

---

[8] http://www.autoblog.com

You started with a single post. You spent nothing, but even if you had, it would have made little or no difference. But you initiated an interesting or valuable conversation. Someone influential recognized you, and now you have greater influence.

- **Feed the network.** This expression once referred to using provocative advertisements such as Apple's 1984 SuperBowl screen-smashing commercial. Such ads can still work, although there seems to be a real paucity of ads worth talking about these days. On the other hand, blogs let you feed the network at far lower cost and as a more credible source. Let's look at GM's Lutz again. His first blog was about GM's Saturn, which scores high in customer service rankings. He posted just prior to a big auto show where a spiffy new Saturn was introduced. The blogosphere exploded with conversation on the fact that Lutz was blogging, on the fact that he responded to comments on whether the new car was real or prototype, and so on. At last count, there were about 100 comments under his posting and almost an equal number of links to it—mostly from average people who enjoyed joining and extending a conversation with a prominent Fortune 10 executive. The automotive media also picked up on the news. How did this posting, which probably required less than an hour of executive time, feed the word-of-mouth food chain compared with a Saturn ad? If Lutz were quoted in an official press release, we doubt it would have been noted, but his blog was news. By the way, there is a new Saturn TV ad campaign. Do you recall seeing it? Neither do we. What fed the network better, the blog or the expensive ad campaign?

Vardi was right. Blogging is indeed word of mouth on steroids. Unlike major league sports, where steroids have caused a multitude of scandals, word of mouth on steroids builds credibility, enthusiasm, and customer evangelism.

4 Direct Access

"Freedom of the press is guaranteed only to those who own one."

—A. J. Liebling

Most businesspeople see media coverage as a benefit. Until blogging, the common wisdom was that press coverage was the most credible way to bolster the company name, products, and reputation, and it remains a tremendous benefit to most organizations. Many companies invest significant dollars into PR campaigns, with media coverage a primary objective. Yet more often than is usually noted, people and companies are disappointed by what is written about them. A colleague involved in a hotly disputed local issue recently told us, "If I read something on a subject I know, I usually find significant factual inaccuracies and I often find the reporter took an unfair or ignorant slant. Often that slant favors my side, but it's still wrong."

Some executives in positions where the spotlight constantly glares can get coverage that others find enviable, and they just don't want it anymore. These executives complain that the press abridges what they have to say in ways that distort their original statements. They assert the press does a shoddy job of checking facts before publishing, manipulates direct quotes, and takes obstinate stances when mistakes are brought to light. One well-publicized example can be found in the hollow-sounding words of CBS News President Andrew Heyward standing by its story with the declaration, "I have full confidence in our reporting," which were echoed stubbornly before the network had to admit that Dan Rather's "evidence" against George W. Bush's military record were probable forgeries.

Blogging provides the first adequate toolset for enabling executives and businesspeople to get their messages out directly to their audiences—and to hear back from them, something that does not happen through the media or other relay mechanisms.

Some top executives and personalities can get coverage whenever they want. But that doesn't mean they will be either satisfied or more clearly understood by readers of that coverage. A few have turned to blogs, which allow them to have direct access to their target audiences, to guarantee that they will get to tell their side of the story, in their own words.

While top executives have the power to take on the press, direct access to key audiences is essential to most people in business. Well-known executives don't mind head-to-head challenges to the press. In fact, several use their blogs to show how much they enjoy it, or so they told us.

The situation is more complicated for executives in smaller companies. They usually do not get as much ink as they want—and then when they do get it, the story is often reduced or minimized. Blogs offer them the same option of getting direct access to their publics whenever they choose to post. During more than 20 years in PR, co-author Israel served mostly startup companies often in relation to their crucial initial launches. On many occasions his clients were distraught over what they felt was unfair, overly brief, or inaccurate coverage. Israel's observation was that editors took dismissive and even arrogant attitudes when confronted with mistakes. They resisted printing retractions or doing corrective follow-up stories. They told clients to write a letter to the editor, which is rarely, if ever, as well read and never as prominently placed as a news story. Even in the letters, clients did not get their say. Editors edited and condensed the complaining letters themselves. The letters also were published weeks later, long after the damage was done and too late to fully correct it.

Blogs do not completely solve this problem, but they have already proven to be powerful tools for directly accessing company constituencies without having to buy a company printing press. Blogs are a whole lot less expensive as well. And they change the balance with a certain elegant irony. "While a journalist is writing about my blog, I'm blogging about his journalism. This is change," Jonathan Schwartz, president and COO of Sun Microsystems, told us. This obviously recalibrates the tilt on the playing field in ways that have not previously happened.

Bob Lutz, General Motors vice chairman, told us he was "looking for a direct line of communication with the world" through his blog. In his first posting, he declared, "In the age of the Internet anyone can be a journalist." He feels his blog, GM FastLane,[1] enables him to do that. Dallas Mavericks owner Mark Cuban was even more direct: His blog "was in response to the media primarily. I was tired of four-hour interviews being turned into 500-word reports that mischaracterized the interviews. I sat down with *Fortune* magazine for what I thought was a serious interview and it turned into something completely different. Those types of situations were the catalyst for me to start blogging."

Cuban's blog often admonishes sports journalists for inaccuracy, lack of intelligence, and laziness in their coverage, not just of his Mavericks basketball team but in covering sports in general. He doesn't hedge. After a TV reporter speculated on a lack of chemistry between the Mavs coach and players, he wrote: "ABC Sports should take immediate action against Jim Gray and suspend him from working until he apologizes."[2] Early on, his blog wielded armloads of anecdotal and statistical evidence of poor officiating, and he claims that his efforts have resulted in improved referee standards in the National Basketball Association.

Dave Winer, often called the father of the blog, related a horror story to us about *The Guardian*, a London-based newspaper that published an article involving syndication by a reporter who had been part of the story. Winer said the reporter quoted himself as an "observer" and failed to disclose his involvement. When Winer confronted the newspaper's management charging inaccurate, prejudicial, and misleading journalism, he said the editors turned a deaf ear. Although blogging's father did not start blogging to bypass the press, he has long been quick to express frustrations with the way he has been covered.

The executives we interviewed indicated, in one way or another, that blogging was among their top priorities. Cuban kept posting even as his team entered a tense playoff season. Lutz was embroiled in controversies following the company's loss of $1.1 billion, the reduction of his responsibilities, and an advertising boycott of the *Los Angeles Times*. Amid all that, Lutz not only took

---

[1] http://fastlane.gmblogs.com
[2] http://www.blogmaverick.com/entry/1234000340034879

time to answer people's questions, but kept blogging after only a four-day hiatus. He posted a three-part series called "The Sun Keeps Coming Up," which started with "Every so often, we all have to do a bit of a sense check, just to make sure that the sun will indeed rise tomorrow. And, amidst all of the gloom and doom surrounding GM lately, I'd like to give yet another alternative viewpoint." He then posted a series about new GM cars that excite him, even as some newspapers hinted that the controversial executive would step down.

The press was also reading his blog. As his postings increased in frequency, the editorial speculation about his imminent departure steadily diminished.

Each executive treats blogging a little differently. Each came to it through a different route, and each represents a diverse culture. At this level, these guys do not waste time. Each obviously sees the value in taking the time to post and, to varying degrees, to join in on conversations. In each case, direct access to audiences is a key motivational element.

GM in the FastLane

At our deadline, Bob Lutz was the only Fortune 10 boardroom executive who was blogging. His goal, he said, is to "engage the public regarding our products and services. The blog has become an important, unfiltered (emphasis on 'unfiltered') voice. Now we have . . . a direct line of communication. [The blog] has become indispensable."

That direct line was being well used when we interviewed Lutz. At the time, GM had just announced it would cut off advertising to the *Los Angeles Times*, the largest newspaper west of the Mississippi. Gary Grates, a GM Communications vice president, took to FastLane to argue GM's case in persuasive terms. The comments there, which appeared to be unfiltered, were overwhelmingly supportive of the GM position. In fact, at least one member of the automotive press had chimed in with supporting comments on the blog.

Lutz declined to discuss the *LA Times* incident specifically, but much of what he had to say seemed relevant to it. He told us, "Blogs can be . . . an equalizing force when dealing with media criticism. It is fantastic because blogging is a self-regulating media."

He declined to broadside the media in general, saying that "There certainly are knowledgeable journalists in the media, who—on balance—report fairly and only after having carefully checked their facts. Regrettably, many others feel compelled to jump on the bandwagon all too easily, taking hearsay and superficial impressions for factual evidence and often coming to the wrong conclusions. That can be very damaging to the business. Recently, a negative article was published declaring one of our vehicles a flop. Within a few days, a third-party blogger analyzed the article and discredited it with the facts."

Direct access, Lutz emphasizes, is a larger issue than just bypassing unsupportive reporters. According to Lutz, his blog has started to chip through the crust of GM's stodgy image by demonstrating some passion in corporate leadership and "a willingness to listen to everyday people."

"Anyone who calls us averse to criticism or thin-skinned obviously has not read the blog," Lutz told us. He said that FastLane shows that GM's leadership advocates an "honest, transparent culture." Communicating with us during highly adverse times, the vice chairman noted that readers have been a source of encouragement, and reviewing hundreds of comments would indicate that is indeed the case. "It shows how much passion people have for cars and trucks. It also serves as a reminder how many people are pulling for GM. It's terrific." He added that comments are a "source for ideas that could impact new cars" although he served up no examples.

Lutz uses staff to manage the enormous flow of comments. They send him email digests that eliminate some redundancy, but they don't censor the negative comments. The highly mobile executive peruses the summaries in airports and in-flight through his trusty BlackBerry handheld computer. He finds the comments "fascinating."

The blogging community sometimes admonishes Lutz for answering comments in a group posting rather than joining in on direct conversations. Still others complain that Lutz never links to other bloggers, and he admits that he simply doesn't have time to hang out in the blogosphere with developers and other groups. Some say that the lack of interactivity removes the authenticity from the conversation.

We think otherwise. Lutz demonstrates transparency and a desire to listen. His language may sound more corporate than Blake Ross at SpreadFirefox, for example, but Lutz *is* more corporate than your everyday developer. To most people, he comes across as both transparent and authentic, two essentials for successful blogging. Lutz also scores highly on the two most fundamental rules for blogging about a subject: passion and authority.

Lutz's breach of perceived blogosphere "rules" demonstrates the inevitable fact that blogging, as it enters corporations, will adapt to corporate cultures without bastardizing the essentials. Lutz sounds corporate enough, but he doesn't use corpspeak. We can't picture him getting help from a ghostwriter, and his occasional typos and grammar gaffes give the reader a sense of an intelligent executive writing in a hurry.

And he is a guy in a hurry. Yet he takes the time to blog even during the busiest of times. Direct access is what makes this investment worthwhile.

Moving the Whole Damned Compass

Sun's Schwartz, by contrast, immerses himself deeply into the blogosphere. He has good reason to do so. It's where tech developers and financial analysts hang out—two primary audiences at Sun. He started his Jonathan Schwartz Weblog[3] in 2004, two months after becoming president of Sun Microsystems.

We asked Schwartz how he became so adept. "I type fast and I talk a lot. Good bloggers are chatty and are into relationships." The blogosphere lets him hang out where he can meet people good for Sun. "When I started seeing who was reading me I was stunned. It was our customers and the analysts. Everywhere I go, more and more people tell me they are reading my blogs."

He asked rhetorically, "What are my other options to reach developers? Take out a *LinuxWorld* ad? My readership is bigger than theirs is."

Schwartz made blogging a Sun strategic initiative, encouraging other employees to join in. Less than a year later, more than 1,000 of Sun's 32,000 employees were blogging, making it, by percentage, the "bloggingest" of all companies. Schwartz argues that having so many employee nodes into the blogging network is a key reason the company is experiencing "such a strong turnaround in developer relations." We asked if blogging had really moved the needle. "It's moved the whole damned compass," he retorted.

Schwartz's posted musings usually relate to Sun, but they include whatever he feels like saying. One blog started by discussing his son's haircut, meandered through a Zen reference, and then explained that Sun had made a mistake by installing sidewalks before observing routes taken by employees, who often strayed from walkways. "Sun's culture encourages people to cut their own paths," he observed. This is an important point to communicate, he

---

[3] http://blogs.sun.com/roller/page/jonathan

feels. "We are in a global war for talent. We have to prove we are a more vibrant, interesting, and open company. These blogs reflect the quality of the people and that's the quality of the company."

Schwartz not only blogs several times per week and sometimes per day, but he spends time being part of the blogosphere. "It's a community of communities. I recently had breakfast with Dave Winer. What do we have in common? We both blog." Much more than Lutz, Schwartz sees the blogosphere as an immersive place for Sun. A key to the company's comeback attempt depends on building open-source developer support for Sun's Solaris 10 operating system, which is the vital component to Sun's strategic alliance with Google.

He has predicted that in the near future all software will be free and that surviving companies will need to move the value away from traditional delivery of a piece of software. This is a popular position in the blogosphere and a forecast that, if proven true, could eventually push competitor Microsoft off its seat of control.

Both blogging and open source, in his eyes, are part of a new "Participation Age." We asked him what blogging's role will be in this new era. "It's kerosene on the fire," he said. "The Participation Age has been on the Net since e-mail. Moving from there to blogging is like moving from carrier pigeon to phone. The emergence of blogs means we have passed beyond early crude tools and it results in fundamental changes on how everything relates."

Unlike other executives we asked, Schwartz voices respect for journalists and the editorial process. Still, he lauds the benefits of direct access. He became president in April 2004, when the company was at a nadir in relationships with critical developer and analyst audiences

While many executive bloggers discuss blogs as a way to bypass journalists and thus gain direct access to audiences, Schwartz extols the value of conventional journalism. Journalists "are there because they are independent thinkers who provide fresh insights. Like the rest of us, they may get a fact or two wrong from time to time. But that's not the point. Journalists can jump off the rail that companies are on and take the conversation to points that interest audiences more than corporate spokespeople do. That adds value even if they get a few facts wrong."

From his perspective, blogging's advantage is in its "transparency and authenticity." More than 1,000 Sun bloggers give people outside the company multiple views inside it and an authentic view of the company culture from

the rank-and-file up to Schwartz himself. Schwartz argued that SEC requirements for quarterly reporting are not nearly as revealing as this horde of bloggers talking daily and in public about the guts of the company. "[These
perspectives] are infinitely more valuable than Federal governance regulations. Executives are missing a point. There is no perfect truth despite transparency."

Unlike what we heard at Microsoft, there was no ambivalence about blogging at Sun. Legal never stepped in to assess or fret about risk, and the corporate communications people embraced it from the start, according to
Schwartz. "Most PR teams would cringe, but ours didn't. We have a transparent culture and competitors like HP do not. Our PR team is thinking about
how to use technology and culture as a corporate weapon and blogging does
both." Noel Hartzell, executive communications director for Schwartz, added
that Sun's focus is in building communities and "a key function of the communications team is to be an information gatherer, analyzer and counselor on
participating in these communities. A bad way to do PR is to blast press
releases every Thursday. We help feed the right information into the right
channels. What could be better for a PR organization than blogs?"

Schwartz sees blogging as a watershed bidirectional change:

> I don't read blogs—I read. Blogs are more searchable.
> Technorati and PubSub are more useful to me than Google. It's
> easier for me to connect in a blog-based world. People in
> Morocco and Australia have input into how we grow. I graze
> Sun's blogs and read the comments. If a developer has a percep-
> tion . . . that's valuable, I know about it fast. We get all kinds
> of helpful comments. I just read a comment from a developer in
> Portugal, who thinks we're the bee's knees. It's terrific to see
> that kind of stuff.

Rivals also watch Sun's postings. One competitor we know, speaking off the
record, told us, "We had counted Sun out. We assumed by now they would
be dead or irrelevant. They're back. It's their [expletive deleted] blogs. We just
went into a customer meeting and they were asking us about some stuff that
[Sun Developer] Tim Bray had posted that morning."

Schwartz often tweaks competitive noses, sometimes playfully, occasionally
with vitriol. He recently made direct appeals to the HP customer community

after HP announced a barrage of bad news. He once posted an open letter to IBM's Sam Palmisano in which he chided the chairman and CEO for not supporting a Solaris upgrade, charging that IBM was preventing its customers access to the "most secure operating system available." He knew full well that the letter would do little to endear him to Big Blue. But it was a clever ruse to bypass the company and appeal directly to IBM customers, who rallied to Sun's cause. "Now IBM is much more accommodating," he deadpanned.

Like other bloggers, Schwartz takes risks and gets personal from time to time and, like many bloggers, he finds his foot in an occasional bucket. He once confessed to enjoying kangaroo meat on a trip to Australia, entreating readers not to tell his kids. A while back, a Sun executive sent him a link to a Japanese company that promised blogging would "enhance your physique." Schwartz thought it was "funny, human and culturally interesting." He did a quick post. Later, alarmed colleagues rushed to inform him that had he looked closer, he would have seen some graphically explicit enhanced physiques on the site.

According to Schwartz, "The perception of Sun as a faithful and authentic tech company is now very strong. What blogs have done has authenticated the Sun brand better than a billion dollar ad campaign could have done. I care more about the ink you get from the developer community than any other coverage. Sun has experienced a sea change in their perception of us and that has come from blogs. Everyone blogging at Sun is verifying that we possess a culture of tenacity and authenticity."

Maverick Blogger

When he was 12, Mark Cuban started his first business—selling garbage bags door to door in a working-class Pittsburgh neighborhood. In the 1980s, like so many entrepreneurs, he found his way into the computer industry. He started MicroSolutions, a consulting firm, which he sold to CompuServe in 1990, making him a millionaire. But he was just hitting his stride. Living in Dallas, he wanted to listen to basketball games from his alma mater Indiana University and could not. To solve the problem, he co-founded broadcast.com, a pioneer Internet radio and TV service that showed enough promise to go public. The company was not profitable, but that didn't matter. Yahoo! acquired broadcast.com in 1999, and Cuban became a billionaire. To celebrate, he bought a huge home and, for a mere $285 million, purchased the

Dallas Mavericks, one of the most consistently mediocre teams in the NBA. He invested heavily in the talent to transform the team into the contender, which it has become. Cuban also became the team's most visible and demonstrative fan. As a consequence, he has ponied up more than $1 million in fines for in-your-face courtside antics with referees, and the TV cameras have caught him sharing chest thumps with team members. He once said the head of NBA referees "couldn't manage a Dairy Queen." Then, so as not to offend Dairy Queen managers, he spent a day working in one.

When not clashing with referees, Cuban lets off steam duking it out with the press. His aforementioned duke-out with ABC's Gray is but one example.

His blog is free-ranging and free-swinging, as are his interests. A co-founder of HDNET, which produced "Enron, the Smartest Guys in the Room" and "Good Night and Good Luck," both critically acclaimed and commercially successful, he takes on Hollywood copyright goblins and speculates on the death of CDs as well as Wall Street's naked stock shorters and whatever else catches either his enthusiasm or provokes his chagrin. Cuban did not comment on whether or not this was a wise course for a blogger. He says he does it because he has the freedom to do so.

He told us he blogs about whatever is on his mind about any subject he thinks is important. He started posting "primarily in response to the media," giving us the *Fortune* magazine incident as but one example. He thinks the blog and the Internet have given him the tools to offset what the press has to say about him and his team. He says executives should blog, but only "if they have a vision they are trying to communicate, or if they are very visible in the media."

"I think that any reporter or columnist will be a little more careful when doing interviews with me, specifically, because I do 99 percent of my interviews now via e-mail, so I have a paper trail that is ready and available to be revealed on my blog," he told us. He recently used that record, with lethal effect, to respond to a *New York Times* article he considered unfair.

Cuban doesn't believe that his BlogMaverick[4] has done much to geographically extend his fan base, and he hasn't used it for that purpose. However, we know people in New England, New Orleans, the San Francisco Bay area, the United Kingdom, and Singapore who say they now follow the Mavs because they follow Cuban's blog and it is part of what makes the Mavs a very colorful franchise. Likewise, the franchise staff reads the blog to see what's on the

---

[4] http://www.blogmaverick.com

boss's mind, but he adds, "It's not a management tool of any sort." It seems to us that anything that tells the staff what the boss is thinking is a management tool—whether intended that way or not.

Where BlogMaverick has made a difference, he believes, is how referees behave. He says, "There's little doubt about it. The league handles officiating in a far more professional manner than prior to my arrival. They approach it like a real business unit now. They didn't in the past."

Where Cuban has taken a "maverick" view compared to other executive bloggers is on the issue of employee blog policy. While other executives inter-viewed for this book encouraged company blogging, Cuban does not. He advises executives considering a blog to "make sure you are the boss. I don't think I would encourage executives who work for me to blog. There can be only one public vision for an organization. . . . The boss and subordinates don't always see eye-to-eye and having more than one message going out via blogs can be very counter-productive."

When we posted this interview on our *Naked Conversations* blog we used in writing this book, this comment drew fire. "He misses the whole point," huffed one commenter. "His idea is that his blog is a big stick that he can use to poke the media. That's a petty point of view," observed Microsoft blogger Randy Holloway. "In my humble opinion, this kind of forced hierarchy is counter-productive and artificial," wrote Michael Hyatt, CEO of Thomas Nelson, the ninth largest publisher, according to its web site. "Man would I pass on working for this guy," wrote freelance journalist-editor Curt Hopkins, whose credits include *Newsweek* and Reuters. "I hope you cite Cuban as a bad or misguided example for blogging."

We are not going to cite him as advised. While we prefer Cuban's policy to be otherwise, he is someone who has always been interesting because he makes his own rules. We find his blog consistently interesting.

Bypassing Media Mythology

Dave Winer's style is the antithesis of the stereotypical corporate CEO, but for many years he was head of the innovative software company UserLand. His confrontational style is legendary and not always well received. We've heard him described as an "iconoclast," "curmudgeon," and "annoyingly cantan-kerous." Yet those same people admire Winer's brilliance and hold reverence to his pioneer roles in the births of both blogs and RSS syndication.

We include him here because his antipathy toward the press is also legendary. The press has written that his desire to bypass the media motivated him to invent blogs. Those accounts, he said, are but another example of why he holds the press in low esteem. "I did not start blogging to get around the press. That is yet another example of the press not letting a few facts get in the way of telling a good story. The press reports mythology, not facts."

According to Winer, the truth is that his discovery of the power of blogs is less dramatic and more one of accidental discovery. He was working on a collaborative project called *24 Hours in Democracy* while serving as an editor for the online version of *Wired* magazine. He was enmeshed in this massive national project with a huge number of moving parts, "Sort of a tech-sector moon mission," he recalled. "I needed a way to organize the web site and started putting things in reverse chronological order with links to other sources. I thought: this is way cool. I think I'll come back to this approach after this project is over and check it out some more."

He had been publishing DaveNet, an e-newsletter with a significant following in the technology community since the early 1990s. In his view, DaveNet was in essence already a blog because it was him speaking in his own voice about whatever interested him. But spam had pulverized e-mail as a distribution mechanism, so Winer turned to a new medium—personal web sites, where he created Scripting News.[5] He played with the reverse chronological order that is now standard blog format, and it worked well. Distribution, however, remained a problem. E-mail was tainted, but making people visit a web site was awkward. His followers couldn't tell when he had updates, so they had to keep going online and looking, which was time consuming.

He started tinkering with some enabling software called XML as a way to "syndicate" his web site postings, coding a few new features into what would become RSS (Really Simple Syndication). He made the format more applicable to blogs and added it to Scripting News so people could "subscribe" to his site and have his postings delivered to special folders in their e-mail software. This would make reading these personal weblogs much more efficient than surfing the web. The average computer user could stay current on more than a hundred RSS-enabled sites rather than 10–12 web sites. (Some "super readers" like co-author Scoble actually follow more than 1,000 RSS feeds.) Such efficiency bordered on the revolutionary. Also important, RSS was a "clean"

---

[5] http://archive.scripting.com

way to deliver to e-mail—without spam. These features made Scripting News the first real weblog in both form and substance.

Probably by coincidence, Netscape was also playing with XML at the same time and even had its own RSS, although Netscape claimed it stood for RDF Site Summary. What happened next depends on whom you ask. It was clear that Winer and the Netscape people shared a caustic chemistry. Many reports of what happened have been unfavorable to Winer. In his version however, Netscape contacted him for a sit-down, at which Netscape refused to change its version. "I got angry. 'Why don't we just both do it the same way?' I asked. It's infinitely better to have one way to do it rather than two. I went for a walk and thought it over, and said 'Okay, why don't I throw out what I've done.' I took their format and changed mine to match it." Then, Netscape made some changes to incorporate some features unique to Winer's version. This awkward collaboration resulted in RSS 2.0, a single standard generally accepted by users.

This collaboration gave Winer the direct voice he wanted, and he set a tone that has also shaped the blogosphere. He thinks blogs should represent "the unedited voice of an individual. It's not an organization speaking. It's informal. It's 'Come as you are. We're just folks here. We're not concerned with typos or grammar errors,' which remind readers that it's just a human speaking." Winer would argue that this informal style has far greater appeal than the more polished stuff of corporate communications teams. "I don't like sterile, politically correct writing. I like writing that stimulates ideas and new thinking."

He also loves writing to bypass the press. He has written at length and with chagrin about the way the media have condensed and misquoted him. He told us that nearly every article he has seen on podcasting (audio blogs) has been erroneous, that nearly all articles regarding his early role are "spun in the most dramatic way possible," and that the media do not like having done to them what they do to others.

"They don't want the light shone on themselves, which is ironic because journalists are experts at shining the light on others. . . . This is why we have blogs. We have blogs because we can't trust these guys," he told us.

Winer also believes his blog is an incredible research vehicle, giving him direct access to people who write the source material on all sorts of topics. If he has a question, particularly a technical one, he asks it on his blog and says it gets answered in about five minutes. "These guys just swarm. They love showing off. It's really cool. Sometimes showing off is the generous thing to do." However, he added:

> *The hard part is when I make a mistake. What you really have*
> *to do is say [on your blog], "I made a mistake." I don't always*
> *agree when people say I made a mistake and it sometimes gets*
> *flamey, but you have to take each one seriously. There's a check*
> *and a balance. The press is now in this flow whether they*
> *accept or appreciate it or not. Their words and expressions are*
> *now part of this flow. And they often don't like it. Bloggers are*
> *a very big group. There are millions of us and we are looking*
> *very carefully at what they [journalists] do.*

He added, "You certainly need a blog to bypass the press. Without blogs we could not connect people together where everyone gets a chance to speak. You can get things done with blogs you can't with the press, who tend to believe that you need to work inside a big company to have an answer."

We asked him what he thought about executive bloggers. He told us, "It's going to be a long time before every executive is blogging. I'd love it if it happened faster. That would mean we created an upheaval in the way things are and the way organizations work. Certainly, a company that has an exec who blogs is going to be seen as more approachable and customers will want to buy more products. Company bloggers will have a better idea of what's happening and [will] make decisions that will make the company more profitable because of their interaction with the blogging community."

Winer is more interested in people who blog than in companies who blog. "The act of creativity—only a person can do it, a company cannot," he concluded.

Doing It in Private

Direct access is larger than bypassing the press or even your own communications organizations. One of the most interesting is one where the blogger would prefer we didn't know about what he's doing. Intel CEO Paul Otellini writes Paul's Blog to talk with and listen to 86,000 employees worldwide, privately, from behind a firewall. This is a different form of direct access, and employees are unquestionably a key constituency for a global CEO. There are also some risks, he discovered, in sharing your innermost thoughts with 86,000 professional colleagues.

"Why am I doing this?" he wrote in his first post in December 2004. "Well, it seemed like a good idea to be able to create an ongoing vehicle to share my thoughts and observations on Intel and our industry with our employees and to allow you an opportunity to have a platform for your thoughts or responses." And respond they do. In reviewing two months of posting, we got to see numerous responses to Otellini's comments. All were polite, but several were challenging and served up some dissent.

Otellini first agreed to discuss Paul's Blog with us, but then declined. A company spokesperson told us, "All things considered, it is a private blog and he prefers to keep it private." How does one do that? Perhaps that's impossible. The postings we read came from an unauthorized article in the *San Jose Mercury News*.

But so far, that has been the only breach. His predecessor, Craig Barrett, wrote an executive newsletter to employees that was also characterized as "confidential." It was leaked so often that observers began to believe it was intentionally being used for that purpose. We find it encouraging that there has been but a single violation for Otellini after nearly a year. If building a trusted network for direct sharing and challenging of ideas was his object, we would have to say it appears he's achieving it.

Private collaboration makes up a significant portion of business blogging. Anil Dash, vice president of business development for blog authoring company Six Apart, estimated in July 2005 that 32 percent of its customers had private blogs and that the total number of private bloggers has increased by 500 percent in 18 months. But Six Apart doesn't know how many of these are business users and how many are individuals using it for family photo albums or planning reunions. Nor did he have access to the actual number of bloggers. "Frankly, we are too young a company to have this kind of data. We just know that private blogs are big and growing fast," he told us.

Other companies using private blogs include IBM, where there are reportedly more than 3,000 internal blogs used for collaboration. Corporate Blogging,[6] the Dutch blog, reports that at Holland-based Macaw, "all employees have their own internal blog. They get it when they get their network, intranet, and e-mail accounts. Not only do they have blogs—they use them. Ninety percent of the 110 employees are internal bloggers." At Six Apart, all

---

[6] http://www.corporateblogging.info/2005/04/company-where-all-110-employees-have.asp

new employees get a blog, and then they are aggregated into a master blog that lets all employees track conversations that interest them. Disney Studios reportedly is a heavy user of collaborative private blogs. Even the U.S. Department of Homeland Security is alleged to use a private blog in the western United States as the speediest form of information sharing.

Not all of us, however, have the problems of NBA team owners and GM boardroom executives. We don't have a trail of reporters following us around, getting our words and thoughts either right or wrong. But people in business need direct access to audiences. And when companies of all sizes post, or just get mentioned in the blogosphere, it often becomes the shortest route to media coverage as well.

In fact, direct access may surprise you into discovering you have given an accidental interview. Blogger-marketing consultant BL Ochman[7] pointed out the new phenomenon of the "stealth interview." It seems some editors have taken to following blogs, extracting quotes from them, and then reporting a story as if they actually had conducted interviews with people whom they had never contacted.

Unless you work for a private or public intelligence operation such as Homeland Security or have a job couched in enormous privacy, or have a company whose behavior is unethical, chances are likely you will benefit from direct conversations not couched in terms devised by committees of lawyers and marketing consultants.

Most companies, of all sizes, will be wise to follow Winer's advice: "Come as you are." Talk as you talk. Let people who matter get to know you through a blog and listen closely to what they tell you.

---

[7] http://www.whatsnextblog.com/archives/2005/04/misquoted_in_th_1.asp

5 Little Companies, Long Reach

"A small key opens big doors."

—*Turkish proverb*

The famous people interviewed in the preceding chapter are very different from most of us. Unless this book fares infinitely better than we imagine, we anticipate no pack of journalists trailing us around eager to quote or misquote whatever we say. For those of us who have businesses that are less than globally monolithic, blogging is our best option to have our own words heard worldwide. It also gives us the opportunity to listen to people we might not otherwise have met.

Whereas Mark Cuban and Bob Lutz have the luxury of choosing to bypass the press by blogging, most people in business have trouble getting their names in the newspaper to begin with, and their budgets often cover little more than Yellow Pages ads. Blogging gives such small businesses global reach at extremely low cost.

Even though this chapter's title speaks of "little companies," some blogging companies discussed here are far from tiny; they are well-established and branded entities with multimillion dollar budgets. We include them because they are not global powerhouses, and they face the uphill challenges of building larger and more loyal user bases. Stonyfield Farm is the world's largest organic yogurt maker, and the Fellowship Church is among the five largest independent churches in the United States. Still, they are not generally considered household names.

Researching this chapter was one of our favorite parts of writing *Naked Conversations*. We have a special place in our hearts for the chutzpa and resourcefulness of entrepreneurs—not just those involved in startups, but people in all sorts and sizes of businesses who demonstrate passionate ingenuity. We think the companies discussed here illustrate the power of blogging as a communications channel.

The Man Makes the Clothes

Thomas Mahon and Hugh MacLeod were bending elbows (in a London pub) together and commiserating. Mahon was a tailor—not just an ordinary tailor, but a Savile Row tailor. Some, with finer wardrobes than our own, would tell you the artisans of that particular street make the world's finest suits. But in Europe, as in the United States, the demand for custom suits costing as much as $4,000 was at a global nadir in late 2004 when this drinking debauchery took place. Worse, the office rent on this fabled London street was steadily rising through the well-maintained roof.

MacLeod was no tailor. He was an ex–advertising executive who had grown cold to the work and cultures of ad agencies. Of late, his creativity had been channeled into edgy ink cartoons that mostly made fun of the ad culture from whence he came. His living was derived, in part, from selling edgy, expletive-riddled cartoons in books, on t-shirts, and on the back sides of business cards. Admirers followed him through his popular Gapingvoid blog,[1] where he posted his ink-drawn cartoons and commentary.

Mahon and MacLeod shared two affinities: the aforementioned bending of elbows and the need to enhance their income. Said MacLeod, "Thomas wasn't interested in blogs and I wasn't interested in suits I could not afford." The idea for a blog displaying the passion and authority required to make some of the world's finest suits "sort of started by accident," MacLeod told us. "We didn't have a vision or anything like that." But, over drinks, MacLeod started filling Mahon's head with "*Cluetrain* and blogging stuff," and slowly Mahon got interested. They formed a partnership. Mahon would make the suits. MacLeod would sell them. Mahon would blog about what he knew. Hugh would coach him and use his blog juice to direct traffic to the new blog.

---

[1] http://www.gapingvoid.com

Mahon, wisely, didn't try to sell suits on the new blog. Instead, he showed his knowledge and love of the craft. He explained the labor and why the cost was justified. Hugh assured him that people who cared would find the site. Mahon entered his first post in his new blog, English Cut,[2] in January 2005. By April, hundreds of bloggers had written about and linked to English Cut.

In the entire world, we would guess there are perhaps 10,000 people with both money and desire for Savile Row suits. They reside in diverse, fashionable locations, often thousands of miles away from Savile Row, yet Mahon faces the economics of a local merchant. His ad budget might cover a phone book insertion, but little more. His business has been built mostly by word of mouth, and he has long been traveling to New York City a few times each year, in part because he likes Manhattan and in part to serve a smattering of American clients. If he sells two suits each time he goes, the sales pay for the trip. If he sells three, he eats and gets to pay rent. A five-suit trip is a bonanza. When Mahon was in New York in December 2004, he sold only two. When he returned 10 weeks after starting a blog, he sold 20 suits and eight sport coats, more than he had sold before in an entire year.

But more than that happened on his latest New York City visit. Via blogging, MacLeod had become e-mail buddies with David Parmet,[3] a career public relations consultant who had found himself unemployed after pushing too hard to get his agency to include blog-related services. MacLeod had posted about his situation on Gapingvoid under the headline: "Would somebody please hire this guy?" Then, recalled MacLeod, "I just asked David out of the blue if he would fancy trying his hand at generating PR for English Cut." Parmet might have resisted, but he had a secret soft spot. "I had always had a thing for Savile Row suits, ever since I saw Bryan Ferry wearing them on MTV." Parmet signed on after learning that Mahon had been Ferry's suit-maker. By e-mail, he committed to escorting the British tailor, whom he had never met or spoken with, to meet several senior editors at some of the world's most influential media companies. In return, Mahon would compensate him, not with dollars or pounds sterling, but with a classic, well-fitting suit that perhaps he could wear to his next job interview.

Why would Parmet, a seasoned pro, take such a risk? He was unemployed, but not yet desperate. He knew that his real customer was not the client but the editor, and he was hanging his credibility on the line for someone he had

---

[2] http://www.englishcut.com

[3] http://www.parmet.net

never even met. "Perhaps through blogging, we had built a mutual trust for each other. When Thomas and I finally met, it didn't take long before we felt we were old friends," recollected Parmet. It turned out to be a risk worth taking.

The media loved the story. CNN did a magazine piece in May 2005 and the Sunday *New York Times* magazine section covered English Cut in September 2005. This media coverage extended Mahon's position as the world's most famous Savile Row tailor, but the blog had already achieved that in its first few months. For Mahon, his blog opened doors where previously there had only been walls. Measuring from one New York trip to the next, English Cut had increased Mahon's business by at least 300 percent in less than 10 weeks. In Manhattan it had increased by nearly fifteen-fold.

Mahon is an example of a local merchant gaining global reach through blogging. He speculates he could now go to any major city in the world and be known well enough to sell a fair quantity of elite threads. All he has to do is post that he will be in a certain city at a particular time and the customers will find him. It's still a word-of-mouth business, but blogging has scaled it to global levels.

There are lessons for a great many local merchants in Mahon's story. Being first was essential to Mahon's success. Being the second blogging tailor may not be nearly as remarkable. Showing passion rather than salesmanship was also essential. Blogs such as Mahon's, like some ad campaigns, may have limited time in the spotlight. We are already seeing evidence that the excitement and novelty of Mahon's blog have leveled off from the original excitement it generated.

It doesn't matter. Thanks to blogging and a resourceful drinking companion, Thomas Mahon today is the world's best-known Savile Row tailor. And thanks to the increasing number of inbound links, the site continues to improve its rankings on search engines.

The Connection King

Every industry has them, and you probably know a few in your own sector. They are professional connectors, people who know everyone and have their finger on the pulse of what's happening. They help people find jobs, make deals, and form partnerships. They know about new products and services before they're publicly introduced.

In blogging, ActiveWords CEO Buzz Bruggeman is the Connection King.

Everyone who has met him understands why he's called Buzz, and perhaps the term "buzz marketing" was named after him. At conferences, he works the room like a political candidate. He keeps an ongoing e-mail dialogue with scores of people, each influential in some way or in need of a favor. He totes a bag filled with early versions of the latest gizmos, which he hands out generously. Bruggeman connected the authors of this book, played a key role in inspiring Dan Gillmor to write *We the Media*, and was probably quoted as an "informed source" in an article you recently read.

In short, when you really want to know what's going on in the PC industry, Buzz Bruggeman is the go-to guy.

Although he's generous by nature, he's hardly the Mother Teresa type. There's strategy and just a touch of reciprocity involved. ActiveWords is a highly regarded software utility company whose product gives users neat little navigational shortcuts to measurably increase productivity. The company reports 100,000 downloads from its site on a six-year marketing budget of less than $15,000. Blogging, Bruggeman thinks, played a role in about half the downloads. As with English Cut, blogging has been fundamental for ActiveWords in facilitating an impressive quantity of national press clips including the *New York Times, Business 2.0, PC Magazine,* and *PC World.* Bruggeman also reports that blogging has significantly contributed to landing a couple of company-changing deals.

But Bruggeman, by his own estimation, is no uber-blogger. He posts to his two sites a few times a week, not per hour as do leading denizens like Doc Searls.[4] Searls has described Bruggeman as a "C+ blogger and an A+ blog reader," a description Bruggeman finds apt.

Our point in discussing Bruggeman here is to demonstrate that you don't need to spend your life posting and answering comments for blogging to help your company.

Bruggeman found the blogosphere because he had to. A few years back, he realized that ActiveWords didn't know much about marketing software, and he "decided we'd better figure that out fast." The company needed press coverage, particularly product reviews, but it had no money for a PR agency or marketing staff. So Bruggeman, a former lawyer, decided to become company evangelist. But try as he might, it was excruciatingly difficult to get traditional journalists to listen to him. Cold calls to business editors got colder receptions,

---

[4] http://doc.weblogs.com

if any at all. E-mailing product editors in an attempt to get them to download only got his correspondence relegated to junk mail folders.

Bruggeman represented a promising new company with a useful product, but he was an outsider to the somewhat insulated tech influencer community. He kept circling the perimeter looking for an entry point, but couldn't find one. He started attending tech conferences and hanging out where he could be closer to people who could make a difference for ActiveWords.

Then blogging came along, and he was struck by differences. "In the traditional media, I couldn't easily get to the guy who wrote the article, but I could get to the most influential bloggers. When I reached out to Doc Searls and Dan Gillmor,[5] they responded." He shifted his company's focus over to the blogosphere. "People have an incredible desire to create and be heard and have a voice and blogging gave it to them," said Bruggeman. He built relationships by figuring out what everyone's passion was. He funneled material on subjects that interested each blogger. On Searls's advice, he started Buzzmodo,[6] his business blog. He often found reasons to link to better-known bloggers.

Bruggeman found his way into the center ring in April 2002. As Gillmor recalled in his book *We the Media*,[7] Qwest CEO Joe Nacchio was on the dais at the prestigious PC Forum, a tech industry executive conference. Gillmor wrote that Nacchio was complaining about difficulties in raising capital. Searls and Gillmor were blogging on it in near-real-time from the audience, and neither was impressed. Then these two A-list bloggers received e-mail from Bruggeman in Florida within minutes of their original postings. Bruggeman linked a Yahoo! Finance web page showing that Nacchio had cashed in more than $200 million in stock even as his company's stock price headed downhill under his stewardship. "I immediately dropped this juicy tidbit into my weblog with a cyber-tip of the hat to Bruggeman and Searls did likewise," wrote Gillmor. The event's host, Esther Dyson, would later write that "around this point, the audience turned hostile." Apparently, attendees were following the two bloggers. Sitting 2,000 miles away, Bruggeman had altered the course of an elite private event and damaged the future of a CEO he had never met. Nacchio was already in trouble with his job, but after PC Forum, he found an edgier and more hostile press and not long afterward was ousted. Gillmor wrote that he considered the event watershed to his own understanding of blogging's power.

---

[5] http://bayosphere.com/blog/dangillmor

[6] http://buzzmodo.typepad.com

[7] http://wethemedia.oreilly.com

Later that year Bruggeman teamed up with author-blogger J.D. Lasica to cover another tech conference called PopTech. Both had ulterior motives. J.D. was interested in interviewing speakers for his book *Darknet: Hollywood's War Against the Digital Generation,*[8] and Bruggeman wanted to get a free pass into the conference. Both got what they wanted, but the blog itself surprised them. "Every time we posted, we'd get about 200 hits, two-thirds from people outside the conference. We realized we were extending the reach and participation of the conference."

Today in the tech sector, most events are covered by blogs. While a couple of years back bloggers had to pay to get in, now they are being pitched by conference producers to attend. More than traditional journalists, bloggers change an event by participating, adding global reach and input. We imagine that in a short while other events in other industries will start being blogged as well.

Bruggeman credits Jim McGee[9] with one of the best explanations to blogging's surprising power. Bloggers, according to McGee, are the agents that tech companies tried and failed to produce with artificial intelligence. Those agents were supposed to go and fetch useful information and retrieve precisely what users wanted, but the stuff never worked, in part because computers lack common sense. Bloggers have become the intelligent agents. They have common sense and add knowledge of their own. They run around the Internet and the real world finding all sorts of stuff and sharing it interactively through blogging.

This new generation of intelligent agents is willing to go to work for their fellow bloggers, as Winer mentioned when he discussed the instant answers he got to blog-posted questions. When Bruggeman posted his thoughts that Microsoft might never have intended its Outlook application program to serve as a third-party development platform, he received more than 20 comments from "some of the industry's smartest people, who piled on ideas of how the question I posed was right or wrong. Without a blog, I would never have had access to that kind of intelligent capital. It's like every blogger can hold an interactive symposium," he marveled.

Bruggeman has also learned to keep his oil and water separately contained. He used to mix his business commentary with impassioned, left-leaning political views. One day someone wrote in: "I love your product. I hate your

---

[8] http://www.darknet.com
[9] http://www.mcgeesmusings.net

politics and I will pray for you." Out of Buzzmodo, Bruggeman spun a new blog called Buzznovation[10] that gave him a venue to air his views, while keeping constructive and business-like tones on the other.

Like other successful bloggers, he avoids selling on his blog. "It just won't work and you lose credibility. People will be smart to avoid the temptation," he said. He mentions ActiveWords only in about one in four Buzznovation postings.

Amy Wohl,[11] who has been an information industry analyst and writer for more than 25 years, calls Bruggeman "the Energizer Bunny of the High Tech industry. Since I've met him, he's introduced me to more ideas and people than I can count. And I thought I had a huge Rolodex! I'm amazed that more entrepreneurs don't try to follow in his footsteps."

Naturally Curious People

The Dallas-based Fellowship Church was founded in 1990. Each weekend, about 20,000 people worship at 10 services. Fellowship obviously understands evangelism's power. Brian Bailey is the church's Internet manager. His evangelism has been of the technical variety, and the result is that Fellowship is rapidly adopting blogs in myriad ways to improve internal and external communications.

Bailey's blog, Leave it Behind,[12] covers much of the same "geeky" stuff you might find in Scobleizer. It's where he has particular passion and authority. Through blogging, he's become Scoble's friend, and like Scoble, he was first turned on to blogging by the ubiquitous influence of Dave Winer.

Bailey started Leave It Behind in April 2004, naming it for a U2 song about letting go in the here-and-now for the eternal. It's a personal blog, addressing diverse subjects. While devoted to Christianity, there's little discussion of it on his blog. "Preaching is not my calling," he told us.

Even so, Bailey has been spreading the word on the power of blogging for years, at first to ambivalent ears. He tried to start an internal knowledge-sharing blog back in 2001, but it was tabled, he quipped, because "the return on ministry wasn't yet clear." He started his blog quietly at first, not mentioning it to his boss, Terry Storch, Fellowship's chief operations and technology pastor. After all, it was not church-community directed. "I would be very

---

[10] http://buzzmodo.typepad.com/buzznovation

[11] http://amywohl.weblogger.com

[12] http://www.leaveitbehind.com

disappointed if all of my readers were Christ-followers. My goal is to gather a diverse group who enjoys being exposed to different thoughts," he told us. He said he is "obsessed" with finding commonalities between people.

But at Fellowship his tech evangelism has paid off bigtime. When Storch learned of Bailey's blog, he saw the value and started his own.[13] A year later, blogging was pervading just about every aspect of the church, according to Bailey. Blogs had been added to two of the four web sites that Bailey managed, and RSS syndication was being added to a good number of pages. There were a couple of departmental blogs, with an inter-departmental blog in the works. There were plans underway for blogs from the church to volunteers and from volunteers to each other; the list of other potential blogs was rapidly expanding. Nearly 20 church employees were blogging on a variety of subjects.

Christian evangelism is certainly among the primary objectives. "Our goal is to use every tool possible, including technology, to meet each person where they are. Fellowship is an intense, challenging, and infinitely creative organization that never loses sight of what's at stake," Bailey told us.

Except for a two-week hiatus, Bailey has posted at least once daily since he started, and he remains committed to maintaining the regimen. "The only way to prove the value of a weblog and see what the true impact would be was to dive in."

He sees three areas where blogs have impacted Fellowship:

- **Internal.** This is where the most dramatic change has occurred. Blogging has improved multiple communications levels. The church vision has added transparency to how ideas develop.
- **Personal.** Bailey feels that his blog has made him wiser by exposing him to new ideas. He has become better known and, by writing every day, more articulate. Like others, he says he's learned to listen better to people with opposing views.
- **Community.** The increased openness has given people a closer sense of connection with the church, whether they are members, "curious seekers, or leaders of other churches with whom we exchange ideas and advice."

Bailey believes blogs can be useful at multiple organizational levels. "I see weblogs as completely natural—a written transcript of the thoughts,

---

[13] http://www.terrystorch.com

conversations, ideas, mistakes, and victories taking place every day in every organization. What isn't natural is sharing that with the rest of the world."

Because the best blogs take risks, he advises, "Get out of your comfort zone. An organization must be willing to tolerate some mistakes and criticism, knowing that the risk is worth the innumerable benefits of open communication. Blogs encourage honest conversation within an organization, pushing both change and growth."

He advises companies to understand what blogs are and are not. "I don't think you can launch blogs as a new corporate initiative in the same way you introduce a new health plan. You need to locate the people in your organization who enjoy writing and have a passion for your product or service and want to be evangelists. How do you begin? My advice is to find the naturally curious people and let them start." As a result of our interview with Bailey, our publisher, John Wiley & Sons, contacted him. He and Storch have contracted to write *Blogging Church*, a book about the new technology in the Christian evangelical world.

Mr. Treo

Andrew Carton may be blogging his way out of the consulting business. He didn't intend it that way, but that's how it was heading when we interviewed him in May 2005. He had founded a consulting company specializing in digital entertainment convergence and had launched a successful business blog[14] as a platform to support his ideas in that area. He was doing quite well, but wanted to reach a broader consumer audience, when "I stumbled upon my Treo smartphone. This was my Eureka moment. I had some very specific ideas about the type of information that I thought was lacking elsewhere and that I wanted to develop." He wanted to make it fun, "not just about tech specs and no endless babbling on my life with Treo, but a destination where people could learn something while being entertained." So he started his Treonauts[15] blog, and out of it a standalone business is growing.

Treonauts grew quickly from a blog that initially had a few hundred daily visitors to average more than 160,000 unique visitors per month—nearly 10 percent of the number of Treo smartphone users worldwide. The blog name

---

[14] http://blog.alteraxion.com
[15] http://blog.treonauts.com

has become a user brand. Treo users worldwide have taken to calling themselves "treonauts." Many regard Carton's blog as the leading third-party source for information and analysis on the Treo. He is quoted just about everywhere that the smartphone is covered, despite the fact that palmOne and PalmSource, the companies that make the hardware and software, respectively, treat Treonauts as merely a fan site.

Equally rewarding may be the revenue Carton has generated. Treonauts partners with leading merchants, who have developed co-branded online stores in conjunction with the blog, one for software[16] and one for phones and accessories.[17] The revenue generated was only $50 in the first month, but more recently it's been as high as $20,000.

While Carton still runs his consulting business, he told us, "I am now almost entirely dedicating my time to Treonauts and the business of blogging. Both [are] endeavors which I plan to continue to be involved in for some time to come." Blogging has not only transformed his business, but his life, he said.

According to Loïc Le Meur, Six Apart's general manager and executive vice president for Europe, Africa, and the Middle East:

> Andrew is doing what Palm should have done for itself but wasn't bright enough to do. He gets 300,000 page views per month. He takes a neutral approach to Palm and writes with great accuracy. He asks people to vote on the features they want and to determine what should be in the next Treo. The Treo press turns to him more than anyone else for expertise. He has become Mr. Treo. This stuff threatens the brands because this guy has more followers than the brand site and more Google juice, and it's not mass marketing. What's the value of one guy who has all the customers on his blog? The Treo companies just don't get his enormous value.
>
> I am extremely private, and from the very beginning, one of the hardest things to do with the blog was to completely expose myself to the world. It felt a bit like standing naked on a podium at first.

It seems to us that his naked conversations are paying off.

---

[16] http://software.treonauts.com

[17] http://store.treonauts.com

From Kitchen to Nuclear Lab

It was one of those slap-yourself-on-the-forehead ideas—so simple you should have thought of it yourself, but you didn't. DL Byron, founder of Textura Design, Inc.,[18] actually did think of it and called it Clip-n-Seal.[19] If it's not yet in a retail store near you, chances are it will be soon. Byron fashioned a couple of pieces of plastic into a rod-and-clamp mechanism. Clip-n-Seal enables you to put two sheets of plastic around something—anything—and meld the plastic wrap to form an airtight seal around it.

In 2003, he started marketing it from his blog for the kitchen and for biking and hiking excursions. End users came, as he had hoped, but something else also happened. Other potential users found him, industrial users including hazardous waste and nuclear labs, Scuba, aerospace, dairy farms, body bags and organ donor deliveries, commercial coffee bean packaging, and a great deal more. Online distribution was bolstered when Amazon.com began offering the product. Brick-and-mortar specialty stores started stocking it on their shelves. When we interviewed Byron, he was in talks with Target, the number-two retail chain. Clip-n-Seal has gone well beyond the inventor's vision into industrial applications. In two years, the company has shipped more than 40,000 units all over the world, at a retail price of $4.95 per unit.

According to Byron, as the company grows in adoption, markets, products, and brand, it may need to stretch beyond the blogosphere, even though blogging has built it to what it is today. "New markets came to us" because of blogging, he said, and those industrial applications have changed the business. The company now uses innovative marketing to attract more commercial customers. Textura Design is currently running an industrial design application contest for Clip-n-Seal and has changed the wording on some of its Google ads to address industrial audiences. But, Byron added, "I doubt any of our industrial customers care that we have a blog or even know what that is. What's important is that they could find us, they got to know us on the site, and our product meets their needs. It's not about the blog. It's about the product."

Byron sees the day when Clip-n-Seal may have to turn to traditional advertising to reach prospects that are untouched by the blogosphere. "Blogging is still a small market and we need to remember that," he observed.

---

[18] http://texturadesign.com
[19] http://clip-n-seal.com

Blogging, however, is important enough to have changed the focus of the company. Byron, whose career has been web-centric since 1994, said Textura Design has shifted its core focus from design to blog consulting.

We wondered where Clip-n-Seal would be without blogging. Byron's answer: "[It would be] one of the millions of inventions that never made it."

Seven Cows, Five Blogs

When CEO Gary Hirshberg founded Stonyfield Farm in 1983, it was a small, folksy, people-friendly operation. Stonyfield began as an organic farm school in pastoral Wilton, New Hampshire, with its chief assets being seven cows.

Stonyfield, now in nearby Londonderry, is no longer what you'd call a small business in the sense of ActiveWords or English Cut. It has grown into the world's largest organic yogurt company, with 2005 revenues estimated at about $200 million. Stonyfield sells about 18 million yogurt cups a month, plus mountains of natural ice cream. While continuing to operate independently, the company is mostly owned by Groupe Danone, a French food products company operating in more than 40 countries with stock listed on the Dow Jones Industrial index. Nevertheless, when you go to the Stonyfield Farm site[20] and read any of its five blogs, three of them written by Chief Blogging Officer Christine Halvorson, you get the sense of the same folksy organization started more than 20 years earlier. The company has made great effort to maintain a trustworthy, accessible image. It has become the meaning of the brand.

To achieve this position, Halvorson says the company does far less traditional print and television advertising than other food companies. "It's only recently that we did paid advertising at all," she told us. Stonyfield's central focus is in innovative "guerilla marketing" tactics. Stonyfield attends and sponsors community events distributing food samples. The company sponsors "Strong Women Summits" because women are the primary customers and Stonyfield wants to demonstrate participation in matters of female concern. For example, Stonyfield has programs to put healthy snacks into public school vending machines. Since the beginning, Stonyfield has used packaging as a communications tool. Yogurt cup lids are used to spread "whatever messages we think are important—and those are often related to saving the

---

[20] http://www.stonyfield.com

planet," Halvorson said. Blogging fits with all of that because "we've always been a company with a particular point of view," she said.

With all that in place, Stonyfield had both culture and strategy conducive to blogging. Hirshberg discovered blogging during the Howard Dean presidential campaign, at a time when he was concerned that growth would force his company to lose its customer intimacy. He told *BusinessWeek* magazine that he saw the campaign was using bloggers to do with voters precisely what Stonyfield had been trying to do with customers since the days when the company was still milking its own cows and writing "Let us hear from you" on the back of yogurt containers.

Hirshberg hired Halvorson, a career writer, from a Monster.com ad. In addition to the three blogs she writes, Halvorson also edits and posts The Bovine Bugle,[21] written by one of the company's contract organic dairy farmers. Baby Babble[22] is a collaborative effort by six Stonyfield parents of very young children and babies. Halvorson recruited the latter team because she is not a parent and could not speak from personal experience.

We wondered why a company whose brand connoted simplicity and an interest in saving the world needed five blogs. Halvorson explained that the company saw itself as serving five market niches: women, people concerned about junk food in schools and healthy kids, people concerned about organic food production (including organic farmers), parents of very young children, and other customers.

Halvorson feels the ongoing dialogue has increased awareness, loyalty, and perhaps the customer base for Stonyfield. "We know the readers . . . are enjoying them. The Bovine Bugle, which discusses everyday life on an organic farm, inspires nostalgia while providing insight. The Baby Babble inspires parents—or at least gives them a place to rant and find like-minded parents. We hope we are entertaining, [and] that folks are finding us from other blogs or accidentally stumbling upon us," Halvorson told us.

"It's hard to quantify, but we assume we've garnered some positive impressions among our readers and that's what counts most, not necessarily our ROI. . . . We've gotten a lot of positive feedback from professionals in the marketing community about what we're doing." However, the PR community, she noted, watches Stonyfield with a wary eye because blogging messages, delivered without controls, are different from the way PR has been done traditionally.

---

[21] http://www.stonyfield.com/weblog/BovineBugle
[22] http://www.stonyfield.com/weblog/BabyBabble

She advised companies thinking about blogging not to bog down the process with excessive policies and procedures. As so many other bloggers advised, she said to blog often, be authentic, and of course, be interesting. And one other thing—have a thick skin. "Bloggers aren't necessarily nice," she warned.

Feeding on a Downhill Business

With a year-round population of about 2,000, North Conway, New Hampshire, sounds as hometown as Londonderry. But it rests near some of the most popular—and treacherous—ski slopes on the eastern seaboard, proximate to New England's apex, Mount Washington; the town is surrounded by hiking and cross-country trails, not to mention breathtaking fall foliage and rushing whitewater rivers. While skiing dominates, the town enjoys appeal as a four-season sports vacation destination. The regional tourism publicists have dubbed the area Mount Washington Valley, and on peak weekends the population swells to as much as a half million.

These visitors bring prosperity and gentrification with them. Weekend and seasonal second homes dot the lower slopes. Famous-maker factory outlets have come in and brought in sedentary shoppers from bigger cities.

If you're a tourist, Horsefeathers is the kind of local eatery townies send you to for a good dinner. It's a neighborhood-type restaurant, where much of the staff knows most of the regular customers. Brian Glynn and Ben Williams opened Horsefeathers in 1976, and it earned its way to status as a local favorite, where you can grab a burger at the bar, eat in one of two dining rooms, enjoy live entertainment, or book a private party upstairs. Many of their "regulars" are actually in town only for a week or two each year, but they return year after year. Patrons chat about sports, slopes, weather, and how the town has changed.

But fast-food chains and franchises have been inundating the town. While they're not direct competition for Horsefeathers, every family car that drives through a McDonald's or grabs a flat box from Pizza Hut is one less table to serve in some local establishment. Horsefeathers depends on the loyalty of repeat customers, who represent 60 percent of its $3 million in annual business. Williams, who handles the front end of the restaurant, needed to keep customers loyal enough to "not wander down the street to try something new."

A few years earlier, the partners started an e-newsletter to keep in touch with customers in their primary homes, so that when they returned to North Conway, they'd still feel part of the community. It worked for a while, and the list built to 2,000, but then spam made group mailings and newsletters less effective.

Of course, Horsefeathers has a restaurant web site, just like every other restaurant. But according to Williams, theirs was dull with a few pictures and a menu that never changed—just like every other restaurant web site. "Customers would look at the site once and seeing nothing new, never return." So Williams decided to try create the Horsefeathers Restaurant Blog.[23] Taking a strategy that Bruggeman could have recommended, he focused on a single purpose: retain customers. "We had no desire to sell sandwiches via PayPal," Williams told us. Nor was the blog aimed at telling strangers they should come and eat. Word of mouth from happy regulars would do that.

The blog strives to extend the sort of conversations online that you would have with Williams if you were at a Horsefeathers dinner table or sitting on one of the 13 barstools. Williams blogs about local happenings such as ski and river conditions. Recent postings profile a local archery range and offer some historic tidbits on perilous Tuckerman's Ravine, where extreme skiing began. He never hypes Horsefeathers itself. "No one wants to hear how wonderful we think we are," he said. He posts often and that helps the restaurant appear prominently in search results, which likely helps in new customer acquisition. Google helps put Horsefeathers on the tourist "must see" list.

In the blog's first year, it received more than 50,000 visitors. "For us, this is a huge number. On an average day 150 to 200 people will electronically check in at our home base. We have as many people visiting Horsefeathers.com every day as we have seats in the dining room. The busiest day is always Thursday and the heaviest traffic occurs right after lunch. You have to think that these are our customers checking in to see what's up for the weekend," he speculated. While business is growing, the blog has allowed him to cut his advertising budget. The only downside to the blog that he can see is that what it saves in advertising revenues it costs him in time. "But I have much more fun, and it's much more effective," he told us.

Five Success Tips

While the diversity of the businesses in this chapter is apparent, so are the similarities. In case after case, we heard successful business bloggers give five tips that seem to work for each of them.

---

[23] http://hihowaya.blogs.com/weblog

- **Talk, don't sell.** Blogging was born in an environment of anti-pitch sentiment. People visit blogs to see what others care about and know. Over time, they will either come to trust you or they won't. If you talk to them, they get to know you. If you sell to them, they'll just leave—if you're lucky. If you're not, the blogosphere will buzz with allegations that you are abusing the new communications channel. The adverse effects of this on your reputation may be more enduring than you might think.

- **Post often and be interesting.** Treonauts' Andrew Carton told us that he forces himself to blog at least once daily. He sometimes finds himself spending the better part of the day thinking of something interesting or useful to say. This doesn't mean you have to become a writing factory. Many bloggers just link to other blogs in the category where they are trying to establish their own authority. Adding a one-liner spruces it up and means others will often link to you on their way to the original source. Of course, as we stated, posting often helps you with search engine ratings, and being interesting is what motivates others to link to you.

- **Write on issues you know and care about.** We cannot say it enough: A good blog is passionate and shows authority. It may be unwise to sell on a blog, but showing what you know and what you care about is part of why you should blog. If you do it right, then as Carton and others you'll meet in future chapters will attest, you can sell items from a blog. People will buy from you because what you write is useful and interesting to them and they come to trust you.

- **Blogging saves money but costs time.** A good blog reduces or eliminates the need for both advertising and PR support of goods and services. Our friends at Firefox get many more downloads from Blake Ross's SpreadFirefox blog than they did from their two-page ad in the *New York Times*. Companies get coverage from blogs that other PR tactics cannot attain even for tons of extra billable hours. The good news is you save money—unless you take into account what your time is worth.

  Being a good blogger takes time. You need to join the conversation by reading other blogs, linking to them, and putting comments on them. You need to research what you write about, and check and recheck your facts. This takes time, and the people we spoke to who quit blogging all cited time as the major reason they stopped.

- **You get smarter by listening to what people tell you.** As Dan Gillmor emphasized in *We the Media*, "My readers are collectively smarter than me." So are your customers. Ernie the Attorney, whom you'll meet in Chapter 6, talked about how negative comments used to irk him when he first started blogging and how he wanted to win the argument. Over time he learned to listen even to the nastiest comments. He learned where people are coming from. You learn about things you do that might make customers angry. Microsoft's Mike Torres drops by any site discussing his MSN Spaces. Because he shows he's listening, people become more polite. When we think about why there is such a strong anti-corporate sentiment these days, we think the demonstrated unwillingness of big companies to listen to what everyday people have to say is one of the blockbuster reasons, and blogging can help, bigtime.

A Blogging Plumber?

In our research, we had hoped to find a local plumber or general contractor who blogs. We didn't, but we expect we will in the not-too-distant future. We see huge benefits. Let's say you are a local plumber—an independent, without the word "Rooter" in your company name. You have few options in promoting yourself or your business. You can take out a Yellow Pages ad, but when people look in the Yellow Pages for a plumber, they are usually in a hurry. They will see whether you took out a large ad or just entered your name and number on a single line. The potential customer will know nothing about you, your reputation, your knowledge—nothing but your name and number.

Now, let's suppose you are a blogging plumber. For the near future, you may have the opportunity to be the first blogging plumber in your community. You can demonstrate your authority. You can offer tips for how to keep pipes clean and water hot, how to change water purification filters, and how to prevent roots from blocking drains. It may be the best blog in the world—but how will people find you? Not too many blog surfers go looking for a local plumber—except in a crisis.

Well, more and more people go looking for local resources online at places like Google Local. They type in the names of restaurants, dry cleaners, and even plumbers. When they do, the plumber who blogs will be the first to come up, and that tradesman's blog will show his expertise and knowledge. The blog will let people know the plumber as well as—if not better than— they want to. More important, the blog is a trust-building mechanism. Compare what you would know about a blogging plumber with what you know by reading a Yellow Pages ad. Whom would you call in an emergency?

Local merchants and franchises can also benefit from admirers. For example, Scoble has blogged rave reviews about Victor's Celtic Coffee Company in Redmond, Washington, purveyor of his personal favorite cup of java. The company faces nearby competition from the likes of Starbucks and regional favorite Tully's. Scoble blogged about Victor's, which sent some traffic into the coffee shop. Someone else linked to Scoble's blog, which sent some more business that way. If you Google for coffee in Redmond, guess who comes up first—four rankings above Starbucks? We think this has implications for local businesses everywhere and consultants anywhere.

We didn't find our local plumber, but we think someday soon one will take the plunge.

6 Consultants Who Get It

"Consult. v. To seek another's disapproval of a course already decided on."

—*Ambrose Bierce*

Consultants are a special breed of business professionals. Their best work is often braided into the fabric of other company products, services, and brands. They are most often contracted when a company is anticipating or undergoing change. They are supposed to have special expertise in a definable area, and they are expected to care about outcomes beyond their own compensations.

Most consultants don't have the money for big self-promotional campaigns. They might have a web site and a Yellow Pages ad. Some might sponsor a local sports team or niche market event, but they depend for the most part on word of mouth to amplify their reputations. Even if they enjoy lucrative practices, nearly all consultants need to build a personal market presence if they want to grow their businesses. Even if they are part of a large organization, when consultants leave, they take their reputations with them.

Consultants, by nature, are often the sorts who like to try out new things, including technology. They like also to demonstrate professional knowledge, and they like to be the first to tell you about new things that will be good for your business, be it an independent dry cleaner or a blue chip conglomerate. Very often consultants are technology enablers who evangelize new solutions into established institutions.

They are important to blogging for two reasons:

- Consultants who blog are building reputations that make them category leaders, whether that category is defined by geography or niche. Their opinions are becoming more important in influencing markets.
- Consulting expertise has started to evangelize and deliver blogging into other businesses. They are now seeding blogging into corporate strategies the way they previously germinated PCs and web sites. We believe they will play key roles in the phase of blog adoption that has started to occur.

In Europe and North America we found a great many bloggers who consult businesses. Consultants are wisely using blogs in decidedly different ways than they use their web sites. The consultant-bloggers gaining the most notice are building reputations, not selling services. Many we spoke with emphasized that they started blogs because of a need to express themselves, rather than as an action item on a business plan. Some go out of their way to avoid self-promotion. Many were quick to point away from themselves and to others in their field. All the consultants we talked with seemed more eager to extol the benefits of blogging over their own marketable attributes.

For some, blogging has changed their community status because of recognition generated by their blogging. Some are now finding themselves enjoying personal levels of prominence they had not previously imagined. Through their blogs, a great many people are getting to take a series of small, frequent glimpses at who these consultants are and how they think—and in some cases, the reader may become a customer. But at this point, the blogosphere is a better place to market your reputation than sell your goods, and in the end that will prove more valuable.

While some consultants may plan for this new prominence, for most it's more like what happened to Blake Ross and Joe Hewitt at Firefox. They just started something because they had passion and talent. They wanted to share it with a few friends. Or like what happened when Ernest Svenson, a New Orleans–based corporate lawyer, just felt compelled to start blogging. Fame— or something akin to it—followed.

Ernest and Open

Atty. Ernest Svenson is better known as blogging's Ernie the Attorney.[1] He has an eye for irony that has fine-etched some of his blogs. He didn't want us to interview him at first, saying "I don't blog to market myself. It isn't about self-promotion. I just hate the thought of being seen as 'Mr. Marketing Guy.' I think that sort of stuff fails on blogs." Instead, he told us, he writes to discover "insight about myself. People just want a story: What's the deal? Just tell me how it works. The best thing you can do, if you want to market on a blog, is *don't*. Just talk."

While other lawyers may pontificate on lofty issues, Svenson speaks of simpler things in a wry, self-effacing voice. A case in point was one Christmas Day shortly after his marriage ended when he and his two teenaged daughters were heading to Panama to visit family. A freak New Orleans snowstorm delayed the first leg of the trip, making them miss a connection and leaving them stranded. They wound up staying the night at the Houston Airport Hilton, taking holiday dinner at the Kettle Restaurant, "Home of the $7.98-all-you-can-eat Buffet." You might expect dark and morose reports on the blog, but Svenson stayed upbeat, expressing the joy of discovering the hotel's free WiFi and posting photos of his son and a New Orleans snowman he built that day and e-mailing them to the traveling portion of his family. A legendary Macintosh champion, Svenson posted photos of airport monitors displaying the familiar but ominous Microsoft "Fatal Error" warning.

You feel for him, but he makes you smile. More importantly, he demonstrates consistent transparency and authenticity. Ernie the Attorney is not trying to sell you legal acumen. He is allowing you to see and know a real person experiencing a real-life vignette. Over time, you realize the guy is smart, funny, and seems pretty trustworthy. If we ever happen to find ourselves in New Orleans after it is rebuilt and in need of an attorney, we know where we will turn. We've only been face to face with Svenson twice, but because of his blog, we feel as though we know and trust him.

Svenson's blog covers diverse subjects, but he doesn't wander far from the intersection of technology and society. Unlike co-author Scoble, he is not always a technology champion. "Sometimes technology is like spam trying to intrude into people's lives, making slow adopters feel left out. Mostly, I observe how technology affects people, and often it just adds a lot of stress,

---

[1] http://www.ernietheattorney.net

even as it promises to make people's lives easier. It isn't doing that if people don't know how to use the stuff."

We were talking with him on his cell phone, and as he told us, "Actually, I love technology," the phone went dead as if to illustrate his point.

When he started blogging in early 2002, Svenson wrote about sports, life, angst over the untalented New Orleans sports teams—almost anything but the law. What with the "Ernie the Attorney" handle, however, blog visitors expected legal commentary. He still avoids discussing his practice, but to accommodate site visitors, he has begun to talk about how laws change society. He also beat the drum for Federal Judge Richard Posner, whom Svenson admires for delivering objective, clear opinions. His most gripping material was posted after Katrina, when he and his family became homeless. Ernie posted via SMS relay and while living briefly in a tent city.

While blogging has landed Svenson a few referrals, there's been no great windfall. Although a few individuals have sought him out because of his blog, his firm's core practice is large corporations. Over time, such enterprises also may turn to blogs to know people prior to contacting or contracting them, but not yet.

Svenson may not have planned it that way, but blogging has boosted his legal community stature. More than 1,000 people visit his site daily, including a couple of judges on the New Orleans bench. They've asked him to serve on a committee to determine courthouse WiFi options. He is invited to speak at conferences a few times a year, and recently was invited to join a group of prominent lawyers in a new blog called Between Lawyers[2] at Corante, the popular blog publishing conglomeration.

He feels that blogging has helped him evolve. His circle of friends is global. He marvels at how blogging has taught him to listen more closely and tolerate opposing views. He used to argue with people who posted opposing comments. Now, he's learned to do his best to understand. While blogging might help him in his legal practice, he says that on a larger scale "it helps me get through life."

Collaborating with Competitors

In the preceding chapter, we wondered if there was room for a second English tailor blog after Thomas Mahon's. Our opinion was that the next tailor would

---

[2] http://www.corante.com/betweenlawyers

need a fresh angle. Being first always helps, and it's no different in the blogosphere. There are lots of blogging lawyers, and the prominent ones keep finding new things to say or fresh approaches.

One of the best known in the category is Lawrence Lessig,[3] a Stanford law professor who has become the perceived guru on the issue of intellectual property (IP) in the Digital Age. Does that mean that the IP turf is now staked out, prohibiting other lawyers from addressing it? Actually, no. Blogging invites others into topical conversations and in many cases encourages collaborative efforts.

We were a bit surprised by the number of lawyers collaborating on blogs, perhaps because we perceive the profession as being among the most competitive. It is part of their business to argue on one side, trying to defeat the other. Perhaps that's why so many lawyers enter politics.

But in at least one case, we found blogging got three erstwhile competitors to collaborate. Attorneys Stephen M. Nipper,[4] Douglas Sorocco,[5] and J. Matthew Buchanan[6] are all patent lawyers with a particular interest in blogging's impact on intellectual property issues. Each started blogs within three weeks of the other and then discovered each other through blogs. In a short time, they found themselves to be trusted colleagues, exchanging e-mail, talking by phone, starting collaborative wikis (a form of social software usually used for internal communications that allows groups to collaborate by editing each other's words on an Internet site), and eventually launching a podcast. Even though they had known each other only a short time, they found that they had become trusted friends with a common interest in dealing with how intellectual property attorneys relate to and treat clients. The result has been the creation of Rethink(ip),[7] a collaborative blog addressing how lawyers and clients should work together on IP issues. All this collaboration began before the three actually met in real life, which happened at a conference. They have merged and refocused their wikis into one so they can collaborate in greater length and depth than one would want to find on a blog.

---

[3] http://www.lessig.org/blog

[4] http://www.inventblog.com

[5] http://www.okpatents.com/phosita

[6] http://www.promotetheprogress.com

[7] http://www.rethinkip.com

Hallow Thy Customer

The author-consultant-speaker combo has been around for centuries and is still in widespread use. There are many blogging consultant-author-speakers. For example, author Seth Godin[8] blogs and frequently speaks at conferences and to business groups.

Ben McConnell and Jackie Huba became disenchanted with the one-dimensional broadcast aspects of their advertising careers back in 2000. They stepped out on their own and refocused their thinking onto word-of-mouth evangelism—not the pushy viral or buzz marketing stuff, but the strategic concept inspiring a company's best customers to become product champions.

They started a business designed to evangelize customer evangelism.

The two took a while to think it through and put their ideas into a book, *Creating Customer Evangelists: How Loyal Customers Become a Volunteer Sales Force*, which they published early in 2003, just before blogging started to accelerate. *Creating Customer Evangelists* advised six key corporate actions:

- Continuously gather customer feedback.
- Make it a point to share knowledge freely.
- Expertly build word-of-mouth networks.
- Encourage communities of customers to meet and share.
- Devise specialized, smaller offerings to get customers to bite.
- Focus on making the world, or your industry, better.

The advice predated blogging, but they note that blogging facilitates each of the six points. Their blog is memorably titled Church of the Customer: How to Live in Customer Heaven or Rot in Customer Hell.[9] They are working on a sequel that will incorporate the significant enhancements to the topic made by blogging and examine the possibilities of open-source marketing.

McConnell and Huba told us blogging is the best tool so far for enabling companies to convert customers into word-spreading evangelists, a powerful mechanism for true believers to spread the word about what you do and why other people should believe in what you are doing. To them, word of mouth is a fundamental tenet of "two-way marketing, which supplants the traditional command-and-control practitioners who declare 'We are the

---

[8] http://sethgodin.typepad.com
[9] http://customerevangelists.typepad.com/blog

company. Here is the message. Now consume it.' It's the boarding school approach. Shut up and eat your meat," McConnell told us.

Huba added that two-way marketing is essential to evangelism. Word-of-mouth tactics may backfire if they are one directional. She's wary of "organizations that set out to do something viral or generate buzz. They often end up coming across as cheesy." Quick buzz may generate nice, temporary hits, but Church of the Customer is looking at a bigger picture. "We are more interested in companies trying to create long-term, sustainable word-of-mouth. Sometimes innovations such as Firefox or ICQ create buzz because they offer obvious benefits. But evangelism should be about matters that are enduring. It's about changing the world."

Blogging creates an emotional connection in ways that press releases cannot accomplish, "providing a forum for a real person to talk and others to engage in that discussion. It's a great way to get feedback—one humungous, knowledge-sharing sounding board," McConnell said.

McConnell and Huba sense that blogging in business has only just begun. While awareness is rapidly building, uncertainty and doubt remain in the minds of decision-makers, whom McConnell positions "at the toe-in-the-water stage." At speaking engagements, the two often poll audiences about blogging. Only 30 percent have heard of blogs, fewer have read them, and only about 5 percent have heard of RSS, they estimated in June 2005.

The top question they hear is "What do you do about negative comments?" "People are scared to death of anyone, anywhere saying something that might be construed as negative. This, of course, is highly irrational. It doesn't take into account that your company has supporters, who have a higher level of credibility and can shoot down unfair and untrue comments."

As an example, Huba referred to Lutz's GM FastLane blog. When he posted regarding GM's decision to withhold advertising dollars from the *Los Angeles Times* because of negative coverage, an early comment was strongly negative. Lutz left it up. Over the next day, however, at least 30 customers, voicing support, smothered the naysayer. "This demonstrated the power of customer evangelism," Huba argued.

They see today's blogging situation as running a parallel course with business Internet adoption in the middle 1990s. Adoption went slow at first. Companies wondered aloud what they could possibly do with a web site, but then a tipping point was reached, and virtually every company found that it needed to have one. Huba and McConnell see a time when business blogs will become just as pervasive. "I see no reason for any company not to blog—unless they're sleazy. Every company needs a feedback system, and the easiest way to do that is through a blog. It's almost like a truth serum," she said.

They also believe blogs will evolve over time from their current status as single-page diaries. Company blogs will become more integrated with existing web sites, which in turn, probably through RSS, will become something more interactive and blog-like.

McConnell sees a metaphoric interplay with a church congregation being collectively smarter than its preacher. The company preacher may study a lot about a certain position. He or she may have a lot of knowledge on a subject, but the collective wisdom of the congregation is probably far greater than the preacher can attain via personal research and study. Therefore, it's up to the preacher to be able to tap into the collective knowledge and then lead the followers to newfound and greater glories.

McConnell had one parting thought for company preachers and their choirs: Don't bother with the atheists. Focus on the agnostics, where there's hope for conversion.

Designing with Grace

We personally know only three people in the design industry, each unacquainted with the other. Each is a fan of Design*Sponge,[10] Grace Bonney's elegant blog. Bonney is a furniture design industry consultant, freelance journalist, and sometime PR practitioner. Her blog isn't about self-promotion, but about design—all sorts of design. She uses few words and many pictures. A casual scroll takes you on a virtual tour of the latest innovations in everything from plastic bags and handbags to wall art and tabletop conversational pieces to furniture, magazine holders, lamps, and just about anything else being designed and offered to chic and/or elegant homes.

A while ago, Bonney was just another underemployed Manhattan-based consultant. Now she is recognized as a design industry "invisible influencer." A mention in her blog can very well map the shortest route to coverage in the most influential traditional media columns such as the *New York Times*.

Bonney demonstrates blogging's power in niche markets where we expect blogging to play an increasing role. People like Bonney with passions for all

[10] http://designsponge.blogspot.com

sorts of subjects are beginning to emerge. Because of the efficiency of Technorati and PubSub searches, like-minded people can easily find niche experts.

You don't need huge followings to influence a niche; you just need the right readers. Suppose you had a political blog, for example, and you had only three readers. They just happened to be the heads of government in the United States, China, and Russia, and each read your blog every day, trusted your writings, and adjusted their own courses accordingly. How many more readers would you need to be an influence? Now reduce this scenario into a business niche, and you can easily see the promise to people wishing to influence niche markets. Bonney may not end up with tens of thousands of daily visitors, but she is influencing the influencers of her niche.

Bonney told us, "My blog has given me the inside track on my industry, my market, and [my] audience. I feel extremely in tune with all three. It's a fantastic way to share your point of view, engage in your community, and meet wonderful new people all over the world who love the same things you do. I suggest it with my whole heart. It's brought so much joy to my life."

Spreading Internationally

Canada-based education and parenting consultant Alyson Schäfer provides another niche market example. She advocates reforming child discipline methods, so she started a blog[11] at her husband Ken's urging. She took the chance, although anxious at first that she would be just giving away her best thoughts to potential competitors. She reports that she experienced an immediate increased demand to speak and consult. Her blog also drew the interest of a publisher (Wiley Canada) that approached her and, over coffee, offered her a book contract.

There are also consultants whose business becomes the blog itself. Marco W.J. Derksen is a marketing consultant who started blogging in 2002 with Marketing Facts,[12] a Dutch blog about interactive marketing and new media. Over time, Marketing Facts expanded into a group blog. Traffic built to more than 2,000 visitors per day and more than 120,000 page views per month. Heartened by this, Derksen quit his day job in April 2005 to form Upstream,[13]

---

[11] http://www.alyson.ca

[12] http://www.marketingfacts.nl

[13] http://www.upstream.nl

a consultancy on how businesses should blog. He is among the first Dutch blogging consultants, and his new business generated coverage in local marketing magazines and local newspapers. He doesn't think businesses like his will be news for long. He told us blogging is heating up in the Netherlands and across Europe.

But someone in a good position to know cautions that heat has not yet reached ignition point. Six Apart's Loïc Le Meur, himself Europe's most popular blogger, thinks business adoption has just begun to yawn and stretch. "All the consultants in Europe still don't know what to create in order to wake up the market."

Says Derksen, "The gap between the product managers, [the] CEOs, and the consultants is huge in Europe, and changes are slow. Brands and corporations all wonder what to do with blogging and why they should bother." He predicts that they will come around to see blogging's benefits when some unanticipated event will motivate thousands of consumers to express themselves on one product, as has happened a few times in the United States. "Brands will finally understand that traditional marketing becomes less important than word of mouth."

Still, for some it's becoming a living.

Did They or Didn't They?

There is an emerging group of marketing consultants who are consulting companies on blog strategies. The most successful blog themselves and offer blog counseling in a mix of services to businesses. Several made clear that their hearts belong to blogging, and they hope their careers will follow accordingly. Two of note are BL Ochman of New York City and Toby Bloomberg of Atlanta, Georgia, coincidentally a cousin to New York City's mayor.

At one time, Ochman owned and operated one of the top 100 independent PR firms in the U.S. The advent of the Internet led her to believe it was time to retool. She took 1995 off to study it. When she returned, her first client was Just for Men Hair Color. After a political reporter observed that presidential candidates Bill Clinton and Robert Dole were each appearing at different campaign stops with different hair colors, Ochman built a web site where visitors could view them displaying black, brown, red, blond, and gray tresses and vote on which color best-suited each. Three-fourths of voters said both should change their hair colors, a coup for Ochman's client. "We got a ton of media coverage and I was absolutely hooked on the promise of Internet marketing and PR."

Ochman's experience opened doors. "I started writing for Internet Day and other online publications, and clients came from my articles. That's how I got consulting work from Ford, IBM, Preferred Hotels, and other big companies." These days, she helps companies sell online by writing and optimizing content for search engine pickup. She coaches clients on blogging and performs various functions connected with online marketing and communications. She hopes blogging will become her full-time work, "with maybe a little consulting on the side." She wants to sell more of her own reports, run seminars, and build her blog's circulation to the point where ad revenue will support it as well as her 4,000-subscriber newsletter.

Ochman started her blog What's Next[14] in early 2004, and despite the time it sucks out of her workday, she loves blogging's ability to expand her access to information. She said several new clients have found her through What's Next. "Clients I work with these days understand that they really need help to do business effectively online. They know from reading my blog that I am up on what's happening online, and they trust me sooner because they know me better from reading the blog," she said. The blog has also generated speaking invitations for her, as it does for so many prominent bloggers.

And there's another benefit. "It's fun. It has introduced me to a lot of smart people. Blogging forces me to keep learning and expands my horizons," she told us.

Additionally, Ochman's blog directs traffic to her web site, where she sells her privately published book *What Could Your Company Do with a Blog?* containing 85 examples of companies using blogs in their marketing. Over a four-month period, she sold 300 copies at $97 each directly from the site. She's also sold 500 copies of an article called "Press Releases from Hell and How to Fix Them" and is planning to update it to include "Blog Posts from Hell."

Ochman is not convinced that all businesses either should or will have bloggers. "It takes more time and effort than might be obvious. Many executives would rather have a root canal than write every day," she observed. (In a painful twist, Israel actually *had* a root canal the day after talking with Ochman. He would have preferred to have spent the time blogging.) Also, she said, "I've worked with CEOs who were lousy communicators. Who wants to read their blogs if [they] are going to be close-minded, lousy writers? The businesses that should blog are the ones that are willing to be open and

---

[14] http://www.whatsnextblog.com

honest. That eliminates a lot of companies who still think that they can control all messages and ignore feedback."

Consultants who blog need to get over an inclination to hold cards close to their vests. "If you're afraid to share ideas, you shouldn't blog," she stated flatly. "One time someone asked Walt Disney if he wasn't worried about telling so many people about his ideas. And Disney said 'Those were last year's ideas.'"

Her conclusion: "If you are paranoid about your ideas being ripped off, don't blog."

Is Blogging Marketing?

Toby Bloomberg, founder and president of Bloomberg Marketing in Atlanta, has focused on online integrated marketing strategies since 1997, "when the Internet was still a mystery to many businesses." Now, she consults corporate marketing departments and sees blogging as a value-added addendum to the existing corporate marketing mix.

Bloomberg told us, "Blogs add one more tool to a marketer's repertoire. As with any marketing program, to be effective, blogs must be integrated into a master marketing plan. From a business perspective, are blogs the saviors of marketing and might companies die on the vine without a blog? I think not."

Bloomberg's own Diva Marketing Blog[15] shows all the elements we found in successful blogs. It is transparent and authentic, showing passion for subjects she knows. She posts frequently and Googles well. This gets her lots of media interviews and speaking engagements. Bloomberg's blog has given her a strong brand.

There's one twist: Her passion for blogging is as a marketing tactic. This revealed a different perspective from that of most bloggers we asked. In other aspects, Bloomberg seems to sing in harmony with today's blogosphere. "How much closer can a customer get to a brand than talking with the CEO or the people who are the heart of the brand? The emotional value that is associated with a blog can help inspire trust and credibility. Blogs can be a powerful experiential marketing tactic," she told us.

"Companies who do not include blogging as part of an integrated marketing plan will miss out on significant opportunities and be at a disadvantage as competitors adopt blogs. Because they help organizations get closer to

---

[15] http://www.divamarketingblog.com

customers and customers closer to brands, blogs are a powerful tool that few can afford to ignore. Bottom line: If your target audience wants a blog, you had better blog," she advised. She also has thoughts on overcoming time drain: Have a corporation set up a blog for multiple bloggers, sort of time-sharing the effort.

She foresees blogging's eventual ubiquity in the lives of everyday people. "The technology will bring an ease and depth of global interaction that is definitely world-changing."

She shares the view that any company can benefit by using blogging to open the communications doors wider—at least any company that doesn't have harmful secrets buried or that enforces a suppressive culture. She told us, "If the company culture is manipulative, employees are not treated with respect, and customers are thought of as commodity items, then that company should not blog. That company should close its doors."

Bloomberg is convinced that blogging's home in the corporate structure is the marketing department. "Every marketing director I've ever met is looking for innovative ways to create stronger customer relationships. Blogging is one of the best tools to accomplish that, so I recommend all companies explore the possibilities. Especially for service and consulting firms, blogs are an excellent way to establish and promote thought leadership."

She envisions a business-like evolution for blogging already in motion with a "rapid progression as marketing/business blogs move from a shoot-from-the-hip attitude to a structured and strategic approach."

While standalone blogs will continue to give news and views very much as they do today, she believes blogs will integrate into larger marketing strategies similar in the "sophistication we're seeing with e-mail strategies. Marketers will also develop short-term blogs that only run the length of a campaign."

Additionally, she predicts a rapid evolution of niche blog communities where blogs will feel like portals enhanced by additional social networking software to allow real-talk conversations. Blog ads are also in her crystal ball, taking a slice away from web site ad revenues. As people turn to aggregators to read blogs, bloggers who include ads on their sites will have to find ways to drive readers to their blogs. Perhaps they'll add links or white paper downloads accessible only on the blog. Industries that are shying away from blogs such as healthcare will find ways to come to terms with regulations and the type of information that they can comfortably disseminate. It's only a matter of time before blogging is incorporated into job responsibilities, Bloomberg said.

Brave New or Same Old?

We disagree with Bloomberg on a few key points. Most fundamentally, when we envision business blogging as an integrated component of today's corporate marketing departments, it feels about the way a shirt feels when it just doesn't fit right. Trying to fit blogging into a typical marketing department gives the same sense of discomfort to us. Blogging just doesn't integrate well with other so-called "marketing solutions."

In technology, three large companies have experienced the significant proliferation of blogging into their culture: Microsoft and Sun Microsystems. The two cultures adopted blogging differently, but both companies' blogs continue to bypass their marketing departments. Some of the most influential bloggers like Bob Lutz, Mark Cuban, and Scoble tend to ignore the process and controls exercised by their marketing departments anyway. Ernie the Attorney almost declined to talk with us for fear he'd be labeled "Mr. Marketing."

But before we bristle and shun Bloomberg's arguments, we need to step back a bit. So far, blog championship has remained rooted deeply in the technology community, where all tech transformations begin. It will not always be this way. In fact, Bloomberg is evidence that the center of the blogging revolution is in fact in motion. It's very much like the early days when the Internet community's nexus was in the Unix developers' community, when freeware distribution was all that "netiquette" permitted, and Usenet newsgroups provided all the interactivity one would ever need. In those days, it was considered socially unacceptable to even utter the word "advertising" among Internet enthusiasts. But over time, as technology got easier to use, adoption accelerated. The business community adopted web sites slowly at first, but by the time of the tipping point in 1996, it was hard to recall the look and feel of the 1994 Internet. Many technologists would argue the change was for the worse, but such change was essential for the massive adoption that has become the Internet Age.

Now, here comes blogging. Rules for socially acceptable blogging behavior have been loosely defined, but as we will discuss later, rules and guidelines are indeed necessary, just to give bloggers, managers, HR, legal, marketing, and other concerned departments the comfort of tangible and universally imposed rules. We have little doubt that some deceptions have already occurred because you really can fool some of the people some of the time. Blogs will change over time. Marketing will find a way to loop itself in. While we shudder at how this may result, there is hope it can occur without tainting the authenticity that most blogs exude.

The fundamental argument of this book is not to eliminate marketing, but to change it into something more conversational. Bloomberg calls this "corner grocery store relationships," a thought quite close to our description in Chapter 3 when we talked about the way customers used to relate to the corner butcher, baker, and candlestick maker.

Where we differ from Bloomberg today is in our perceptions of the collective hearts and minds of today's marketing decision-makers. In Israel's 25 years of consulting them, he did not find every marketing director interested in "building stronger customer relationships," as Bloomberg said. In fact, among his reasons for getting out of the PR business was his sense that too many marketing departments had reduced their interest in customers to sticky eyeballs and columns of analytical spreadsheet numbers. Perhaps Bloomberg has enjoyed the benefit of meeting a better class of marketers.

For a long time, we considered calling this book *Blog or Die*, an idea that the collective wisdom of the blogosphere convinced us was lame. But unlike Bloomberg, we do see companies that we think will wither on the vine, and the cause of atrophy will include marketing departments that just don't get the transformational change in progress and continue to do what they've always done.

In our vision, blogging changes marketing more than marketing changes blogging. Marketing changes from what it has become over the past 50 years—the stuff that Godin calls Interruption Marketing—into something new, more efficient, and far more effective, which our friends at the Church of the Customer call "Two-Way Marketing."

7 Survival of the Publicists

"What we've got here is . . . failure to communicate."

—*Captain*, Cool Hand Luke

There was a joke circulating the PR industry in the late '90s:

Q: Why do lawyers like PR consultants so much?
A: It gives them someone to look down on in the ethical pecking order.

Things haven't improved much in terms of how people view PR professionals today. The 2005 Edelman Trust Barometer, an annual worldwide survey, reported that PR people rank far down the list of credible spokespeople, just above athletes and entertainers and just below lawyers.

This finding is hard to shrug off. Here is this central component of the image-building business, perceived to have more cracks in it than the portrait of Dorian Gray. PR people generally see themselves as communication facilitators, but many observers view them as gatekeepers or spin masters. When the *Naked Conversations* project was first announced, Israel (who had practiced PR for more than 25 years) received e-mail from someone he'd never met telling him, "Your book will undoubtedly suck. You're a PR guy. Every time you open your mouth you lie."

How did this industry end up with such a tainted image? A long string of scandals helped. By reading the papers, one can get an impression of an ongoing collusion between PR agencies and large organizations intent on deceiving the public. There's also a language barrier. PR people are accused of speaking in an oxymoronic mix of risk-avoidant and hyperbolic language that most people don't trust. In addition, PR folk are considered flak-catchers who stand in front of the press to take heat and deflect it from clients. The result is that a large number of people see the PR practitioner intentionally blocking the path to the truth, someone who guides company spokespeople to manipulate the message around the actual facts to the advantage of the company and at the expense of the public's right to know.

Bloggers enjoy the opposite reputation. They write in the plainest of language, so unrefined that postings sometimes scream for a good edit. They are prone to tell it like it is, even if "it" is unflattering to the companies they represent. Whereas the PR practitioner's loyalty is assumed to be to the client, the blogger's loyalty is perceived to be to the public at large.

We are, of course, talking about perceptions here, not realities. The reality is that some bloggers are not saintly, and some embellishments slip past the wary eyes of blog-watchers. Likewise, not all public relations practitioners deserve the harsh rap.

In fact, we see two schools of PR in practice today. One is the incumbent school of "command and control." This school argues that companies should keep communicating in the same manner and with the same rules that they have always practiced and perhaps a dab of makeup to cover up the warts of their profession. Some of the smartest in the field are rapidly transitioning from traditional to more conversational practices, creating a new "listen and participate" school of thought in PR. This latter group plays by rules that are in striking contrast to the command-and-controllers. We think this transformation into two schools is important to the field because the profession appears to us and many we spoke with to be in upheaval and facing a change-or-perish challenge, denied by many and embraced by a few up until now. In fact, we firmly believe that many members of the command-and-control school will soon find their futures will be in the restaurant service industry.

By contrast, many of the Listen-and-Participators blog, and they're good at it. They understand blogging has already disrupted the status quo of their professions and have adapted to the change, to the benefit of both their clients and themselves. Most still embrace a good number of traditional tactics, which in many cases makes sense. But you can see their hearts and minds transitioning to new forms of communication, including using blogging to change the rules of the game from a one-way monologue to a two-way conversation.

Where Swords Cross

Press releases are perhaps the single point where the swords of the blogosphere and traditional PR tactics cross. Press releases are typically generated by a mid-level PR person and then edited by one or more members of the marketing and executive teams in committee fashion. If the company is publicly held, major releases must be passed by Legal. Sometimes a dozen pairs of hands have tweaked a release before it is distributed via e-mail and news distribution services. Some take weeks to produce, and each reviewer has a need to insert adjectives, embellishments, and cautions somewhere into the document.

The blog process is entirely different. A single person has a thought, then posts it. There's rarely a committee involved. If she's smart and wants to be credible, the blogger discloses what her interests are and how she knows what she's publishing to be true. People read and decide how much of it they trust. They ask her questions through comments or even e-mail. Then they may add relevant, fast-breaking news as they get wind of it.

Blogs and press releases are also fundamentally different in how they get amplified. Press releases are amplified by the people who send them and the budgets that support them. Blogs get amplified by the people who receive them based on how interesting or valuable they consider the information. The story becomes amplified by the receivers—not the senders. Word can travel fast from one blog to the next, occasionally faster than business or news wire services.

The press release is a bread-and-butter issue for PR agencies. They write them, distribute them, and then smile-and-dial editors and analysts in attempts to get the "news" in them published. However, a great many people are now questioning their value. Arik Hesseldahl, a Forbes Online editor, told us, "I just don't use press releases. I don't know any editor who does." Even the companies that produce them are ambivalent. An internal communications officer at a Fortune 100 company told us he didn't read his own company's press releases. "They're just a bunch of crap," he told us. "But we do have some really cool blogs going on." Press releases and the new blogging option are among the cornerstones of the Listen and Participate new school. This is a big issue among press practitioners these days, and we will revisit it again later in this chapter.

But the blog challenges to PR go well beyond the press release. Some veteran practitioners, such as Waggener Edstrom's Frank X. Shaw, who runs the

Microsoft account, understand how traditional practice must adapt and see blogging as vital to an emerging PR practice. According to Shaw, blogging has made it a "smaller, faster world." He told us his agency used to have a few days or even a week to react to a major news story from the time he heard about it to the time the major media would react to it. This provided sufficient time to plan, meet, and decide on a course of action. Today, he and his staff typically have about four hours to respond, from start to finish. To speed the delivery of a message into the channel, Waggener Edstrom e-mails it to Microsoft's bloggers, who then may choose to serve as part of the global news distribution network or not.

As we said, many PR professionals make damned good bloggers, and we found examples in most areas of the profession. Here are some of the ones who seem ready to offer useful advice.

Fascinating Conversations

Richard Edelman, president and CEO of Edelman PR, the world's largest independent PR firm, is in a position to evangelize blogging into powerful offices where blogging's relevance to date has been generally discounted and where most of today's blogging denizens don't get invited. Edelman oversees a worldwide organization of nearly 2,000 employees in more than 40 offices on four continents, and his agency's Edelman Trust Barometer, based on yearly surveys of 1,500 "opinion leaders" worldwide, is now in its sixth iteration.

Until recently, Edelman was virtually unknown in the tech sector, having built his reputation on international services. Soon after starting his blog, Speak Up,[1] in September 2004, he heard blog-community complaints that he came across sounding like a corporate executive, which, in fact, is precisely what he is. He concedes his posts are too long and infrequent, but said, "I feel as if I am part of the revolution, not simply standing on the sideline observing." He gained some "street creds" after he posted a condemnation of rival company Ketchum PR when his competitor was caught in a "pay to play" collaboration with conservative columnist Armstrong Williams. His main point was that PR agencies should employ a more stringent ethics set than Ketchum had used.

In fact, over time, Edelman's language has gradually loosened, and on last check, he was edging toward greater brevity and frequency. Where we find

---

[1] http://www.edelman.com/speak_up/blog

him most interesting is in the fascinating conversations he writes about. While many bloggers post about shared pizza with each other, Edelman seems to be globe-trotting to break bread with diverse thought leaders. In May 2005, for example, he posted three consecutive reports of meal-side chats with blogger-philosopher David Weinberger[2]; Julie Gerberding, head of the U.S. Centers for Disease Control; and Oh Yeon Ho, CEO of South Korea's OhmyNews,[3] an interactive newspaper that probably influenced the unexpected outcome of South Korea's last presidential election.

Edelman advised PR agencies to have their clients speak for themselves instead of using outside celebrity or PR spokespeople and for agencies to be transparent on who's funding campaigns. Regarding the blogosphere, he commented that PR agencies had better understand how it works and what it does.

Does today's PR practitioner face the same fate as the last century's blacksmith? According to Edelman, perhaps. "Certainly many of today's practices are already headed for the scrap heap either because they undermine integrity or because bloggers will supplant them," he said. They include such practices as buying one's way onto a video news release issued by a "credible" reporter, negotiating to see interview questions in advance in return for an exclusive story, and making partial disclosures that hold back certain key facts.

His list reminded us about just how much house cleaning some PR firms need to undertake. "I think those of us in PR have to improve our own game. We have to be very much part of the conversation by reading key bloggers in each relevant product category, [to] be prepared to contribute to the conversation by smart posts and to keep key bloggers updated by having relationships akin to those we have with reporters."

He agrees with our view of public relations in sea change and told us:

> *Blogging is not a passing fad. Any brand, business or organization that fails to grasp [that] fact may very well be. It's essential to any company seeking to connect in a spontaneous, continuous fashion with its publics. It affords a window into a company unlike any other—more credible because it lacks the dimension of control, more sustainable because it is rooted in reality, more powerful because it can be connected to comments*

---

[2] http://www.hyperorg.com

[3] http://english.ohmynews.com

> *of others having primary experiences with a company's product*
> *or service. Smart companies will take heed of what they learn*
> *from online critics, amending the product or process by being*
> *committed to continuous improvement from whatever source.*

The Edelman agency encourages its clients to get on the blog wagon, designating mid-level employees as bloggers "so that the company's R&D or marketing or service units can gain profile outside of trade media or business publications. In fact, good word of mouth in the blogosphere leads to coverage in the offline media."

This has all happened, from Edelman's perspective, because "traditional marketing has entered its twilight years." It's premised, he said, on an old model of persuasion that worked from the '50s through the '80s, where

> *[M]arketers could reach 97 percent of the target audience with*
> *three ads in prime time on network TV. They relied on a pyra-*
> *mid of authority in which elite audiences such as investors,*
> *regulators, retailers, and elite media received advance notice of*
> *company plans. A large commitment to advertising and appro-*
> *priate monies for slotting allowances guaranteed favorable*
> *treatment at retail . . . and the consumer, lured by the ads,*
> *would purchase, especially if a big name celebrity is in the ad.*
> *The big idea—keep everything under wraps until the last*
> *moment before the ads break—give an exclusive to the* Wall
> Street Journal *and you are home free.*
>
> *So now a smart company has a different approach—call it*
> *the "paradox of transparency." Co-create your brand with key*
> *consumers. Talk to critics at NGOs [Non-Government*
> *Organizations] in advance to reach an understanding. Use*
> *your employees as your first line of offense. Use a real person*
> *as a spokesperson or maybe the winner of a reality show like*
> *American Idol. Create synergy among the promotions and talk*
> *across the silos, but offer real dialogue, not hot air.*

Edelman advises practitioners to get out of the way of the conversation. In his chat with Weinberger, the *Cluetrain* co-author contended that bloggers generally distrust PR people because they prevent their clients from speaking openly. Weinberger, who now consults Edelman, wants PR people out of the middle to ensure veracity. But Edelman argues PR people can play facilitator roles by opening windows into corporations and serving as prods to action. "PR should be seen as a spur to true interaction, not a barrier," he added.

Pitching the Pitcher

If you type Steve Rubel's name into Google, you will find him in a virtual tie with Edelman, even though the latter has been at the PR game twice as long and runs an agency 100 times larger than CooperKatz, where Rubel is a vice president. Edelman has also written or co-written a half-dozen books, and the world's largest independent agency bears his name. But Rubel has been blogging longer and posts much more frequently.

Not long ago, Rubel was just another PR practitioner, making a living mostly by smiling and dialing editors on behalf of clients. Now his blog, Micro Persuasion,[4] is wildly popular and is even indexed as a source for Google News. Rubel is often the first to either break news or point to another blog that does. He's among the world's most frequently interviewed bloggers and speaks at conferences more than 50 times a year. *Media* magazine named him one of the 100 people most influential to the media—along with Bill Gates and Oprah Winfrey.

The editors he used to dial up now call *him*. A large number read Micro Persuasion as a primary source for fresh leads. When he caught wind that the blog aggregator company NewsGator was acquiring a competitor, he blogged about it. Within an hour, dozens of other bloggers repeated Rubel's scoop, amplifying the news. Most linked back to Rubel's original post. By the next morning, NewsGator founder and CTO Greg Reinacker found himself talking with press from all over the world. A press release had not yet been issued.

Another irony is that other PR practitioners at rival agencies now pitch Rubel to mention their clients on his blog. When we talked to him, it was clear he was enjoying the attention, but he consistently deflected the conversation over to his clients' blogs and to what other agencies can and should do.

The first of his clients to follow his guidance into the blogosphere was the Association of National Advertisers (ANA)—composed of such Fortune 500 companies as Proctor & Gamble, Sears, and Disney. With Rubel's coaching,

---

[4] http://www.micropersuasion.com

ANA CEO and President Bob Liodice started blogging.[5] This was at a time when mainstream media (MSM) still regarded the blogosphere as the purview of lonely teenage diarists, so CooperKatz sent out a brief announcement about the new blog's launch. The *New York Times* picked up the story, wrote positively, and gave it prominent play. Now the press regularly goes to Liodice's blog to report on what he has to say, and the blog has become the central conduit of the ANA's public voice.

By encouraging his client to blog, Rubel also changed his traditional PR role into listen-and-participate. Instead of positioning himself as a gatekeeper in the middle of the conversation, Rubel connected the parties directly to each other and then stepped back to let them talk on their own. This is contrary to the way agencies traditionally work. Agencies lose billable hours when they engineer themselves out of the conversation. By relinquishing traditional command-and-control tactics, CooperKatz established a new facilitative role, one more valuable to clients and the press, if not more lucrative to themselves.

Recently, CooperKatz elevated Rubel to head up a newly formed practice addressing blog and social media activities, naming it Micro Persuasion after his personal blog. Among Micro Persuasion's first new clients was Vespa, the motor scooter company, which followed his advice to initiate two blogs that feature real Vespa owners posting about their daily experiences. The scootering bloggers were selected by an online call for applicants at Rubel's suggestion. Rubel posted several blogs at Micro Persuasion and attributed the idea to the book *Creating Customer Evangelists* by Church of the Customer's Huba and McConnell.

Another Rubel client, WeatherBug—a software utility program for the meteorologically obsessed—claims blogging has helped it in several ways. WeatherBug's parent company, AWS Convergence Technologies, had at one point partnered with another company, resulting in WeatherBug being identified as a spyware carrier. According to Rubel, WeatherBug has since been vetted as a clean application, but his client was left with a reputation problem to overcome. "WeatherBug used a blog[6] as a central communications tool to dialogue with some of its biggest critics," said Rubel. Now, he claims, many of the best-known and most-trusted bloggers have since extolled WeatherBug's virtues.

Through Rubel's guidance, WeatherBug also pioneered event-related blogs. The first was Groundhog Day, and it's now an annual event blog on which the

---

[5] http://ana.blogs.com

[6] http://blog.weatherbug.com

company straight-facedly reports on shadow-sightings and their implications. In 2004, when four hurricanes hit Florida, WeatherBug instituted information-sharing blogs that the media cited as a primary news source, as happened again in 2005 with Katrina.

The Micro Persuasion practice is CooperKatz's fastest growing unit, and CooperKatz has started to develop specific blog-related products. One of these is "Blogwatch," in which junior agency team members monitor blogo-sphere mentions of their clients, their products, and their markets on a daily basis, determining if postings indicated that client risks were normal, high, or elevated. This approach is inexpensive and useful for clients, and it provides high-margin incremental revenue for the agency. It is now, in various forms, a common practice in a growing number of PR firms.

Rubel believes all agencies can prosper while providing clients powerful services through blogging. For example, noting 1,500 bloggers at Microsoft are now putting out volumes of content daily, he suggested that Microsoft's PR agency could pluck the 100 most interesting entries every day and aggregate them into a master blog, making it easier for Redmond-watchers to find employee-generated content. He says he's happy to help other PR profession-als. "The best PR people have always been connectors. They've often had to be like Plasticman, stretching between clients and press. Blogging is the best connection tool ever invented," he said.

Moving It Down the Avenue

Renee Blodgett runs a one-person PR shop from a home office. She also sees the beauty of small in her clients. Saying she loves a family-type relationship with clients, she told us, "I love putting companies on the map." She recently moved her operation from Boston to San Francisco. There were some pains, but she lost no clients, demonstrating the diminution of geographic relevance for business services.

One client, the news aggregator NewsGator,[7] required her to live and breathe in the blogging community. She started Down the Avenue[8] in November 2004, covering technology, marketing, public relations, politics, media, and life. While it's well written, that is not why we found it unique. As

---

[7] http://www.newsgator.com
[8] http://www.downtheavenue.com

far as we can tell, she was the first PR consultant to use her blog to directly extol the virtues and milestones of her own clients. That was bound to happen, but Blodgett managed to do it without offending the blogosphere's noncommercial sensitivities.

She told us she writes about her clients "in the same way I write about someone who makes an impact on me or those around me. If I'm thrilled about news that a client will speak on a prominent panel, received an industry award, or landed in *USA Today*, it's validation that what they're doing is positive, [that] we're on the right track and have something compelling to say." But Blodgett braids her client-related virtues into other postings, sometimes favorably discussing competitors. It's not that different from how Buzz Bruggeman gingerly handles ActiveWords plugs on his blog, taking care to mention his company only about once in every four postings.

There have been no challenges so far, no negative comments about it, no critical blog postings elsewhere. "The key," she told us, "is to maintain full disclosure that they are clients within the post." She encourages other consultants to do the same. "With a powerful vehicle like a blog, it's a natural fit for a communications consultant and frankly, a 'must' in my opinion."

Parallel Evolutions

Neville Hobson and Shel Holtz are friends, and they collaborate together on a popular podcast—an audio blog—covering the PR industry. Blogging seems to have made both of them overnight stars after more than 25 years' hard work each.

Both spent much of their careers employed by large organizations and then started their own practices and then blogs. One thing that separates them is geography. Hobson is British, living in Amsterdam. Holtz is a Californian. They also share the view that blogs are important evolutionary tools but disagree that "everything has changed," reminding us of our conversation with *Megatrends* author John Naisbitt.

Something changed for Hobson, and he did have to adjust. A business consolidation left him out of a job. Always believing that technology is the communications industry's greatest enabler, he started blogging daily in 2004. "I did my thinking in public," he told us, in the hope that it might, "enable me to connect with others who had similar mindsets. My blog played an instrumental role in my deciding to go my own way rather than find another traditional job."

Holtz was a reporter before serving 20 years as an agency and corporate communications executive. One day, he brought an idea to his employer that some intranet technology he had designed could save clients significant dollars. His boss didn't want to lose the higher revenue from reselling the existing solution, which cost more and did less, so Holtz left to form Holtz Communications + Technology in 1996. He thinks online technology has been among the biggest changes during his career. Holtz argues that PR quality has increased on its own, for reasons far more comprehensive than the blogging phenomenon. He sees less fluff and more quality content these days in corporate communications. Today, he said, most companies are communicating material of substance to employees and other audiences, and corporate PR executives serve at higher levels in the organization. Often, the top-level communicator has been placed proximate to the CEO and is included in senior-level meetings.

Holtz warned us not to overrate blogging. He sees it as merely one more milestone along the online communications continuum, perhaps no more significant than when instant messaging emerged. Yet, he shares with Edelman our perception of a sea change in progress. "Control of message, targeting of audiences, measurement of effectiveness—it's all changed. And, most strikingly, most communicators don't know it yet."

Hobson's self-employment came a decade after Holtz's, and he sees blogging as what got him into it. He launched exclusively from his blog NevOn,[9] using neither brochures nor flyers—not even a web site. "My blog is my persona. It's where my new business relationships begin. Others get to know me before we meet. Blogging has produced new professional relationships, which have led to new clients," he said. It also altered his life. For example, he reads online news in tandem with finding out what other bloggers say on a subject. "I connect with those opinions either through joining in conversations on other blogs or writing comments and opinions in my own blog where others may comment. It makes for amazing connections. It has convinced me there's a new way of working where a blog is central and that by doing it that way, relationships have a new form of trust as their foundation."

His practice enables him to bring blogging into corporate environs where it did not previously exist. When we interviewed him, he was helping an unnamed global telecommunications company to develop a blogging platform

---

[9] http://www.nevon.net

to serve as a primary channel between internal marketing communications and public relations staff and external agencies in Europe.

Holtz sees his own work as a practice in transition, with a long-view memory of how the practice of PR has changed. Until 10 years ago, his life was filled with the joys of blue-lines and press checks for corporate brochures. Now that stuff has gone the way of Gutenberg's press. The online "change has been stunning. The introduction of many-to-many communication has had a dramatic impact on the communication environment. From a strategic point of view, online communication has turned all the models and assumptions under which we operated upside down," he told us.

Today, Holtz still performs traditional communications consulting services if a prospect asks him, but said, "I don't promote these as prominently as my online-focused services." Holtz sees blogging fitting progressively into this chronology of online activity. He sees his blog as an extension of a subscription-based newsletter that he's written for years.

Despite his attempt to put blogging into perspective, he admits that blogging has dramatically and irrevocably changed his business, but "not as dramatically as some of the more zealous blogging evangelists would have us believe. For one thing, I don't believe PR ever [had control of messages]." Instead, he sees a more significant change on the other end of the equation. "The audience has been amplified exponentially. Blogs affect organizational communication in terms of transparency, tone, channel, [and] influence. There's not an element of PR that won't be affected by blogs."

He also told us he had to laugh when we wistfully argue that blogs could replace press releases. He argued that new media don't kill old media, and history is on his side. Rock music did not kill opera. Nor did TV kill radio—but radio did have to adapt its content. He concedes, however, that blogs are "unquestionably, transformational." Press releases are the official, authoritative, final statements of record by an organization, and they can be distributed in compliance with securities regulations. "They may be lowly, but they have a place," he argued.

This all may be true. But press releases may have all the impact on getting news coverage that the WeatherBug groundhog has on authentic weather prediction. Let's take another theoretical look at what we think might eventually happen at General Motors as it continues to find ways that blogging can help it climb out of the perception holes it finds itself in. Suppose an engineering team starts blogging about a new car they are designing, with a new environmentally clean fuel system and the ability to go from zero to 60 in 6 seconds or so. Suppose this team blogs about their work, without revealing IP and patent secrets, but they transparently discuss the trial and error involved. They describe the tests that fail, followed by the ones that pass. They describe the collisions with marketing and sales during development. This blog goes on for a couple of years, until the new car is ready to officially launch. At that point, the traditional PR people kick in with a huge, graphically striking press kit, filled with exciting photos and zippy language. The PR is quickly followed by a huge ad campaign that even includes the *Los Angeles Times*. But when you read the blog and compare it with the controlled media kit press releases, there are certain subtle differences in what you see. Which will you believe? The blog, written by a team you've come to know over two years, or the glitzy media kit written once again in corpspeak?

Personally, we think it's a no-brainer.

Shut Up and Listen

As head of the Voce Communications Digital Advocacy (DA) practice, which focuses on online communication, Mike Manuel told us his job is to help companies listen and understand what's being said, see where opinions are being formed, and figure out who their core influencers are. He helps clients, particularly Yahoo!, determine the best way to get into conversations.

His advice: "Shut up and listen. Listening is hard for companies, and ironically, it's hard for communicators too, especially the command-and-control types accustomed to . . . well, talking. It's really in our professional interest and the interest of our clients to take the time to . . . determine how the blogosphere is—or is not—impacting public opinion and brand perception. And you do this simply by listening."

As the lead for Voce's DA practice, Manuel worked with Yahoo!'s Search division to understand how online discussion was impacting its perception—and to formulate a strategy that would allow the group to have a louder voice in a noisy marketplace. Among the results was a Yahoo! Search team blog.[10] The blog lets visitors get to know and talk with product team members. This approach has the same obvious humanizing benefits that we reported on at Microsoft. Manuel worked in the background for the blog's planning and development. He's clearly proud of the result, suggesting the Search Blog can serve as a model for other corporate blogs.

---

[10] http://www.ysearchblog.com

Yahoo! Search also uses blogs and wikis internally to share insight and information into online discussions. "We use tools like blogs and wikis to help structure all this data in a meaningful way so that it's digestible and actionable for a variety of points in the internal food chain. This is all part of what we call a listening engine," he explained. Manuel also is involved in planning Yahoo! 360, a blog tools service now live, which was still in early beta when we spoke to Manuel. He declined to discuss unannounced client products. This was not to our surprise.

In a larger light, Manuel sees three major trends being driven by blogging:

- **Blogs are democratizing the media.** Whether it's the Trent Lott scandal or the Dan Rather cover-up, the blogosphere is actively watching mainstream media—and participating in news cycles for the first time. Previously, audiences couldn't take active parts because there was no easy way to be heard. Now they can be heard through blogging almost instantly. Manuel feels this directly impacts both journalists and communicators.

- **Blogs are driving corporate transparency.** Manuel said he's seeing trust erode with the MSM and corporate brands. "Trust is the only capital you have in the blogosphere and to build trust, companies need to become transparent in their practices," said Manuel. This eliminates command-and-control options and gives audiences "the power to scream back."

- **Blogs are challenging traditional PR practices.** The rules of engagement are different with the blogosphere, but the fundamental principles behind solid media relations still arguably apply. For example, Manuel said, "Blasting out the same product announcement to bloggers and journalists is just a recipe for disaster."

Dissenters on Two Sides

When we published an early version of this chapter on our *Naked Conversations* blog, we were assailed with unfavorable feedback that was split into two camps. One group argued we had been too kind in what we wrote about PR practitioners in these case studies, and the other argued we had been too harsh in our criticism. That gave us some sense of balance.

Among the latter group was Trevor Cook, a director of the Sydney-based PR firm Jackson Wells Morris. He left comments dissecting the draft chapter point by point. We asked him to submit comments for inclusion in the book. We were expecting to have him tear into us, and we were prepared to print his comments. But we found ourselves agreeing with his central premise: "Blogging and podcasting offer exciting communication opportunities, but they will not completely displace existing media nor will they change the traditional role of public relations. From a PR point of view, blogging and podcasting are important because they allow practitioners to communicate directly with audiences, free of the mediation, constraints, and pitfalls of traditional media."

However, we think that if Cook defines the "traditional role of PR" as we do—as a command-and-control system disliked or even hated by those whom it targets—then he is dreadfully wrong. We further take issue with Cook's next point: "Many of the aspects of PR that people lament—spin, bland messages, and corporate speak—are simply efforts to negotiate the media's privileged gatekeeper role without getting trampled by journalistic elephants. The media is driven by the need to create revenue-producing audiences and, unfortunately, the best way to do that is with stories highlighting conflict, scandal, shock, and lots of other negative stuff. The desire for big audiences also leads to coverage that lacks depth or nuance." In short, he argues that because the press is bad, the PR industry needs to be bad to serve it. We think that if the press is so useless, Cook's clients should blog and thus bypass all the spoilers of simple truth that Cook sees in the middle.

Blog or Die?

When we contemplated the current status of the PR industry, we were reminded of one of the few passages that we really loved in Steven Covey's *The Seven Habits of Highly Effective People*. He metaphorically described a jungle in which a management team is hacking its way through the thick, vision-blocking undergrowth. An executive comes in, reviews the team, and then climbs a tree to get a broader view. He calls down with alarm: "Wrong jungle!" The senior manager glares back up at him and replies, "Leave us alone. We're making progress."

The point is that organizations have inertia that continues them along the course they are traveling. They don't like change. Systems that are in place have worked so far, and there's no reason to upset the status quo.

The command-and-control school of communications has been successful doing what it does for more than 50 years. Its practitioners still get press coverage. They are happily hacking their way through their jungles. They don't see that customers don't believe what they are being told and editors don't write what's in the release. The esteem of corporate spokespeople is at a low point.

Blogging is indeed just a tool, a mere dot, as Holtz suggested, on a longer continuum. But it is a revolutionary tool, and those who just keep hacking along in the undergrowth will remain blind to the big picture until it is too late.

8 Blogs and National Cultures

"We are all so different."

—Dr. Alfred Kinsey

"We are all alike."

—The 14th Dalai Lama

When we started searching globally for blogs in languages other than English, we were puzzled by what we found. We had expected Germany to be prominent, being the most populous European country and a leader in engineering and IT, but it turned out to be far less active than its smaller neighbor, France. Likewise in Asia, we were surprised to find business blogging far more prevalent in Japan than in China.

We found there was a reason for the disparity, something important that we had overlooked until Loïc Le Meur, a Six Apart, Inc., executive, who assisted us heavily in researching this chapter, summarized these apparent disparities with a single word—culture. "Some countries are conducive to the openness required in a successful blog. Others are less conducive," Le Meur told us. "We French are accustomed to expressing our thoughts as individuals out in the open. So are you Americans. On the other hand, Germans tend to be more reserved." Le Meur runs Six Apart's European, African, and Middle Eastern operations. He is also arguably Europe's best-known blogger, writing in both French[1] and English,[2] and speaks to a great diversity of companies regarding blogging.

This issue of culture was one of many surprises that confronted us as we researched *Naked Conversations*. Until our chat with Le Meur, we had not begun to grasp its importance in shaping who blogs and where.

Virtually Touring Europe

As Le Meur escorted us through our virtual tour of the European business blogosphere, we found, as we did in English-speaking countries, that the most interesting blogs resided in very large and very small companies. Among the very large was the impressive blog of Michel-Edouard (M.E.) Leclerc, one of France's best-known and most popular business leaders.

Leclerc is president of the *Association des Centres Distributeurs E. Leclerc*, a co-op association of about 600 small and large retailers, mostly in France. The E. Leclerc Association's strategy is to negotiate tough and in volume with suppliers so they can pass low prices on to customers. The Association was established in 1949 by M.E.'s father Edouard Leclerc, who owned and operated a single retail shop in Brittany. The elder Leclerc then began to organize like-minded retailers across France. The Association imposed rules of operation including voluntary limits on markups. The father's ideas were well received by retailers and even better received by their customers. The Association includes food markets, restaurants, gas stations, pharmacies, travel agencies, jewelers, clothing stores, dry cleaners, toy stores, shoe repair services, and sundry other merchants. It is also a leading advocate in pro-consumer legal reform. There are few French citizens who do not shop at one or more Association stores and fewer who do not know Leclerc. He was mentioned so often as a candidate in the last presidential election that he had to go on television to declare he would not run.

According to Jeff Clavier, a French citizen and blogger[3] who founded Silicon Valley–based SoftTech Venture Consulting, "The whole idea was not for Leclerc to become a super-rich billionaire like the owners of many

---

[1] http://www.loiclemeur.com

[2] http://www.loicLeMeur.com/english

[3] http://blog.softtechvc.com

Association competitors, but to give the people the best products at the lowest prices." There are definite political implications. The Association has become a low-cost threat to high-margin monopolies, and the urbane, Sorbonne-educated Leclerc has become its face and voice. He has campaigned effectively on behalf of consumer rights, playing the driving role in several acts of consumer legislation. He holds a degree in economics, and it is clear from his blog[4] that his interests are on global social issues. You won't find him directly promoting E. Leclerc agendas. In fact, the blog is run separately from the Association, and he uses it to present his insight and opinion on politics; French, European, and global economic issues; the rights of the handicapped; help for tsunami victims (the Leclerc organization donated more than two million euros); French hostages; a poetry book he admired; overproduction of French wine; and the quixotic nature of the Italian economy.

When Leclerc started blogging in early 2005, the French blogosphere was quick to criticize him. Among constructive bloggers was Le Meur, who put up a long post[5] in the form of an open letter. "Mssr. Leclerc," he wrote, "I don't know you and please don't take this personally, but here is what you would get from a real blog rather than on this website that you have made and call a blog." He then enumerated the flaws of Leclerc's page, including its lack of RSS feed and Permalink capabilities, providing Leclerc with a public lesson on basic blogging. "I was hoping somebody who reads my blog could reach Leclerc," he recollected, but doubted anything would happen.

Two days later, he was driving in Paris when his cell phone rang. "I hear: 'Hey Loïc, this is Michel-Edouard Leclerc's office. When can you meet with him?'" In one of those Marshall McLuhan moments, Jeff Clavier, sitting in Silicon Valley, had read his friend Le Meur's post and showed it to his wife, who had worked for Leclerc for eight years. She forwarded the post to her former employer—along with Le Meur's phone number. Leclerc directed his assistant to call Le Meur, who managed not to drive off the road when he received it. Less than 48 hours after panning one of France's most influential luminaries, Le Meur found himself sitting across from him in the latter's executive office.

"Well, explain to me how a blog is so different from a web site," Leclerc challenged, and Le Meur went to Google and typed in Leclerc's name. Le Meur's recent negative posting came up first. Leclerc stared blankly at the

---

[4] http://www.michel-edouard-Leclerc.com/blog/m.e.l
[5] http://www.loiclemeur.com/france/2005/01/micheledouard_l.html

Google screen, his jaw slightly dropped: "How did you manage—on a search for my name—to get your name to come out above mine?" Le Meur said, "I told him that because he didn't have a real blog, he had no Google juice. But if he converted this thing he had started into a real blog, his name would eclipse mine."

Amazed, Leclerc paid heed. Over the protests and mutterings of his marketing advisers, who feared negative comments, Leclerc now lets visitors post their unfiltered thoughts. "I was really impressed with Leclerc, more than I thought I would be. He showed me a paper diary where he had made one entry every day for 20 years. He was already a blogger. He just didn't know it and the tools were not yet there. Leclerc said he wanted to be closer to the people. His blog seems to be the perfect tool for this." Leclerc now uses all blog functionality and posts loyally every day. He has accumulated juice on Google and authenticity in the blogosphere, and Le Meur's post has fallen off Google's front page.

Observed Clavier, "Despite being one of the most visible French executives, Michel-Edouard has remained very approachable and genuine. That's why I am not surprised that he got the 'blogging thing' so quickly. His blog is an enabling platform for larger scale genuine conversations."

Both his diary and his approachability came across in our interview with him. Leclerc told us that he still takes his hand-written diary with him wherever he goes and the blog is merely its extension.

Said Leclerc, "In order to save energy and capitalize on already formulated answers, I decided to create a personal site. My colleagues, younger than me and more expert on the Internet, convinced me to blog in order to be more interactive and more in line with the current events." He said it serves two purposes. On a personal level, it is a space where he can structure and organize his ideas, helping him clarify his vision. On a professional level, it provides an efficient mechanism in which he can communicate with people who are interested in the organization.

Leclerc is an enormously busy person, perpetually in meetings, at conferences, or in transit. "I am constantly questioned about my organization and how I view the company, the economy, and social relations." The blog is a place where the questions most frequently asked of him can be answered, and anyone who wants to know can go to read them.

Leclerc has learned and changed because of the blogging experience, he told us. "Blogging is thinking in front of others. It is accepting that you are open to their comments, their suggestions, and criticism. This exhibition in front of the public leads to . . . humility. You need to be prepared to make amends, to review an argument, or reformulate it. You also need to be intellectually strict. When you lead a huge company, you create expectations that you did not want to create. My blog is in the public debate. It is up to me to be as credible as possible, [to be] coherent, and not to contradict what I say in my blog with the company's actual practices."

Leclerc said that when he first started blogging, it felt like an intellectual game, but over time, a sense of responsibility set in. "All these comments ultimately constitute a kind of social recognition. With the increase in audience, you become a little bit of an addict. It pleases your ego. And it is here that you measure your responsibility. If you don't take care, a blog can not only be a tool of influence, which is good, but also a tool of manipulation. I personally consider that due to the fact that I am well-known, I am required to be even more responsible in what I write. Of course, that prevents neither humor nor polemic," he said.

Although he finds unevenness in the quality of comments he's received, he told us they "oblige me to polish up my arguments. These are good tests before I take the floor at conferences. I was, for instance, very fond of reducing the VAT [European Community Value Added Tax] for products that most respect the environment (organic, fair trade, etc.). I thought that would boost their sales to the detriment of products that pollute more. But comments kept insisting the idea would be nearly impossible to implement and I moderated my position." Another time, Leclerc used his blog to take on a French Member of Parliament (MP) who proposed banning merchants from bagging up buyer's goods in non-biodegradable sacks. Leclerc suggested recyclable bags as a more pragmatic alternative. Both cases elicited heavy comment traffic. The MP moderated his proposal, "showing the influence blogs can have on people in power, " Leclerc told us.

He added that he did not wish to be "a slave to his blog." He reads all comments each morning and then reserves a half-hour at some point in each day to blog. He spends much time traveling throughout Europe and disdains bringing a computer along. Instead, he hand-writes his blogs into his diary, on planes and in trains, and then uses an old-fashioned Dictaphone for his secretary to transcribe and post. On weekends he makes his own entries, but said that, "I enjoy concentrating on the content more than sitting in front of my screen online with other Internet users."

Although Leclerc's blog began as a personal experiment, the Leclerc Association had begun experimenting with blogs in a couple of ways. In the public area, Leclerc told us the Association is employing tests inspired by "our friend Loïc Le Meur" to improve customer interaction. He predicted the results will prove that blogs are superior to opinion polls in helping understand what customers want. While the blogosphere often talks about companies being transparent, Leclerc was the first to observe that the customer also becomes more transparent through comments than in survey results.

Internally, the Association is using blogs to determine best practices in each merchant category. For example, Association grocers discuss the best way to display fruits and vegetables to get customers and grocers to interact more conversationally.

We asked him about European business blogging, which he described as being in the "crazed" early phases and where comments can be harsh.

> *There's a lot of zapping. But the phenomenon already regulates itself and you see the implementation of a kind of market segmentation. There are the blogs of young people that, better than chat, enable them to exchange ideas, music and to create a more intense associative link (around sports for instance). In the world of companies or in the environment of arts or culture there are many corporate initiatives. But what I see is that apart from corporate blogs or festivals, the managers, the animators, or the artists create in parallel their own blogs disassociated from the first ones. Blogging enables one to have a greater humanization of communication.*

Polls that came out during our research on Leclerc indicated he would again be the front-runner if he chose to be a candidate for French president. We wondered if we were interviewing the next head of state and could not help but insert the non-blog question into the conversation. He began:

> *I like public debate. I have a passion for political questions. With my job, I happen to be at the head of an extraordinary observatory of social life. I am managing a network that works with 8,000 industrial suppliers, around 30 banks, and all the administrations. My group is located in several European countries and I buy goods everywhere in the world. Thanks to*

these links, to our networks, and to the work of our executives, I have gained a certain vision of society. And I try to enrich the public debate. You should not leave the political expertise only to political professionals. I personally made the choice never to be at a loss for words and to say what I think. This is why my fellow citizens choose me by an overwhelming majority in the opinion polls. They like people who spend their energy for society. They applaud a certain kind of courage. And I am extremely flattered by this.

But he would rather blog than be president.

I think I am more legitimate and efficient in my economic activity. Within 20 years, [my group has] succeeded in changing the French legislation, which was quite dusty. We obtained a court decision against the oil monopolies. Thanks to our actions, there is free competition for cosmetics, pharmaceuticals, and branded textiles. I did a lot for the practical transition to the Euro currency and [lowered] prices. One of the major questions today is the environment. I fight for the development of fair trade, for energy conservation, and for a reduction or recycling of packaging. If I were a Member of Parliament, maybe I would be heard a little bit. But as a manager of a company who expresses himself with all the strength of a commercial network, I can make my ideas much more credible. Yes, it is on the practical level that I feel myself the most effective. On my blog, as in all types of media, I can convey more positive ideas than if I would have been a mayor or an MP representing a district.

For us, the Leclerc interview was a highlight of the *Naked Conversations* experience. We are in no position to comment on French or world politics, but we wish we saw the vision and humanity displayed by Leclerc in the people who stand for election there, in our own country, or anywhere else for that matter.

At the Heart of The Strawberry

Le Meur estimated there were at least 10,000 French business blogs in June 2005, with adoption rates accelerating in both large and small business organizations. One of our favorite small business stories is about a company that probably could not exist without its blog. In fact, the blog is at the heart of the matter.

La Fraise, or "The Strawberry,"[6] is the passion child of Patrice Cassard, a self-educated former web games and communities developer based in central France near Lyon. He's crazy about t-shirts, rarely wearing anything else on the upper half of his body. To him, t-shirts are a "tremendous way to express oneself, not just in designing them but in wearing them. T-shirts allow you to convey a message, or to stand out from the crowd," he said. But retail shop after shop, he noted, stocked the same commercially churned, mass-produced piles of folded cotton—hardly the stuff of free expression or passion.

Convinced he could do better, but not quite certain how, Cassard decided to start his own online t-shirt shop—and simultaneously, his blog. He confessed that he originally started the blog to feel less lonely as he immersed himself in startup efforts. He would just share his experiences with anyone who might be interested. He quickly discovered there were a great many interested people, and they were more than a little willing to share their feelings on t-shirts. Readers started sending him designs. Others then started voting on which designs they would buy if the t-shirt were actually produced.

When a design musters enough votes, Cassard compensates its creator with 300 euros (just over $350) and manufactures them. He almost always ships t-shirts on the day they are ordered. The blog is central to every aspect of the business except the physical shipment and credit card processing, making it highly efficient while charging customers less than they might pay in a brick-and-mortar store. The blog also gathers a bigger crowd than most retail t-shirt departments. He averages 30 comments per post, and one recently drew 345. In May 2005, his average monthly sales were between 1,500 and 1,800 units. Revenue averaged about 36,000 euros (almost $45,000), with growth trending upward each month.

Le Meur usually references La Fraise as a proof point when presenting to Europe's largest companies. "Often, they laugh at me. They say, 'We are a

---

[6] http://www.lafraise.com

multinational corporation and you bring us this t-shirt guy?' I say, 'No, wait. Before you throw me out of the room, our t-shirt guy has figured out how to put the customer at the center of everything, rather than out on the edge. The customers have more product ideas than he does and he prospers by listening to them. They decide what he manufactures and markets. What could this strategy do for you?'"

Sometimes these companies still throw Le Meur out of the room. But increasingly, they want to hear more. He advises those who will listen: "If a blogger has enough passion, the blog becomes the central place on the Internet for that topic. Companies understand the importance of Google, but they don't yet get how blogging fits in. If the corporation doesn't do this for themselves, then someone else will. That is why Andrew Carton's Treonauts blog [covered in Chapter 5] is so much more influential on the Treo company web sites and their marketing materials. They can no longer take it away from him."

Slow Driving on the Autobahn

With a population of 80 million, Germany is about one-third more populated than France. But whereas France had more than 3.5 million bloggers in June 2005, Le Meur estimated that Germany's bloggers number only 200,000, and fewer than 100 of them are business bloggers. Most, predictably, are consultants.

One prominent business blogger of note is Marcel Reichart, managing director of marketing and communications at Hubert Burda, one of Europe's largest media companies.[7] Deutsche Telecom, owners of T-Mobile in the U.S., has a blog[8] for its German T-Online service, but posting is sporadic, comments are not allowed, and it looks more like a static web site than a blog. The Fish Market,[9] an e-commerce company, has a charming, heavily trafficked blog. The site would probably not fare as well in the U.S. because it is so highly commercialized, but it seems to be successful there. Frosta,[10] a well-known German food company, has also started a blog.

SAP, the German-based global enterprise software behemoth, claims to have the largest German business blog, directed at nurturing its global

[7] http://marcellomedia.blogs.com/mrb
[8] http://www.community.t-online.de/c/34/68/72/3468720.html
[9] http://www.fischmarkt.de
[10] http://www.blog-frosta.de

community of SAP users. We cannot be certain of the size claim because much of it is behind a firewall. However, several senior SAP executives, including board member Shai Agassi,[11] blog at least sporadically. The company does seem to be encouraging company employees to start blogging. Agassi told Le Meur that he advises employees, "If you blog, you exist and you start gathering a community around your expertise."

We were disappointed when BMW declined to discuss its blogging plans. We think it would be an ideal company to blog because so many of its customers are passionate evangelists. We have rarely talked to an owner of a BMW who did not advise us to buy one. We think the company would learn much from its existing customers on how to make its vehicles even better. If blogging can move the needle for the likes of General Motors, we can only speculate as to what it could do for BMW.

One irony—eBay enjoys a huge and growing presence in Germany, which is further evidence that people there trust Internet technology. The country may be a passenger in that slow lane so far, but when they put their pedals to the metal, as anyone who has experienced the Autobahn can attest, the Germans are capable of moving amazingly fast.

How can blogging take off in France and lag in Germany? Le Meur points out that while the French, like Americans, are quick to express their feelings and aspirations, German businesspeople tend to be cautious in what they publicly disclose. German author and freelance journalist Jochen Wegner,[12] speaking at Les Blogs, Europe's first blogging conference, said that culture is key to why there is so little going on in Germany. "It is not natural for Germans to share their views and talk about themselves."

Siestas in the Blogosphere?

Compared with Spanish-speaking countries, Germany is exploding in the blogosphere. Spanish, the second most popular language in the Western world, is the language of only about 50,000 blogs total, according to Blog Census, an organization that tracks blogs by language. That's fewer than probably exists on North America's West Coast.

---

[11] http://www.sap.com/community/pub/private/mendocino/blogs.epx
[12] http://selbr.de

According to Mariano Amartino, an Argentina-based blog evangelist and community-building consultant, "Spanish-speaking companies don't blog." He estimates the number of them worldwide at about 10—one each in Mexico, Costa Rica, and Uruguay, and double that in Spain and Argentina. Amartino is probably responsible for the creation of about 20 percent of them through his consulting business. We also suspect he forgot to count his own,[13] which is perhaps the best-known Spanish language business blog by an individual. When we posted an early version of this chapter on our book blog, several readers told us that our estimate *had* to be too low. But try as we might, we failed to find any additional business blogs in the Spanish language. In fact, we are cheating just a bit with the few examples that we do discuss here.

Amartino helped Argentina-based Clarin, the world's most popular Spanish-speaking newspaper, to create two blogging projects. In 2003, he helped build Clarin.com,[14] which was probably the first media-owned blog worldwide. When Amartino was involved, the site was receiving 18,000 visitors daily, and they were leaving more than 3,500 comments a week. During our visit to the site in mid-2005, comments had been stripped out in favor of Trackbacks, a trend we found prevalent elsewhere as well. As we were writing *Naked Conversations*, Amartino was helping Clarin with a new project that, he said, "takes into account the value of having real bloggers write the blogs." His new project, Clarin Weblogs,[15] quietly launched and in July 2005 was receiving about 5,000 daily visitors. The key difference in the new blog is that it covers blogosphere issues exclusively. According to Amartino, Clarin wants to build a presence in the emerging Spanish-speaking blog community, riding the wave when the new phenomenon inevitably takes off.

He sees two barriers currently slowing adoption: (1) Small businesses, often skating on thin margin, mistakenly perceive that the cost of all things Internet-related is high, and (2) large corporations still "don't get" the powerful benefits of blogs and continue to dismiss them as irrelevant online teen journals. Amartino sounded far from discouraged, however, because blogging is gaining momentum in the development community, which, he believes, will seed traditional corporations over time.

---

[13] http://www.uberbin.net
[14] http://weblogs.clarin.com
[15] http://weblogs.clarin.com/weblogs

China Dragging

Business is booming in China. So is Internet access, with 92 million of its 1.3 billion people now going online according to Hiawatha Bray of the *Boston Globe*. But while China's 2003 regime change brought hopes of less restriction on market economies as well as human rights, government censorship of the Internet speech in China seems to be headed in the reverse direction.

We heard some big numbers when researching China's blogging participation. The Blog Herald[16] reported that Blog China[17] claimed in July 2005 to have 2 million bloggers, with projections of reaching 10 million by year-end, when it intends to go public on NASDAQ. We have no way of confirming or verifying these numbers, but people closer to the situation have raised considerable doubts. The numbers are much smaller according to Isaac Mao,[18] a principal researcher at CES Labs on e-Learning and co-founder of CNBlog.org, which tracks blogging on a weekly basis. According to Mao, in mid-2005, there were a mere 1.23 million bloggers nationwide, with about 760,000 posting at least once weekly. He considers frequency important in counting active blogs. This number is far below other estimates, but our instincts tell us his number may be more solid.

"The blogosphere here is mostly for personal use," Mao told us. "I don't see many Chinese enterprises supporting employee blogging like Microsoft or Sun Microsystems, but interestingly, some businesses are using blogs for customer relationship-building. Some small businesses are trying to use blogs to market their products and services," he told us. For example, Tao Yao[19] is a blog used to sell hand-crafted jewelry online, with the transaction linked to the Yahoo! China auction site. (Yahoo! is one of many Western Internet companies, along with Google and Microsoft, that have agreed to abide by China's increasingly stringent censorship rules.) Mao notes that blogging gives small Chinese businesses easy access to more customers, and he expects growth to continue there.

We asked if censorship was a factor slowing business. "China's government's control over the media including online web sites is well known around the world. Though they won't interfere directly with business blogging, it's very

---

[16] http://www.blogherald.com
[17] http://blogchina.com
[18] http://www.isaacmao.com
[19] http://taoyao.blogbus.com

easy to be affected, knowing that if they want to shut down or censor some blog hosting site, they can and will." Mao has had first-hand experience. On April Fool's Day 2005, he posted a joke blog saying he had been shipped off to Siberia. It was mysteriously taken down, perhaps shipped off to some arctic wasteland where it remains frozen in cyberspace. When we interviewed him by e-mail, we asked if our conversation might be monitored. "The policies of my government are well known," he discreetly replied.

Japan Rising

Japan, in contrast to China, is experiencing a striking acceleration in both consumer and business blogging, particularly among women. The Impress Group, which conducts an annual survey of Japan's online trends,[20] reported that 32 million Japanese homes had broadband by the end of 2004 and that more than 7 in 10 Japanese had heard of blogs, up from about 40 percent in 2003. According to the Impress findings, 25 percent of women under 30 are active in the blogosphere.

To better understand why Japan was taking off faster than any country east of France, we turned to Nob Seki, Le Meur's counterpart for Six Apart in Japan. We told him we were surprised that a country whose business community is noted for polite formality and conservative dark suits would be so active in the blogosphere, where up-close-and-personal seemed to be the norm. Seki told us that we had only a partial understanding of Japanese culture. While Japanese corporations may retain a top-down organizational structure, he said, "People here are different at work than they are at home. At home, we are informal. It's different when you are in the office, part of an organization. When you leave, you can easily become very personal." In fact, there is evidence that major corporations are loosening their structures after a decade of recession, and through Seki we learned that the legendary Japanese politeness is not always the case.

Most Japanese business blogs, we also learned, are informal in tone, addressing visitors in a style usually reserved for personal friends or family. Japanese people are very accustomed to switching back and forth from formal to informal. "If you are speaking as a company president," he told us, "you are expected to be very formal, but sales people talk to customers and

---

[20] http://www.impressholdings.com/release/2005/025

prospects as if they were their best friends." Many Japanese blogs are sales-oriented—more than would be accepted in French- or English-language blogosphere sectors—and their informal style surprises no one in Japan.

A case in point is a Nissan Motors blog[21] designed to blatantly sell a new city car called Tiida. Its sales-focused tone surprised no one, but what did raise enough eyebrows to catch media notice was that it began with Tiida's product manager proclaiming: "I am Yamamoto from Nissan Motors." This is unusual, Nob told us, because such managers usually don't get to introduce themselves on a personal level to the public. Each Yamamoto posting focused on another snazzy feature of the car and was written in a clear effort to make you want to buy it. The low-cost car has become popular and the blog well accepted. We are told Nissan is considering marketing the car internationally.

Before 2004, nobody in Japanese business blogged. Nobody. When Six Apart opened shop there in December 2003, Seki recalled, "People thought we were crazy. There was no blogging market, and no market was expected." Then it developed rapidly through a series of overlapping phases. First, web site developers bought the blogging tools, stripped out the ones that created an authentic blog, and used the rest to build static web sites at lower cost than was possible with traditional web technology.

Next, e-commerce vendors such as Lloyd's Antique Online Shop of Tokyo[22] discovered that blogging gave them enough Google juice to triple sales. Lloyd's took its existing online catalog and recalibrated. Each post displayed a photo of an item for sale, with a catalog-type description. Lloyd's allowed comments through Trackback, so that the e-commerce sites were technically blogs.

While all this was unfolding, larger companies started watching what was happening. Enterprise players started immersing toes into the blogosphere, with internal blogs replacing intranet applications on the workgroup level. By the middle of 2004, gargantuan marketers such as Procter & Gamble were blatantly marketing detergent to Japanese housewives via a blogsite extension of a traditional advertising and marketing campaign. The blog asked women at home to share their washday experiences. It was, of course, all part of the launch of a new detergent and was enormously successful.

BK1, a large online bookseller—sort of the Amazon.com of Japan—started a site in July 2004, selecting employees to blog about books[23] and letting

---

[21] http://blog.nissan.co.jp/TIIDA

[22] http://www.businessblog.jp/000178.html

[23] http://blog.bk1.co.jp

visitors buy the books by clicking on a shopping cart feature in the blog. After three months, traffic had increased by 10–20 percent and sales had increased 5–10 percent (after adjusting for the impact of a new Harry Potter book that was released in Japanese at the same time). Takeshi Kouno, who designed the site, told us that the blog had solid PR impact because BK1 was the first bookstore in Japan to use blogging, and attention to the blog attracted new customers. What really helped was that bookstore employees introduced new offerings with personal reviews written in the first person. This was in striking contrast to competing online book merchants, who merely offered up title search databases on static web sites. In fact, the company became a recognized authority on how to use blogs to attract customers, and the media have interviewed corporate staff on how to use a blog for business.

Like Pulling Teeth

A small business story we could really sink our teeth into was that of Isshin Dental Clinic in Yokohama, which set up a blog to market into the geographic limits of its community. Its Haisha Blog[24] shows photos depicting smiling, congenial, white-coated staff. (*Haisha* means dentist in Japanese.) Visitors can read answers to frequent questions and patient testimonials. According to Six Apart's Ginger Tulley, who translated the blog for us, the clinic has told Six Apart that it is "a reasonable investment." Reasonable indeed. Revenue jumped more than 80 percent in less than a year. We think the style of the blog is more acceptable to Japanese culture than perhaps French or American, but it is indicative of the enormous opportunities blogs offer to small businesses everywhere. While a web site can probably do very little for a local dry cleaner, the Haisha Blog is indicative of future plumber, baker, and sushi blogs to come to a great number of localities. Each will demonstrate the authority and commitment of the merchants, tradesmen, and craftspeople behind it.

Nifty & Nasty

Nifty Corp.—a Japanese ISP and a subsidiary of Fujitsu—started Japan's first business blog in 2003, aimed at consumers. It was a natural step from Nifty's

---

[24] http://www.haisha.biz/index.html

hosted bulletin boards, which included Channel 2, one of Japan's best known and most controversial. The service allowed unfiltered anonymous comments, with sometimes shocking results. Seki told us, "People could write about anything. It got very nasty." One tragic example was a teenager who announced anonymously on Channel 2 that he intended to commit murder. Then, the next day, according to Nob, he did. Electronic bulletin boards are still in vogue in Japan, with much of the subject matter coming from the depths of the dark side. Their use of anonymous comment has shaped Japanese business blogging, which ardently wishes to avoid such unpleasantries.

When Nifty introduced its blogging service, the company shut down the comments feature, asking people to continue the conversation through Trackback, which is traceable. The experiment succeeded. Not only are Trackbacks being used in decidedly more polite fashion than comments, but the need to have a blog in order to join the conversation ignited consumer blogging. In Japan, it is extremely rare to find a blog that employs comments. Elsewhere in the world, shutting off comments remains controversial because it stops people who don't have blogs from joining in. Likewise, anonymous comments allow "drive-by" participants who post ugly comments and then move on without participating in dialogue. In Japan, Seki sees no likelihood that comments will re-emerge. "Trackback is more polite," he told us. "And you know who you are talking with."

Culture Shaping Blogs

This chapter helped solve one of the mysteries we saw in blogging at the outset. Why do some companies blog while others don't? Why do bloggers at some companies blog well and with abandon, whereas others are tediously bland? Why is blogging exploding in the United States, France, and Japan but growing slowly in Germany, Russia, and China? Why is blogging flourishing at Microsoft and Sun and stifled at Apple Computer and Google?

Is it really just culture? We saw evidence that it might be. But where we got hung up was in variations of our own native tongue and the way it is spoken on the British Isles. Blogging has taken off in England with the general public, but in Ireland it has not. The English are generally regarded as reserved. On the other hand, through literature and taverns, the Irish are generally regarded as a great story-telling people. So why don't the Irish blog? We asked Tom Raftery, whose IT Views[25] is the only Irish blog we follow. Raftery noted that the Irish are also noted for being "quite guarded when it comes to personal and emotional issues. On one hand, we are still quite parochial. On the other, some would say that because of our oral storytelling tradition we don't need a blog to tell the world what we are thinking—just some friends, acquaintances, co-workers, passers by, or complete strangers, a pint of Guinness, or a dram of whiskey, and we have no problem communicating."

More seriously, he explained the most likely reason for Ireland's dearth of bloggers is not cultural; it is that Ireland lags behind other countries in broadband adoption in the home, with about 3.4 subscribers for every 100 households. "Now, if the price of broadband were cheap enough that bars would provide free WiFi . . ." he speculated. But we think it will be awhile before tavern-based WiFi services displace darts as a pastime. In fact, we hope so.

Of course, technology is a factor and always will be. For example, we assume that the reason mobile blogs—blogs generated from handheld devices often featuring photos—are so much more popular in Korea than text ones is that most people there have cell phones but fewer have personal computers, particularly at home.

Still, culture is clearly playing a role in how blogging develops. It can be national, ethnic, corporate, or departmental. Where people are encouraged to speak their mind, and those in power trust the people they oversee, blogging flourishes. There are reasons why political blogging in the United States has taken off wildly, whereas in China it has not.

We imagine the same could be said about why blogging is not prolific at Apple Computer but it is at Sun Microsystems.

[25] http://www.tomrafteryit.net/views

9 Thorns in the Roses

"The only thing we have to fear is fear itself."

—*Franklin Delano Roosevelt*

We've gushed through eight chapters extolling the virtues of blogging. Through the cases we've reported on, we've tried to illustrate a great number of reasons why any company of any size and in almost any country should blog. But we are not prone to Pollyanna outlooks. Wherever there are roses, there are thorns. Blogging has its prickly issues—some real and some imaginary. Some companies and people should not blog, period. For others, determining whether the benefits outweigh the potential drawbacks can be a tough call.

The prickliest thorn is one we discussed in the preceding chapter—culture. When Scoble spoke with Target executives, they told him that blogging was unlikely to start up inside America's fourth largest retailer because being personal in public was just not Target's way.

That's a cultural thing. Besides, Target is currently in a strong position, pulling ahead of most competitors. Cultures don't change in that situation. Target will probably not blog until a weaker competitor in the same category starts blogging, perhaps out of desperation, and the new blog brings it success that cuts into Target's bottom line. At that point, Target may have to change its own culture in response.

Cultures—in nations or in companies—change slowly and often painfully. The thorn that might stick into Target's side ultimately is that other retailers appear through blogging to be more open and responsive to customers. The folks at Target told us they were continuing to watch blogging very carefully, and we assume that this is why.

From our perspective, culture is the biggest thorn—the sharpest and the most threatening. Countries and companies where blogging is prevalent, over time, will be perceived as more open and more trustworthy.

The Echo Chamber

Another thorn is what we call the "echo chamber." Blogging can fool you. You may think you are conversing with the world, when it's just a few people talking frequently, back and forth to each other, creating the illusion of amplification. The echo chamber can deceive a business into thinking it is either more widely successful or further off the mark than it is in reality, because a few people are making a lot of noise. Always remember that the people who comment and link most often are the ones with the most passion on a subject. They don't necessarily represent your target audience accurately.

Such was the case with Howard Dean in his 2004 run for the U.S. presidency. The blogosphere was wild about him. The noise generated media attention and financial contributions. What was little noted during that period, however, was Karl Rove saying that Dean would be the easiest candidate for the incumbent president to beat, that John Kerry was raising more money than Dean, and that the polls consistently showed moderate voters in both parties were uncomfortable with Dean. Blogging's echo chamber threw lots of people off track. It can fool you if you don't watch and listen closely.

Reasons Not to Blog

There are unquestionably people and businesses who have good reasons not to blog. But we also believe that many of the reasons we have heard are overblown. Fear of what *could* happen has become, in our view, the greatest of all barriers to entry. We are certain that for most people, driving an automobile is probably riskier than blogging.

Some reasons—such as fear of accidental disclosures or conflicts with other corporate communications channels—are identical to reasons we heard back in the 1990s for why companies shouldn't build web sites. Others—such as lack of centralized control—remind us of the mainframe days of the '70s, when administrators argued that PCs should be banned from the enterprise. During watershed times, businesses develop a disease called FUD (Fear, Uncertainty, and Doubt). Decision makers, uncomfortable with the disruption, start searching for reasons to stave off change. Incumbents feed those fears with every fathomable reason to maintain the status quo. Each reason contains some element of truth, but just how much is the subject of debate. We'll get to that in a minute, but first, let's look at the aforementioned group that can sit out this revolution—companies and people with good reasons not to blog.

Who Should Not Blog

If you are a genuine bad guy, or are part of an organization of bad guys, don't blog.

We asked *Naked Conversations*' blog visitors, "Who shouldn't blog?" We got some insightful answers. Randy Charles Morin,[1] a software developer, hit the nail on the despotic head with his two-word answer: "Saddam Hussein." He's right. Saddam has always been a command-and-control freak. He prefers monologue to dialogue even in face-to-face meetings. We think Saddam would have been most persuasive in discouraging members of his former organization from blogging. We doubt he would believe that his blog readers were collectively smarter than he is, and we don't think he'd respond well to the "tough love" left in comments and linked blogs. Saddam has a well-documented history of avoiding transparency. Besides, he is going to have some trouble with Internet access at either home or work for some time to come. Saddam, if you are reading this, don't blog. It won't help your situation.

Blogs have so far worked extremely well for companies and people with do-the-right-thing cultures. We think they will fail in cultures that have public-be-damned attitudes. You don't need to be an actual despot to make the list, as former executives at Tyco, WorldCom, and Enron will tell you. But the list

---

[1] http://www.kbcafe.com/rss

is broader than the corrupt. It also includes the tacky. As Church of the Customer's Jackie Huba[2] told us, "Cheesy companies with cheesy products and disdain or contempt for their customers should not blog."

We would add to the list those companies that disdain or mistreat their employees, such as diamond and gold miners, rubber plantation owners, and "employers" of children tethered to workbenches. Such entities would probably find it difficult to tolerate an open employee blogging policy, and conversational marketing is probably not among their company objectives.

An organized crime blog might prove colorful, but we doubt it would be transparent. However, not all vice-mongers need abstain. Two self-proclaimed, top-level call girls maintain well-trafficked blogs. Belle de Jour: Intimate Adventures of a London Call Girl[3] and Jet Set Lara: An International Escort's Travel blog[4] are both highly literate and occasionally enticing. But both authors remain anonymous. Lara displays enticing photos on her site, but she keeps her face concealed. The only testimony we have that Lara is real is that Belle said she was in her blog. Belle and Lara may or may not be authentic, but we have no way of knowing, and this cuts into their credibility. Should they blog? Well, in Belle's case, it seems to have helped her business. She claims she's about to be under contract to begin a regular column in a British tabloid.

Additionally, companies that intend to victimize customers and supporters, such as fraudulent charities, Ponzi and other pyramid schemers, and sundry con artists should not blog. We suspect, however, that some con artists have already found their way into the blogosphere, and the challenge will be for other bloggers to be vigilant in flushing them out. Bloggers need to ask hard-nosed questions when their colleagues make claims or issue pleas for financial assistance. For example, in the aftermath of the tsunami tragedy of late 2004, millions of dollars were raised through a large number of relief funds, and to date it remains challenging to certify that the money was distributed appropriately. Similar deceptions were suspected again after Katrina devastated New Orleans.

Security Operatives

Some organizations deal in highly sensitive and confidential information. We cannot envision, nor would we recommend, a federal employee blogging

[2] http://customerevangelists.typepad.com
[3] http://belledejour-uk.blogspot.com
[4] http://www.jetsetblog.com/travel

publicly about a typical workday in a clandestine intelligence gathering operation. Likewise, companies engaged in less dangerous but equally sensitive matters, such as financial consulting, stock brokerages, private investigators, and defense law, might find it necessary to blog prudently or avoid it altogether. Raytheon, Lockheed Martin, and Homeland Security were all mentioned to us among entities that should not blog, and to a large degree we concur.

But even so, the issue may be more that certain material is not "bloggable," rather than that employees at a particular company should not blog. A great many attorneys blog, for example. Steven Streight, a frequent commenter on our *Naked Conversations* blog, said, "I know of a police chief and a city planner and a fire chief who have blogs. Anybody can have a blog. A mafia hit man can have a blog. A garbage collector, shoe shiner, toilet scrubber, whatever. Sure, certain things must be left unsaid, but they know all that. That's old hat to FBI and CIA people."

We should note that in this chapter, we refer only to public blogs. Six Apart estimates more than half of all business blogs are private, and many of the most security-minded companies use them in that light. For example, we were told that the U.S. Department of Homeland Security shares internal information through blogging in its Western region. Our request to discuss how it is being used went unanswered.

Additionally, there are perfectly wonderful companies, whose cultures are just fine, whose employees are happy, but that simply have no reason to blog. One successful company we know has so few customers that they can all meet in a conference room to converse. There are still local merchants who reach all the customers they need through non–technically assisted conversations, and in some businesses the majority of the customers do not use computers.

The Dull Should Not Blog

Some people just shouldn't blog, even in environments where it is encouraged. People who have really awful communication skills should not blog. Employees who hate their jobs, their managers, or their products and services will find blogging a catalyst for early departure. Executive officers who cannot resist making overly rosy predictions may find their blog has a thorny backlash, and the same goes for marketing professionals who cannot resist strings of enthusiastic adjectives. People who find their jobs repetitive or dull shouldn't blog. In fact, people who are dull usually have dull blogs and receive little notice.

People who can't abide criticism will not enjoy the blogging experience. The stronger the position they take, the stronger the comments disagreeing with them may be. Commenters might not agree with you, might not like your work, might have something against your company, or just might not like you personally.

There are also people who just can't resist an embellishment here and there. They do it all the time in conversations, and no one challenges them. They do it in e-mail and perhaps a business conversation, and while people may become occasionally suspicious, for the most part they get away with it. But if a habitual exaggerator tries blogging, he or she is likely to learn it's the wrong venue. The blogosphere is one big fact-checking mechanism. And while a white lie may slip through from time to time, blogging is a venue best avoided for those prone to hyperbole.

Thorns in the Butt

Many of the examples we've provided so far are easy black-and-white stuff, and a bit facile. Most business environments are gray. Very big thorns-in-the-butt lurk in gray areas for both employees and employers. How does an employer encourage blogging on one hand, while on the other prevent employees from embarrassing the company? Technorati CEO David Sifry faced that dilemma when Niall Kennedy, an employee-blogger, altered a World War II poster about loose lips sinking ships to lampoon current corporate anti-blog policy, likening anti-blog executives to Joseph Stalin.[5] Sifry simply *asked* Kennedy to take down the post and Kennedy complied. But what would have happened if Kennedy had refused? Would Sifry have declared that to be insubordination and have fired Kennedy? If he had, what impact would that have on other Technorati employees who blog?

Microsoft is a company that takes obvious pride in its pro-blog culture. But the fact that it has no blog policy, other than "blog smart," has created more than one thorny issue. Some managers are tougher than others toward public transparency. What happens if one who, like Scoble, blogs in an open way, moves into a department that doesn't care for his practice or his tendency to

---

[5] http://www.niallkennedy.com/blog/archives/2005/03/bloggers_seen_a.html

point out areas where the competition is beating Microsoft? Does the blog he or she is encouraged to maintain in one department block that employee's career path in another?

The situation gets thornier when managers are vague, divided, or inconsistent on what should or should not be permitted. Cameron Reilly, a blogger[6] and a podcaster[7] of increasing renown, told us he quit Microsoft after six years as a business development manager because of an issue that emerged after he quoted a colleague on his blog saying, "Five years ago, Microsoft had average products but great marketing. Today, we have great products but average marketing. The biggest problem is—people think it's still the other way around." That post made his boss irate, Reilly told us.

Reilly told us his job was to develop trust in the Microsoft marketplace, which he thought meant he should "speak honestly about the company's business." His boss disagreed, Reilly contended. "I was told that the content of my blog was inappropriate and unprofessional. I was basically given a warning and [told] that if the content on my blog was considered inappropriate again, I'd be terminated." After a brief stormy period, Reilly quit and started his own company. A spokesperson for Microsoft declined to comment on the issue. Policy, we were told, prohibits public discussion of employee termination issues.

Reilly takes issue with Microsoft's loose "blog smart" policy.

> When employers avoid putting clear blogging policies in place, using one of these "just use good common sense" clauses, which can be defined to mean whatever the heck managers want it to mean, there is a problem waiting to happen. My concern isn't so much for the bloggers—it's for the employers. If you leave how the inevitable blogging issues get handled up to the imagination (or lack thereof) of your managers, you stand to lose good people. Bloggers aren't the type to take kindly to bullying. They will leave and start their own company or go work for your competition. The obvious conclusion for employees is that if you don't know what you can or cannot post on your blog, you'd best not do it.

---

[6] http://www.cameronreilly.com
[7] http://www.thepodcastnetwork.com/gday_world

The FUD Barrier

The term "FUD" was coined by Gene Amdahl[8] after he founded Amdahl Corp[9] in 1975. He contended, "FUD is the fear, uncertainty, and doubt that IBM sales people instill in the minds of potential customers who might be considering Amdahl products." IBM people were reminding customers that "nobody ever got fired for buying IBM products," implying that you could get fired for buying Amdahl's.

Since then, the term has become more generic, used generally to reflect corporate inertia to changing existing systems. In fact, a legitimate concern is that blogging doesn't fit easily into functional organization charts. While companies try to squeeze it into communications or marketing groups, it is often an awkward fit.

There has been a lot of FUD regarding blogs, enough to make the prudent manager cautious. Each concern contains grains of truth. But should these grains serve as barriers to all the benefits? We think not. Let's look briefly at the ones we've heard the most about in our talks with corporate managers.

1. Negative Comments

Businesses hate being bad-mouthed. We all hate being bad-mouthed. Church of the Customer's Ben McConnell frequently addresses business audiences. He told us the first question he usually hears after a presentation is: "What do I do about negative comments?" According to his partner, Jackie Huba, "We tell them that people are saying negative things about you anyway and they have lots of places to say it online. Why wouldn't you want them to say it in *your* forum—your blog—where you can address the comments head-on?" As Microsoft's Mike Torres observed, "People are a lot more polite when they know you are listening."

In fact, even the most veteran blogger occasionally expresses angst at what is euphemistically called "tough love" in comment postings. Some commentary seems to be far from loving, but bloggers collectively believe they have become wiser from negative comments. When the comments are unjustified, Huba pointed out, "a company's customer evangelists jump in and defend you." This happened when GM Vice Chairman Bob Lutz was taken to task by

---

[8] http://en.wikipedia.org/wiki/Gene_Amdahl
[9] http://en.wikipedia.org/wiki/Amdahl_Corporation

an auto reviewer's negative comments. More than 30 supporters posted comments defending Lutz while the vice chairman himself remained silent.

2. Disclosing Confidential Information

Nearly all companies have certain aspects that they legitimately should withhold from public consumption or at least carefully time disclosing. These aspects include patent-related properties, financial matters, and personnel information. For example, when Microsoft declined to comment on Reilly's charges, the company was simply exercising a universally accepted corporate policy.

Companies still reserve the right to remain silent, but individual employees have been breaking that silence since the beginning of business itself. Blogging is the newest channel into which beans can get spilled, and from time to time they will. It is most certainly not the only channel in which this occurs. Corporate leaks have been with us for almost as long as have corporate secrets.

According to Stephen M. Nipper, an intellectual property attorney, corporations are concerned about "the possibility that employees might inadvertently disclose trade secrets," but by focusing on blogs, "they are looking for leaks in the wrong pipe." Instead, Nipper advised businesses to look at e-mail, which "tends to be considerably less formal and often sent on the fly without much thought about its content. How many of us can think of instances where we sent an e-mail we wish we could take back?" Because e-mail is sent more casually, he said, it presents a "greater risk to the breach of confidences than blogging."

The opposing argument is that e-mail is just one-to-one, or one-to-a-few, and that the recipient is often a trusted colleague. In contrast, blogs are one-to-many, and you never know who is reading a blog. The audience might very well include the competition. We agree with Nipper, however. A leak to one person can be as fast moving and lethal as a blog. The fear of leaks on blogs is real, but FUD has amplified the dangers to a far greater level than seems reasonable to us.

3. No ROI

After the fear of negative comments, the greatest concern we hear from corporate executives is the contention that blogging takes time yet produces no return on investment (ROI).

The ROI issue is vital to business, but considering it is more appropriate when looking at products and services than when evaluating communication tools. There is no ROI connected with a press release, a web site, or a corporate brochure. Nor is there any ROI attached to the value of a CEO spending three days traveling to and attending an executive conference where he speaks for 20 minutes. But most companies understand the value.

Blogging might be considered part of goodwill, in the same vein as charitable contributions or community services. It also could be considered part of brand extension if you rightfully define brand as how people feel about your company.

If you need to do an ROI analysis on the value of a blog, you might be hard pressed to find it on a spreadsheet. The evidence is all anecdotal, but it seems compelling to us. Take a look at Firefox, for example. The staff at Firefox used a blog as the cornerstone of a word-of-mouth campaign that generated 60 million subscribers in just over 6 months. The blog was incredibly successful, whereas a two-page ad in the *New York Times* generated very few downloads. Blogs may not be direct revenue producers, but they can be extremely good at generating word-of-mouth buzz, and word of mouth remains the most effective way to attract masses of new customers and more sales.

4. Loss of Message Control

A good sales executive will tell you that when she is talking and the prospect is listening passively, the deal probably won't happen. It's when the prospect engages the salesperson in dialogue demonstrating he is "working the issue" that the sale becomes likely. In short, dialogue beats monologue.

The best sales professionals have always understood the value of the conversation. In fact, in the modern corporation, the sales force has often become the last bastion of human interaction with customers, with more and more of the company's customer service being relegated to automated voice processing systems and phone menus. A salesperson may continue to control the conversation, but if he or she is really good at the job, the prospect doesn't realize it.

Bloggers, in fact, *do* control the conversation on their blogs. They pick the topics. They can opt to filter rude, obscene, or otherwise inappropriate comments, so the conversation is under control. But, like a conversation directed by a talented salesperson, blog interaction is open and bi-directional. Legitimate concerns are aired in public. Real complaints are revealed, and the company blogger shows authentic attention to criticism. What happens when someone's conversation is exaggerated or untrue? Other bloggers usually jump in to set the record straight.

5. Competitive Disadvantages

Israel once represented Creative Labs, Inc., the U.S. marketers of the SoundBlaster device that gives most computers audio capability. While he was on a cross-country flight, a competitor's CEO sat next to a fellow company executive—directly behind Israel, whom they did not recognize. For more than four hours, the two loudly discussed their competitive strategy against Creative, while Israel listened quietly and took notes. We think such indiscretions remain more commonplace than loose blogger lips.

Companies fear that their competitors may get insight and information from blogs and turn it against them, and we do not discount this fear. Competitors aggregate information wherever they can. Employees who blog need to understand clearly what they can and cannot talk about, and be particularly prudent in this area.

A few bloggers, including Scoble, have learned there can be a competitive advantage in actually "good-mouthing" the competition—giving competitors recognition when they deserve it. Scoble has blogged about his Apple iPod envy, and his admiration of certain aspects of Google. He has written in praise of the Firefox browser. These are companies or products that compete directly with his employer. It has given him credibility among blog readers, and that credibility has served him and Microsoft well when he has extolled his employer's virtues. There are exceptions, but in general, people believe him because he paints a balanced picture. Could he or another blogger slip and let loose a company secret? It's possible, but unlikely. Most employees seem to understand what needs to be withheld, and we know of fewer cases of confidential information slipping out on a blog than through conversations with editors or in social situations.

When we look at the competitive aspects of blogging, we see one of the most compelling reasons for companies to start sooner rather than later. As was true in the days of the Internet, being first has strong advantages. Thomas Mahon, the first Savile Row tailor to blog, could be considered one of Seth Godin's Purple Cows. His blog, at least at the outset, was remarkable. The next blogging tailors may be just part of the herd of brown cows. The first person or organization in a category takes the lead in the conversation. Your competitor is forced to follow it. She may overtake you, but the odds—and history—are stacked in your favor. As Barnes & Noble learned online against Amazon.com, it's difficult to overtake the front-runner, even if you are the world champion in other contests.

6. Too Much Time—So Few in the Audience

Time is the greatest concern among the successful bloggers we interviewed. The most successful bloggers invest significant hours of their lives to blogging. Peter Flaschner, founder of the Blog Studio,[10] a Canadian consulting group, said, "I've come to the conclusion that any company not committed to the process shouldn't blog. Blogging requires an investment of time. The smaller the company, the greater the investment. A blog started and abandoned can do more harm than good."

Blogging does require a significant time investment—not just writing a blog, but thinking about it, monitoring other blogs, and deleting inevitable spam comments, and if you cannot make that sort of commitment, you probably should not blog.

One alternative for the time-strapped person or company is offered by Elisa Camahort,[11] founder of Worker Bees,[12] who blogs on behalf of a health carrier client[13] concerned both with time and regulatory restrictions. The client prefers to contract her to blog on its behalf, rather than take the time to do one on its own. "It's an alternate way for companies who perhaps don't have the right environment for internal blogging to participate in a more active online conversation," she commented. We have some ambivalence about this form of outsourced blog, but it seems to us better than no blog at all.

7. Employee Misbehavior

Even if you are a saintly boss, some workers will inevitably become disgruntled. Occasionally, one might choose a destructive course. So far, such kamikaze strikes have been rare in the blogosphere. In the first five years of business blogging, there have been more than a billion business postings by many estimates. To date, there have been fewer than 100 incidents reported

---

[10] http://www.theblogstudio.com

[11] http://healthyconcerns.com

[12] http://workerbees.biz/

[13] http://workerbees.typepad.com/healthyconcerns

of employee blogs resulting in disciplinary action or severance, an insignificant percentage it would appear.

Even the most risk-averse people take chances every day. We take risks when we breathe or drink tap water. The point is that the risk of employee misbehavior is so remote, based on what has actually occurred so far, that it seems safe to assume blogging's benefits outweigh its risks.

Ultimately, Culture Decides

In the end, we see culture as the flex point in a business's decision on blogging. Companies whose culture is restrictive should not blog. Companies that operate under restrictive governments or in countries where personal sharing is not acceptable face cultural thorns, and global companies with divisions in disparate cultures, such as the United States and China, have even more to sort out.

"If an organization isn't already in a place where openness and transparency in communication exists and is practiced, then using tools like blogs will be unlikely to do anything positive for that organization. If your openness/transparency foundation isn't there, don't blog," Neville Hobson,[14] the European-based PR consultant and popular podcaster, advised in Chapter 7. We agree.

In the tech sector, cultural impact has caused some ironies in public perception. For example, Apple Computer and Google, two companies that the public has historically held in high esteem, seem to have cultures not conducive to effective blogging. Simultaneously, two companies that have felt their share of scorn—Microsoft and Sun Microsystems—have encouraged employee blogging, giving many the impression of an open culture of trusted and dedicated employees. For several years now, we have spent most of our waking hours in technology-centered business sectors. From our perspective, we see a trend toward reversing these perceptions. There are many technology community denizens wondering why Apple and Google have so few bloggers, and why their employees who do blog seem to write with the dull caution that gives readers the feeling that supervisors are peering over the bloggers' shoulders as they write. We sense increasing questions about the charismatic leaders of Google and Apple, as perhaps too authoritarian, too

---

[14] http://www.nevon.net/nevon

controlling, too fearful of the words and thoughts of the people they employ and the vendors that serve them. And the fortunes of these two companies seem to be slipping a bit, whereas the latter two seem to be rising, as we noted in previous chapters.

Cultures change slowly. If yours is closed, we suggest opening it before shocking the ecosystem with a blog. If your employees feel untrusted, you may need to take steps to demonstrate your faith in them before you encourage blogging. If your culture's communications policy is rooted in command-and-control rules, blogging will falter. If you don't have genuine faith that you can evolve into a better company by listening to what your customers, prospects, investors, vendors, and partners have to say, then a blogging effort will not provide you with its full value. If you don't want to listen—*really* listen—then blogs will be thorny for you and your culture.

If you can't be candid about your company's dirty laundry, then blogging probably isn't for you. If you insist your company doesn't have dirty laundry, then your company may be too boring to write about. Every company has its share of problems. If you aren't willing to discuss them with some degree of openess, then you'll be missing a huge amount of power that the blog could bring to your company. People are hungry for companies that have conversations with them—warts and all. They tend to distrust companies that try to say "everything's perfect here."

We like the somewhat poetic observation of *Cold River* author Jozef Imrich,[15] who told us, "Sunlight is the best disinfectant—all great CEOs encourage transparency and openness as long as sensitive data is not leaked."

---

[15] http://amediadragon.blogspot.com

Blogging Wrong & Right

"The proper Office of a friend is to side with you when you are wrong. Nearly anybody will side with you when you are right."

—Mark Twain

10 Doing It Wrong

"During times of universal deceit, telling the truth becomes a revolutionary act."

—*George Orwell*

No one wrote the official blogging rule book. There are no blogging police, and you can do just about anything you want with your blog. But unless you're a masochist, you will not enjoy the experience if you "do it wrong," and your business will not be the better for the effort.

One simple rule for doing it right is *be real*. If you are going to blog, be authentic. Keep your conversations *naked*. Let people know who you are and where you are coming from. If you don't, blogger vigilantes will form torch-lit mobs to expose your false or character blog, and they will continue their assault until they have driven a stake through the heart of your deception. There may be no rulebook or designated enforcement squads, but the blogosphere is filled with members committed to keeping it a "clean channel," unadulterated by clever, cute, or contrived entries.

If you are coming to the blogosphere from Madison Avenue, or with the heart of a traditional marketer, and you just cannot avoid the temptation to crank it up just a wee bit now and then, our advice is: DON'T DO IT! You will regret it if you do.

Mangled by Tradition

The blogging community has its own culture and ad hoc rules of behavior. Newcomers are always welcome to this fast-growing community, but the welcome mat will get pulled out from under your feet if you do not understand and respect the de facto rules. More than a few people and companies have managed to mangle their reputations by attempting to extend traditional marketing tactics into the blogosphere.

Mazda's brief, unfortunate road trip into the blogosphere serves as an effective cautionary tale. Mazda had some very slick professional footage of one of its cars doing some extreme driving stunts in an urban setting. The footage was filmed for a series of 30-second TV spots that failed to win over the Gen X drivers the company targeted. The company's ad agency reworked the slick footage into a blog allegedly authored by a chronically hip young urban driver. Within hours, the blogosphere caught the deception,[1] and the video became perhaps the first to fail in two media. More importantly, Mazda lost credibility with precisely the audience it was trying to reach. In contrast, Vespa, the motor scooter people, launched VespaQuest,[2] a blog written by authentic urban customers who describe their lives and how scooters fit into it from day to day. The blog is getting warm mention, and its readership has been steadily rising.

Bloggers consistently assault blogs that smack of marketing contrivance. McDonald's Lincoln French Fry is a case study of an established marketing company doing what used to work best—an integrated marketing campaign that starts in one medium and extends into others. It began as a Superbowl ad, depicting a couple discovering a French fry resembling the profile of America's 16th president. For the post-game, McDonald's created a Lincoln Fry blog,[3] which was universally labeled as lame even before Hugh MacLeod got the chance to proclaim it so. Unlike Mazda, which deliberately attempted to deceive, McDonald's wanted you to know the Lincoln fry was a hoax, intending the blog as entertainment. But bloggers—and most visitors—were turned off by the contrivance. They lit up their torches, stocked up on stakes, and spread the word that McDonald's was the latest big company with a lame blog.

[1] http://www.marketingvox.com/archives/2004/10/22/mazdas_blogviral_campaign_falls_flat

[2] http://www.vespaquest.com

[3] http://lincolnfry.typepad.com/blog

The company retreated quickly and terminated the blog, which we think was almost as unfortunate a decision as creating the original blog itself. McDonald's would have been wise to first apologize for the contrivance and then ask bloggers for suggestions about what to do next with the blog. For example, a McDonald's blog would have been a good platform for discussing the company's plans for shifting its high-fat, low-nutrition menu to healthier fare, and bloggers would have perhaps visited a local franchise and then posted what they thought of the improvements. McDonald's bungled the chance to use word of mouth to draw customers into a franchise that has been steadily losing market share for years.

Blogging vigilantism has so far kept the blogosphere the clean channel that is so desired. Bloggers respond well to real people speaking in their own voices, what Dave Winer called "come as you are conversations." They frown on just about everything else.

We named this book *Naked Conversations* because of our belief that authenticity is the core value that makes blogging such a new and different way for businesses to communicate. If authenticity is the defining feature of blogging, then credibility is its benefit. You just won't achieve that with a contrived blog about a French fry.

The blogosphere is changing every day. New people—and emerging technology that we will discuss later—are bringing new ideas that extend how blogging will be used. The rules are changing because no one, thankfully, has the power to enforce them. France's Michel-Edouard Leclerc seemed to address a common sentiment when he spoke passionately of the "humanization of communications" and warned bloggers not to let corporate interests muck it up.

To date, there have been many attempts to muck it up, although so far, reader vigilance has been effective in stopping such incursions. There undoubtedly will be more, by both the well-intentioned and clandestine operatives.

As traditional marketing, communications, business development, human resource, service, and support people edge toward the blogosphere, with an eye toward cheaply reaching millions of people and bolstering their search engine rankings, there will be challenges to keeping the channel clean. Our advice to those who are about to enter is to observe closely what works now. Get a feel for the conversation. Come in listening and watching. Understand the lay of the land before you try to change it. Watch closely those who are being rebuked and why. It is easy to plug smoothly into the blogosphere for the benefit of your business. The blogosphere has shown itself, however, to be harsh on the "muckers." If you inadvertently offend, you will experience what the blogosphere calls "tough love." But it is also a forgiving place, where people and businesses acknowledge mistakes and move away from the contrived and toward getting real.

When Bad Blogs Turn Good

A case in point is Vichy, our favorite case of a bad blog turning good. Vichy, a division of French cosmetics giant L'Oréal, developed a new anti-aging cream. As part of an integrated marketing launch, Vichy's ad agency sold the company on the concept of a blog. From there, a series of missteps left Vichy with at least one foot in a bucket.

The ad agency started with a fictitious author named Claire. This would prove to be a very bad idea. Claire blogged whiningly about needing more sleep so she could still party now that she was over age 35. A studio-produced photo showed Claire as an unwrinkled beauty, pouting studiously into her hand mirror. Claire's language was amazingly similar to the Vichy ad nomenclature.

It took only a few hours for the blogosphere to react strongly and negatively. Comments began pouring in declaring that this was not a blog, that the site had severely limited blog features, that people did not believe Claire was a real person, and that Vichy was foisting a fraud upon the public.

Claire was an example of what the blogosphere calls a "character blog." It is among one of the best examples, it seems to us, of how to do blogs wrong. Characters are used in advertising all the time—in TV, on the radio, in print ads, on billboards—anywhere that models and actors can emulate real people. Claire was not the first blog character. There has been a parade of them. For instance, The Captain Morgan Rum Co. sponsors The Captain's Blog,[4] supposedly written by an illustrated pirate who encourages drinking and carousing in young people "but only in moderation." Considerably more subtle is Gourmet Station's blog, Delicious Destinations.[5] Gourmet Station is an online food and wine gifts web site that features the chronically sophisticated and unisex T. Alexander. Alexander, a fictitious person, discusses epicurean delights at events that never happened in the hope that you will buy food and beverage products for real money. In addition, Denali Corp., a company that

[4] http://www.thecaptainsblog.com
[5] http://www.gourmetstationblog.typepad.com

makes and markets gourmet flavors to ice cream companies, has started Moosetopia,[6] a blog authored by a cartoon moose with a proclivity for travel and bad puns.

"Character blogs are all lame," said Hugh MacLeod, an acerbic cartoonist who writes the popular Gaping Void,[7] Europe's most popular blog, and doles out Lame Blog Awards to deserving sites such as these three. He's not gentle. He's an ex-ad agency exec, and he said he knows "all the lame-ass reasons ad agencies do this kind of stuff. Lame sites aren't made by stupid people," he argued. "They're made by extremely smart people trying to manipulate the consumer into behaving a certain way for their selfish benefit." When he chooses a Lame Award recipient, he told us, the company sometimes fights back in lame ways. When he blogged an assault on a Chanel perfume ad, for example, he was inundated with fake comments. This tactic, called "astroturfing," makes it seem like unrelated people are all up in arms by a particular issue. It is not new. Charles Colson used to astroturf for the late President Richard Nixon. It's an effective ruse in many areas, but it doesn't work in the blogosphere. MacLeod knew when he was being astroturfed because a blogger can trace back to where the comment was written, and all the Chanel complaints were coming from the same Internet address.

MacLeod said his Lame Awards serve a serious purpose. "I'm trying to discourage [lame blogging]. I think non-lame is a much more fertile and rich ground for thoughts and anecdotes." Nearly all the bloggers we talked with agree. While MacLeod may be effectively staving off some, lame duds keep coming. Speaking in October 2005 at the Blog On[8] conference, *Cluetrain* coauthor David Weinberger pointed to a Juicy Fruit gum blog that he termed the worst ever.[9] We think he's right in part because the sugar mongers are trying to dupe schoolchildren and break just about every authenticity standard.

We did speak with a couple of character blog proponents, but they failed to persuade us to their side. One character blog creator argued that he is trying to "expand blogging with innovative creative elements," but from what we can make out, most bloggers just hate them, and the negative viewpoint is entrenched. MacLeod's "Lame Blog" label has become part of blogging's vernacular.

---

[6] http://www.denaliflavors.com

[7] http://www.gapingvoid.com

[8] http://www.blogonevent.com

[9] http://www.juicyfruit.com

Many traditional marketers live in a world of such "integrated marketing solutions" where they intertwine messages and exhortations into combinations of ads, PR campaigns, brochures, and web sites ad nauseam. They argue against the rigidity of blogging's vigilante-type torch-lit assault forces, as did our friends at Vichy. Many traditional marketers are for the most part in a denial phase and refuse to acknowledge the public's deep-seated distaste for much of what they do in traditional channels. The difference is that in blogging, their audiences talk back to them, sometimes in great numbers and with significant force. People might use TiVo to fast-forward past the ad featuring an idiot driving his tractor mower in circles on his lawn, but on the blogosphere they can tell the ad's creators what they think of it. Blog visitors want authenticity. How can you have a real conversation with a character that does not actually exist, or one who might be real but hides his perspective in a cloak of anonymity?

This is not to say that blogs cannot be used successfully to market and sell, as the authors of Treonauts, La Fraise, Blog Maverick, Gaping Void, GM FastLane, and others have demonstrated. In fact, a good blog can and should serve fundamental elements of marketing. A good blog should build trust, interest, awareness, and enthusiasm, just like they teach in Marketing 101. Conversational marketing argues that all of these elements can be built much faster and infinitely less expensively by blogging, by showing the inside of a company to the outsiders who care, as Channel 9,[10] Microsoft's video blog, has done. This is next to impossible with a false or anonymous image.

Let's look at the rest of Vichy's story.

Vichy's marketing team was stunned by the volume and vitriol of the negative comments received on its "Claire" blog. The team might not have understood much about blogging, but they knew when their brand was being bashed, and they could see it spreading. The French press started reporting on the peril of Claire. *Le Monde*, the most popular French newspaper, was unkind in its commentary. *Stratégies*, the leading advertising trade publication, wrote: "Brands that try to disguise themselves as authors are no longer credible. Reading product instructions done up like a blog is silly. Vichy continues to do top-down marketing: the exact opposite of the blogger philosophy."

Vichy called in Six Apart's Le Meur for counsel. The company's first step was to apologize to the bloggers for having offended them. Then it shut down the blog and terminated Claire.

---

[10] http://channel9.msdn.com

A short while later, under Le Meur's tutelage, Vichy reincarnated its blog as *Journal de ma Peau*.[11] The company's very first act on the new blog was to apologize again for the old blog. Then it declared *Journal* would serve customers by listening to them. Unlike the earlier version, Vichy's new blog provided all the functionality that makes a blog more than a web site. Vichy team members introduced themselves with a photo showing real people[12] who looked more approachable than Claire. Very quickly, a dialogue began building, and the earlier irate comments were replaced by more supportive and constructive ones. Trust between company and its market began to build.

Vichy's anti-aging cream is targeted to women over 35. It requires a month-long, four-stage treatment program. Sophie Kune,[13] a French blogger with established independent influence on cosmetics, agreed to work on the project alongside the Vichy team. With Kune's help, five additional women bloggers agreed to undergo the program, with the provision they could post whatever they wanted without interference.

The result of this second effort reversed the first. Volunteers loved the product. Bloggers lauded praise on Vichy for getting real. But *Journal* accomplished more than that. The blog made Vichy smarter about its customers. Lynn Serfaty, Vichy's group manager of international marketing, told us customers asked questions that Vichy had not even imagined. Could the cream be used at the same time as a sunscreen—or for that matter, in sunlight? How about in conjunction with a facial mask? Answering such questions removed barriers to sales that would otherwise have remained undetected. Through the blog, the Vichy team also could prescribe customized versions of the cream for women with particular conditions, which they could then pick up at their local pharmacy.

While the French press had originally slammed Vichy, this second effort garnered editorial praise. The leading financial daily positioned Vichy as a shining star. According to Serfaty, "Everyone at Vichy has learned from this experience," and the result may change parent L'Oréal's future marketing as well. According to Georges-Edouard Dias, head of the L'Oréal e-business team, the Vichy success "confirmed to us that enterprises could be part of the blogosphere, as long as they are willing to play by the rules, having something to share and learn. In a world which has often been organized exclusively around the natural authority

---

[11] http://www.journaldemapeau.fr/blog/index.php

[12] http://www.journaldemapeau.fr/blog/archives/2005/05/merci_pour_tout.php

[13] http://jesuisunique.blogs.com

of a brand, it is refreshing to see that, through conversations, you can actually improve your propositions, and make it more meaningful for your customers."

Vichy learned an important lesson. If you are doing it wrong, the blogosphere will tell you how to do it right, and if you listen, your blog will probably fulfill your goals.

Of Moose and Dork

The people behind Moosetopia and Gourmet Station, on the other hand, insist that their customers love their blogs and shrug off the lambasting they have both received in blogging forums. They consider themselves to be innovators facing the scorn of old-guard bloggers who are trying to impose a rigid vision of what a blog should be.

In the interest of providing balanced coverage, we spent a fair amount of time talking with two of the people behind those blogs: Diva Marketing's Toby Bloomberg, the consultant behind the Gourmet Station blog, and John Nardini, Denali Corp.'s EVP and self-confessed Moosetopia author. We disagree with Gaping Void's MacLeod, who views such marketers as evil incarnate. We like both Bloomberg and Nardini, and we found them truthful and sincere in their arguments. They both talked about the fun they were creating for visitors and the extensions of their brands. They disagreed with our assessment that most people thought their blogs were lame. Perhaps, over time, both will prove us wrong.

However, we see a better way for Gourmet Station to blog. Years ago, Israel worked with an Internet startup called Virtual Vineyards, an e-tailing pioneer and the first to market wine and gourmet food online—not that different from what Gourmet Station does today. The company had real passion for helping small artisan wine producers reach global markets—where they could compete with the mass producers who dominated other distribution channels.

At the time, co-founder Peter Granoff was one of only 13 American master sommeliers (certified experts on pairing wine with food). Granoff was a champion of demystifying wine—removing the elitism that surrounded it so that more people would enjoy sharing the beverage with family, friends, and food. He was the antithesis of the highbrows who sniff, swish, and spit before declaring numerical rankings of a vintage. Granoff displayed both the soul and style of an authentic blogger. The Virtual Vineyards marketing effort centered on Granoff's humanity and passion for wine. It happens that, just as technologists call themselves "geeks," sommeliers call themselves "cork dorks." Virtual Vineyards made Granoff *the* online Cork Dork. The web site centered on "Peter's Picks" and "Peter's Pairings." He started an advice column, which he updated frequently. He labored to personally answer the rising flood of e-mail requesting advice. Just think of what somebody like Granoff, who reeked of authenticity, could do for a Gourmet Station, now that there is blogging to facilitate conversations. Who could move more epicurean gifts— T. Alexander, a fictional character, or Peter Granoff, a passionate authority? Perhaps Gourmet Station is beginning to understand this. Recently, the company started interlacing posts from real people with Alexander's posting.

Likewise, Moosetopia could take the same tack. A blog by an expert who explains the finer points of its product line, such as what differentiates vanilla flavoring from the gourmet version, would demonstrate to customers and prospects that there are real people with unique expertise behind the product. The Denali parent sells to ice cream makers, not end users, and the Moosetopia brand could be used as a branding "secret sauce," just like computer makers use "Intel Inside" to sell their finished products.

Silent Damage

As poorly received as contrived blogs may be, staying out of the conversation entirely is worse. Three well-publicized cases demonstrate just how hefty the tolls can be for ignoring legitimate complaints and concerns even for a few days.

Publicly traded Electronic Arts (EA) is a leader in computer games, with hundreds of popular titles published over more than two decades. In November 2004, someone calling herself "EA Spouse" started a blog called "Electronic Arts: The Human Story."[14] Describing herself as a "disgruntled significant other," she wrote eloquently about unsavory working conditions at EA. To an untrained observer, the blog may have appeared to be insignificant, with few links or other indicators that the author had public influence. The company ignored the blog initially. After all, who could possibly care about the lamentations of one developer's wife? Perhaps EA also shied away because a suit had been filed a few months earlier charging the company with employee abuses, meaning that lawyers, perpetually wishing to avoid risk, would counsel the company to say nothing.

---

[14] http://www.livejournal.com/users/ea_spouse/274.html

Other bloggers, however, noticed and pointed to it through links. As often happens on the blogosphere, more and more people rapidly became aware of the blog and spread the word further, accelerating a word-of-mouth engine into full throttle. Other people began confirming the allegations. The press caught wind and asked the company to comment. EA regurgitated the standard party line of "we don't comment on employee relations issues," so the press covered only the blogger's side of the story. In July 2005, more than seven months after the original posting, we went to Google and typed in "Electronic Arts + employees" and EA Spouse was still the top-ranked item. EA Spouse herself has recently started Gamewatch.org, a watchdog organization for the computer game industry, and EA now faces a second class-action suit charging employee abuses.

So was this PR debacle for EA a blip, or will there be long-lasting implications from it to the company? Let's fast-forward a few years. If you are a young genius game developer, would this company be your top choice for a job? Where do you think recruiters looking for talent to divert into competing companies will go to raid? If you are an investor, and for over a year you have read about the company's unhappy employees and litigation, how secure would you consider your investment? If you are a fund manager, would you include the company in your portfolio?

We don't know EA's side to this story. EA, of course, declined to discuss it with us. We are told the company is more than a little jumpy about any mention of it in the blogosphere, and at this point we don't blame them, but the blame lies not in the blogosphere, but in the company's prolonged silence. EA has passively allowed a deep hole to be dug under it, and it has fallen in.

The first suit has been settled by EA's $15.9 million payment to its former employees, considerably more than the overtime and lunch breaks would have cost them.

We don't practice law and are not qualified to counsel on the litigious aspects of this case. But certainly, a company can demonstrate its concern that employees feel badly about the company, and that it is listening closely and thinking about courses of action, without admitting culpability. When the story first broke, could EA have responded by expressing sympathy and regret about the situation? It could have turned to its own employees and asked how they felt about working there, and perhaps have explained why conditions were the way they were and how the company hoped to improve them. Such actions may have diffused what became a bitter and explosive situation. We think EA will pay a price for its chosen course for a long time to come.

Unlocking Mysteries ▬▬▬▬▬▬▬▬▬▬▬▬

EA is not alone. Kryptonite, Superman fans may recall, is the stuff that brings heroes down. A bike lock manufacturer of the same name had a hard, fast, and expensive lesson on this over a 10-day period in September 2004.

The situation began with an anonymous call to the company by someone who said he had been able to pick the company's popular tubular cylinder locks with a Bic pen. A few days later, the same anonymous claim was entered at bikeforums,[15] an online bulletin board for cycling enthusiasts.

The story soon spilled into the blogosphere, where word spread at an accelerated pace. It soon hit Engadget,[16] one of the most heavily trafficked of all blogsites, which posted a videotape showing a Bic picking a Kryptonite lock.

At Kryptonite, we later learned, the entire 25-member team was working almost around the clock to assess the damage, determine what to do about it, and according to Kryptonite PR manager Donna Tocci, make good to its customers regardless of cost. The company was going by the traditional crisis management playbook. According to Tocci, Kryptonite posted several updates on its web site. Tocci insists the company focused on the problem and ignored the blogosphere "because of higher priorities."

This approach turned out to be a big mistake. By ignoring the blogosphere, Kryptonite gave millions of people the impression that the company had neither sympathy nor remedy for its customers. Bloggers verbally assaulted Kryptonite, spreading commentary and dispatching heavy traffic to Engadget's video. Engadget owner Jason Calacanis estimated the video was viewed by about 1.8 million visitors.

Ten days later, the company appeared to equivocate, announcing it would replace all Bic-pickable locks. Since then, observers estimate the company has exchanged 350,000 locks, at a cost that *Fortune* magazine estimated at $10 million. This is a hefty sum for a company that *Fortune* reported making only $25 million a year.

From the blogosphere's perspective, the company remained stoically silent for an additional 10 months, until Tocci contacted us in July 2005 after we had posted an early version of this chapter to our book blog. Tocci told us that during the crisis, Kryptonite had only limited awareness of what blogs were, how they worked, or how one goes about dealing with them. When she later

---

[15] http://www.bikeforums.net

[16] http://www.engadget.com

tried to get into the blog conversation, she was essentially shouted down, being dismissed as someone who "just didn't get it." She felt the press dealt with her company in a more even-handed manner. "Bloggers are passionate about their views and opinions. They get fired up about one thing or another, positive or negative, and run with it. They don't have to check facts or figures like traditional media," she contended. "It's like the game of telephone. By the time it gets linked 10 times, it's seen as fact and that is what is perpetuated—right or wrong."

We were unable to find copies of the special web site postings to customers that Tocci argued had been prominently displayed during the crisis, except for one that had asserted the locks were still a deterrent—we assume to thieves without Bic pens. Several bloggers told us they had visited the site and saw nothing of the kind, and we simply do not know which side of that part of the argument is accurate. What is relevant is that by Tocci's account, her company did what it thought it was supposed to do. The team met, discussed the scope of the problem, and immediately swung into activities that put the security of its customers' property at top priority. Kryptonite committed a huge sum that had to set the company back on its heels. The team talked to the traditional media and answered customer inquiries by e-mail and phone. But they got blindsided anyway by missing that a new force had come along, and as a result the company suffered lasting damage to its public image. The adverse blog coverage the company received will pop up in search engines for years to come.

A few years earlier, a 10-day response would have been considered speedy. No longer. In January 2005, David Kirkpatrick and Daniel Roth, writing an article[17] called "Why There's No Escaping the Blog" in *Fortune* magazine, led with: "Freewheeling bloggers can boost your product—or destroy it. Either way, they've become a force business can't afford to ignore." Their lead evidence was the Kryptonite story. The bike lock company has become a prominent media example of how to do it wrong in the blogosphere.

Speaking at the Blog Business Summit[18] in late August 2005, Bob Wyman, CEO of PubSub,[19] observed during a panel talk, "You can't really criticize them for not listening to the blogosphere at the time the incident occurred. Kryptonite got blindsided and by not knowing what to do, they showed

---

[17] http://www.fortune.com/fortune/technology/articles/0,15114,1011763-3,00.html

[18] http://www.blogbusinesssummit.com

[19] http://bobwyman.pubsub.com

others who would come after them what to do." We think he nailed the situation, but not everyone took heed, not even other lock makers.

In April 2005, Darren Barefoot,[20] a Canadian blogger, released a video on his site of someone using scissors, duct tape, and a toilet paper role to disable a Kensington notebook computer lock in about two minutes. We're not certain exactly where it originated, but from him the story quickly spread, soon reaching BoingBoing[21] and Gizmodo,[22] two of blogging's most heavily trafficked sites. Kensington, whose notebook computer lock product slogan is "If your notebook's unlocked, your network is too," chose to lock itself out of the blogging network. The company remained silent even when matters got worse. Peter Rojas, then working for Engadget, jumped in with a new angle—a photo of someone picking a Kensington steering wheel lock. Worse, if we are to believe what Kryptonite's Tocci told us, Kensington should have already known it was coming. The problem with Bic pens was never limited to Kryptonite locks; it was a problem with any lock using tubular cylinders such as Kensington also used. We have some sympathy for Kryptonite because what happened to it had not previously occurred. But Kensington, as far as we know, still has not responded. Given the fact that a similar crisis had just cost Kryptonite $10 million, it seems to us that Kensington's proper course was obvious: Join the conversation, and do it fast. The company should have said it was shocked to learn of this problem and that its best engineers would study and solve the problem. It should have apologized to its customers and then made a commitment to put things right.

Speed of response is essential when facing a crisis. Years ago, Johnson & Johnson faced a crisis of far greater proportion than the danger of lost bicycles, when seven people died from cyanide poisoning after someone tampered with a few Tylenol bottles on store shelves and poisoned them. The company very quickly called back all Tylenol, saying it was acting first in the interest of public safety. Johnson & Johnson assumed all responsibility, offering regrets and compensation to the victims of the malicious vandalism and offering a reward for information leading to the perpetrator. It would then invent and develop the tamper-detectable seals that nearly all medicine and food packages come with today.

[20] http://www.darrenbarefoot.com/archives/002657.html

[21] http://boingboing.net

[22] http://www.gizmodo.com

We tell these stories here without glee. We don't like arguing a case of "join the conversation or else." We wholeheartedly agree with Six Apart EVP Anil Dash,[23] who placed this comment on Barefoot's Kensington post:

> *I don't disagree with any of your [Barefoot] points, but boy, I hate that lesson of "Monitor the blogosphere or, sooner or later, you're going to get burned." It sounds like the reason corporations should engage the weblog medium is because we'll extort them if they don't. The real reason . . . is because there's tremendous opportunity for them here. For every lock that gets picked, there are a thousand new customers that could be reached, endless amounts of free market research available and creative new suggestions.*

The Mediocre Way

They may be less dramatic, but the greatest number of people and companies blogging wrong are guilty of no crime greater than being dull—of demonstrating all the remarkability of Godin's brown cows. You may not receive nasty comments, and other sites may not point to you with the kind of indignant wrath experienced by EA and Kryptonite, but being bland will hurt you and the company you represent. It's easy to make this mistake. Write cautiously and make certain you offend no one inside or outside your company. When other sites say something negative or challenging, just ignore them. Pretend the comments never happened. Perhaps they'll go away.

Say what you will about ousted Hewlett-Packard CEO Carly Fiorina, but she was usually interesting. Some of her actions horrified a great number of people who saw value in the traditional "HP Way," which made engineering and quality the highest priorities. Fiorina extinguished the old way in a series of bold moves that polarized employees, investors, the public, and her own directors. When Fiorina was unglamorously sacked early in 2005, we were disappointed to discover that no HP blogger had ventured a personal comment on whether or not her departure was good or bad for the company or

---

[23] http://www.dashes.com/anil

its customers. The first HP blog post we found, posted six hours after Fiorina's forced departure, was written by a corporate road warrior who droned about his hardships in too much business travel. In Silicon Valley, word of mouth was saying that employees were dancing in corporate aisles singing "Ding Dong, the Bitch Is Gone," but corporate bloggers were posting about the rigors of challenging travel schedules. The closest we could come to an HP blogger taking an actual stand was the less-than-profound insight of: "She had her good points and her bad." Another blogger offered assurances that HP still had the customers' best interests in mind. Later, when Fiorina began making the rounds on the speaker circuit, she raised charges of gender discrimination, claiming she once had to attend a strip show because a business associate insisted upon it.[24] No HP blogger of either gender had anything to say on that subject either.

Avoiding controversial conversations that can shape your company's future, it seems to us, is a great way to do it wrong. Competitors make hay of it. When we spoke to Sun Microsystem's Noel Hartzell, Jonathan Schwartz's communications director, he could credibly gloat about Sun's blogs versus HP's. "We have a transparent culture, and competitors like HP do not," he asserted.

Some companies and executives begin dull, but after listening to unflattering comments, they demonstrate that they've paid attention by improving their style and content. Others do not. A case in point is Randy's Journal,[25] by Boeing marketing executive Randy Baseler, who describes himself in the blog in the third person as "the lucky guy who gets to travel the world talking about Boeing's perspective on commercial aviation." As vice president of marketing for Boeing Commercial Airplanes in Seattle, Randy is always meeting with experts, analysts, and airline customers, and talking with aviation and business media, all of which always just adore Boeing. Randy's was among the very first official corporate blogs.

All that traveling must make Randy a busy guy, because when we asked a company representative why Randy doesn't allow comments, we were told that "Randy is just too busy for that stuff." We assume all that flying around makes him busier than GM Vice Chairman Bob Lutz, Dallas Mavericks owner Mark Cuban, and Michel-Edouard Leclerc, all of whom receive comments and respond to them. Randy's Journal is an example of a blog that emulates a corporate brochure, and it's actually pretty good as a brochure. But it is, and

---

[24] http://www.hp.com/hpinfo/execteam/speeches/fiorina/simmons04.html
[25] http://www.boeing.com/randy

has remained for nearly two years, a very bad blog, containing all the drama and personality of an out-of-date train schedule.

We thought this a shame because Boeing is a company of tremendous strategic importance and is embroiled in a clash-filled competition with the French Airbus. You wouldn't know that from Randy's Journal. We would like to be familiar with arguments of why we should support Boeing over Airbus, but this blog does not deliver that.

However, Boeing seems to have learned a great deal from blogger opinions. In mid-2005, it initiated a second blog, Flight Test Journal,[26] which is often downright thrilling. For example, this blog has described what it takes to sufficiently test a new aircraft—in this case the 777-200. The company has also made innovative efforts to join the blogosphere. It recently invited a squadron of bloggers to go up in a 777 test flight if they would blog about the experience. The subsequent postings were universally favorable and passionate.

Good blogs, as we've mentioned, go far to boost employee morale. Adam Phillabaum,[27] who recently joined the aeronautical giant after getting his computer science degree from the University of Idaho, told us, "I happen to work for a company that [once] had a blog that basically everyone thought was lame. Boeing is freaking huge, and sometimes it may be hard to change something in a company this large. But as soon as they heard from the blogosphere that they were lame, it was fixed right-quick. I always thought that was really cool."

Like Elvis on Black Velvet

A good blog cannot just remain neutral, cautious, or tepid. People believe that portraits of companies without internal or external conflicts, ethical struggles, or product development setbacks are about as authentic as a rendering of Elvis on black velvet and as stimulating as a discussion of noncorrosive pipe at a plumbers' convention.

Take the case of Wipro, for example, India's largest technology outsource company. Outsourcing is a controversial subject, and Wipro is in a position to argue the case for it with authority. Wipro could relate stories of companies that have benefited greatly from outsourcing. It could address the anger and

[26] http://www.boeing.com/commercial/777family/200LR/flight_test
[27] http://doingboeing.blogspot.com

frustration of displaced workers, and show the good that outsourcing is doing for other people and companies. It could discuss the benefits of global interdependence. We might or might not agree with the company's case, but we recognize that there is one to be made.

Instead, the Wipro Weblog[28] was written by a team of executives who perhaps have taken a crash course in tedious writing. A typical quote:

> An interesting emerging trend is the global sourcing of multiple
> service lines to one partner: specifically BPO, IT Infrastructure
> and Application services. Organizations are increasingly find-
> ing that leveraging the latent synergy between these areas
> yields far more enduring benefits than a fragmented approach.
> Will this spur service providers to widen their offering?

Each post sounded about like that. In August 2005, the blog was abandoned, which in this case, we consider a wise course.

It is perhaps harsh to single out Wipro because other corporate and individual blogs read just as poorly and their companies have not yet either improved or abandoned the effort. What Wipro missed was the opportunity to demonstrate humanity, and to recognize the inherent friction in what the company does. Such a position would make its blog tremendously interesting to others. People are going to talk about outsourcing anyway. They are going to do so passionately. Would Wipro not be wise to join—and host—a central portion of the conversation?

Forced & Selfish Blogging

Busy professionals who had full plates *before* a company higher-up told them to blog often compose in a style that feels hurried and forced. Such blogs come through often as joyless and rushed—even when the author's expertise on a particular subject is apparent. Tom Foremski, who blogs full time for Silicon Valley Watcher,[29] noted in June 2005 that "Forced blogging comes across as such, and cannot be disguised. You know it when you see it." He

---

[28] http://www.wiproweblog.com

[29] http://www.siliconvalleywatcher.com/mt/archives/2005/06/the_seemingly_b_1.php

sees it occur in a lot of blogging journalists who have difficulties developing a "blog voice"—or maybe several blog voices, depending on the time of day or mood. These are different personalities, and the style is different from the rigid house style of their employers. That's why journalist blogs are better done from home, not hosted on their employer's server, and driven by passion and interest, not by the need to fulfill employee duties.

Google is one of technology's all-time great stories. Someone should write a book about its remarkable technology and company. What's relevant about Google here, though, is the company's long and wonderful history of putting the company first. That's why it is so disappointing to see its official Google blog[30] serve as an example of doing it wrong by blogging selfishly.

Google is one of the world's most successful, respected, and trusted companies—and the owner of Blogger, a pioneer in blog authoring toolsets. And yet its own blog, in our opinion, comes across as self-serving. Google engineers and product managers use the blog to report on how well the company's projects and products are doing. To read it, you would assume the company has never had an unsuccessful effort and that everyone at Google simply adores everyone else.

To read the Google blog, you would think there is no world outside the company and no use for a computer other than to access Google services. The Google blog links mostly to other Google sites, at least as of July 2005. The blog speaks of no company other than Google. It acknowledges the existence of no competitors. It rarely, if ever, joins conversations on issues of search, even ones specifically about Google. In the blogosphere, many are wondering aloud about Google's apparent isolationist blog strategy.

Blog aside, Google is in a very strong position in terms of public perception. Google has more daily visitors than does the entire blogosphere. But by ignoring the new phenomenon, it may discover ignoring blogger complaints can be like ignoring a Chihuahua at your buttocks. It keeps nipping at you until it does real damage. Google had about 40 bloggers when we were writing this chapter. We knew a few of them on a personal basis, and find them intelligent and interesting, but their blogs are not. We cannot help but wonder why. One senior Google manager who read this section recently confided to us "off the record" that company policy is about to change, and employees will soon be blogging with abandon. We'll have to wait and see if it happens. We don't know why he refused to let us name him.

---

[30] http://googleblog.blogspot.com

Apple Computer is yet another company, admired and trusted by millions, that has given the impression it doesn't trust its own employees enough to encourage blogging. Steve Jobs, Apple's chairman, founder, and CEO, has had a long-standing reputation for wanting to sing Apple's praises without accompaniment, and that apparently extends into the blogosphere. We understand that more than 100 company employees blog, but most write on personal issues and on their own time. Fewer than 10 of Apple's bloggers, from what we could tell, have ever even mentioned they were Apple employees. What does that mean? Short term, probably very little, but perhaps seeds are being planted that will grow into bad fruits for Apple over time.

Apple employees steer clear of blogosphere controversies regarding their company when they could argue Apple's side. For example, Apple sued two vendors for breaking rules of non-disclosure on blogs. It won the court case but lost in the court of public opinion reflected in blogs and published reports. More recently, the company saw its stock slip during a technology rally after it ignored rumors that the company had an inventory overload caused by a drop in demand. Even though the rumors proved to be untrue, Apple hurt itself with stonewall policies. The company seems to be taking an overall combative rather than conciliatory policy. For example, when *iCon*, a book sharply critical of Jobs, was published by our publisher, John Wiley & Sons, Apple banned all Wiley books from Apple Store bookshelves.

Righting Wrongs

U.S. pulp magazines of the '50s such as *True Confessions* and *Modern Romance* often used a formula of "Sin, Suffer, Repent" (SSR). The articles always began with a sin, which was the juiciest part. It was followed by a brief middle section that discussed how the sinner suffered—the more anguish, the better. Each article then reached its inspirational conclusion by the author expressing how true happiness was eventually achieved through open-hearted repentance. The Vichy story is a classic example of SSR.

The blogosphere is proving itself an occasionally harsh but usually forgiving place. No company mentioned in this chapter has committed a fatal sin. Each can improve its position by blogging and by adhering to the guidelines for success strewn throughout this book and summarized in the next chapter.

Blogs will evolve over time. Businesses will adapt blogs to their purposes and that, of course, is how it should be. There are no absolute rules on the blogosphere, and no enforcement squads—and we are thankful for that. But there are fundamentals such as transparency and authenticity. We cannot yet prove their durability. But companies that want to do it right in the blogosphere would be wise to adhere to these fundamentals.

And now for some advice on how to do it right.

11

Doing It Right

"The trouble with doing something right the first time is that nobody appreciates how difficult it was."

—Walt West

Our two previous chapters cover the realities and fables of blogging's dark side. If you are still reading this book, chances are good that you have either already started blogging or decided to give it a try. This chapter and the next are dedicated to helping you understand some of blogging's finer points—not the tools and technologies, but the techniques and guidelines that have worked for other successful bloggers. This chapter also identifies many of the little details that can improve the effectiveness of and response to most blogs.

Here are our top 11 tips on how to do it right. We hesitate to call them "best practices," not just because the term has become a traditional marketing cliché, but because blogging is too new and dynamic to have any "tried-and-true practices." Scoble first published these practices, in draft form, on our *Naked Conversations* book blog. Several were improved or expanded by reader comments.

Tip #1: What's in a name?
Search engine results.

When our publisher, Joe Wikert, started a blog called The Average Joe[1] in February 2005, he made a common first mistake. He didn't think through his title.

Quick: What does "The Average Joe" mean to you? Probably not much. It's like wheat flour. No shape. No meaning. A more specific title would make his blog easier to discover by people who might care about his subject and might be interested in his products or services. Based on its name, why would you want to read Joe's blog? How would anyone know it is about book publishing? What could someone possibly enter in a Google search that would return "The Average Joe" as the top-ranked response?

Your blog's name can help you own your market niche. Suppose someone named Paula wanted to make and sell baked goods from her home in San Carlos, California. What's the better blog title: "My Blog About Something Made with Flour" or "Paula's San Carlos Bread-Baking Blog"?

By now, you probably understand how important search engines are to your business and how blogs impact them. A while back, we were looking for a book publisher. So how did we search? Our first query, as we recall, was something like "book publisher blog." We brainstormed for the words to enter that would help us find the right book publisher. A few we recall trying:

- Book publisher problem (or "hate," "sucks," or "avoid")
- How do you get a book published?
- Negotiating book publisher contracts
- Best business book publisher
- Author favorite business book publisher
- How to write a book
- How to get a book author deal
- Getting your book written

Joe didn't have his blog yet, but if he had, "The Average Joe" would probably not have appeared prominently with any of these searches.

Before you enter your title, it's a good idea to spend some time, perhaps an hour, doing some search variations to find out what words bring up results

---

[1] http://jwikert.typepad.com/

similar to what your blog will contain. There are tools to help you come up with searches on your own, as well as tons of sites that'll help you better understand how people searching for information think. Search for "Danny Sullivan" or "John Battelle" and you'll find lots of search-engine optimization (SEO) tricks to help you, not to mention John's excellent book on searching.[2]

But let's get back to Joe. In our search attempts, we noticed four recurring words in our entries: "publish," "author," "write," and "book." Those are the words Joe should want in his title tagline to optimize search engine results. He should also include his name, because blogs should be both personal and unique.

How about this: "Joe Wikert's Book Authoring and Publishing Blog"? Sounds boring, right? But here's what's more important. Go to a blog search service like Feedster. Enter in "publishing" and see what comes back. Notice that the blog title is underneath each post. Now, what's the likelihood that you'll click on a blog with the name "Average Joe"? Compare that to how likely you'll be to click on something that says "Joe Wikert's Book Authoring and Publishing Blog."

Joe can improve the name further. He already has something most of us don't have: authority. He's an executive at a publicly traded book publisher that's almost 200 years old and had 4 of the top 25 best-selling business books in 2004, according to the *New York Times*. Why not reflect that in his tagline?

"Joe Wikert, *Wiley publishing executive who can get you published.*"

When we were searching for a publisher, we would have clicked there in a heartbeat.

As Wikert told us five months later, "I took your advice and changed the title to 'The Average Joe: A Book Publisher Blog.' Shortly after making this small change, I went from almost nowhere on search engines to #1 in the results of a Google search on 'book publisher blog.' I launched the blog on February 19. As of July 15, I've made 82 posts, had 353 comments and 46 Trackbacks, and gotten 43 links from 36 sites.

"How has this helped our business?" Wikert asked. "Well, I'd be hard-pressed to give you any specifics here. I don't know how measurable this is today or will be in the future. I'd like to think that new authors are visiting, liking what they find, and ultimately choosing Wiley as their publishing partner. I've tried to focus much of my posting attention on helping the new author. For example, I see that 'royalty payment,' 'average advance,' etc., are

---

[2] http://battellemedia.com

often the most popular search terms leading people to 'The Average Joe.' As a result, I've tried to talk about every aspect of advances and royalties." We have observed first-hand the effect of Wikert's blog on his business; several aspiring authors have thanked us for pointing them to Joe's blog and expressed a desire to work with a publisher who "gets blogging."

Sounds a bit above average to us, Joe.

Tip #2: Read a bunch of blogs before you start.

Before you start blogging, read a wide selection of blogs, so you understand what's out there. For that, we recommend you get an RSS news aggregator, which is a program that collects and displays feeds from multiple RSS-enabled blogs in one convenient window. (As we mentioned earlier, RSS stands for Really Simple Syndication.) There are several RSS news aggregators available for both Windows and Macintosh, most of them free. RSS is extremely important, and we will discuss it further in Chapter 14. What's important here is that RSS lets you cover much more ground than going to site after site with a web browser. When a blog is updated, an RSS aggregator delivers the updates to your e-mail application, making it at least 10 times more efficient to read than with an old-school web browser.

Blog search engines, or RSS search engines, are the best tool for finding blogs that interest you. We think all of them could be easier to use, but each keeps improving at its own pace. PubSub[3] provides the best results via RSS subscription and has become our favorite as of this writing. Bloglines Citations[4] is very easy to use and understand, so it's a good choice for a beginner, as are Feedster[5] and IceRocket.[6]

Technorati[7] is valuable because it tells you who's linking to whom. That's very important to know. It's a good vehicle to see how each blog ranks. Technorati has also become a central conduit for "tagging," a new system for searching and finding photo and text blogs that interest you. More about that in Chapter 14.

---

[3] http://www.pubsub.com

[4] http://www.bloglines.com/citations

[5] http://www.feedster.com

[6] http://www.icerocket.com

[7] http://www.technorati.com

You also can use an old-fashioned web search engine, such as Google, to locate blogs, provided you remember to always include the word "blog." What you miss in traditional search engines, however, is currency. They sometimes take a couple of weeks to pick up a new blog. That is beginning to change, however. Google Blog Search[8] looks just like Google and is just as easy to use, but it finds only content produced after August 1, 2005. With some RSS search engines, your blog can be listed in a matter of days or even hours.

Let's say you're looking for blogs on quilting. You can do a search on quilting on any search engine and get a snapshot of the current—or past—state of the blogosphere. What if someone starts blogging about quilting later? But if you use an RSS news aggregator, you can subscribe to the search, and anyone who uses the word *quilting* on a blog, from that point on, will automatically show up in your news aggregator. Most bloggers use RSS search subscriptions to search for published content on their own names, companies, or competitors, and for common jargon used in their business categories.

Reading other blogs should help inspire you to write your own—and should give you some ideas of what is already being said and what you might contribute. If you read 50 blogs for two weeks and you still don't feel you have something to write about, you probably aren't going to be a good blogger. But, please stick around anyway. Even if you don't start your own blog, you can see what others have to say on blogs impacting you and your business, and you can be quick to comment whenever appropriate.

Tip #3: Keep it simple. Keep it focused.

Most people enjoy breezing quickly through a great number of blogs. If you want others to talk about you and pass around your information, you should make it easy for them to do so.

With that in mind, it's best to have each post contain just one idea or one set of links. One guy who makes it hard is Mike Gunderloy.[9] His page of links to other blogs works well for people who visit with a web browser, but it's hard on bloggers who try to link to a single one of his entries. On a web browser, Mike's page looks great. However, most influential bloggers watch sites like Mike's via their RSS aggregators rather than using a web interface,

---

[8] http://blogsearch.google.com
[9] http://www.larkware.com/index.html

and when viewed in RSS, Mike's blog shows an entire day as one entry. This makes it very hard to read or e-mail to others. Imagine that an item two-thirds of the way down his page interests you. "Hey, Jane, check out the cell phone link here. Just scroll two-thirds of the way down this entry," you have to write. That just isn't as quick and easy as "Hey, Jane, check out this link."

Tip #4: Demonstrate passion.
Tip #5: Show your authority.

We offer these two tips together because they are separate components but should be inseparable in your blog. A good corporate blog is both passionate and authoritative. Passion alone does not make a point, as many teen diarists have shown. Authority alone is boring, as Randy's Journal, discussed in the preceding chapter, exemplifies.

How do you demonstrate your passion for a topic? One way is to post often. How often depends on how much competition you have and what kind of audience you are trying to build. When we look at Technorati and PubSub lists of the world's most popular bloggers, they all post more often than once a day.

Scoble's list of favorites includes Engadget,[10] Dave Winer,[11] Microsoft's Employee blogs,[12] Misbehaving,[13] Hugh MacLeod's Gaping Void,[14] Joshua Micah Marshall's Talking Points Memo,[15] Glenn Reynolds's Instapundit,[16] Doc Searls,[17] Jeff Jarvis's BuzzMachine,[18] and Daring Fireball,[19] all of whom almost always blog at least once daily.

[10] http://www.engadget.com
[11] http://www.scripting.com
[12] http://blogs.msdn.com
[13] http://www.misbehaving.net
[14] http://www.gapingvoid.com
[15] http://talkingpointsmemo.com
[16] http://www.instapundit.com
[17] http://doc.weblogs.com
[18] http://www.buzzmachine.com
[19] http://www.daringfireball.com

Israel's list includes What's Next,[20] Blake Ross,[21] Ernie the Attorney,[22] the Loïc Le Meur blog,[23] McGee's Musings,[24] Seth Godin's Blog,[25] J. D. Lasica's New Media Musings,[26] and Joho the Blog,[27] as well as Doc Searls.

There is a good deal of diversity in the content of these two lists. What's the same is that both of us enjoy prolific bloggers, most of whom blog at least daily and all of whom blog several times weekly.

However, on days when you feel life's distractions conflicting with your blog's topical passion, we advise taking a break. There are days when you will just not be in the mood. Don't force it. One of Microsoft's most popular bloggers (at least he was until he stopped posting in 2004) was Christopher Brumme.[28] His blog wasn't one that most people would read. He works on the highly technical .NET Common Language Runtime team. He would post only once every month or so, and his posts ran about 11,000 words each. He ignored most of the tips we offer here. Nevertheless, he was very popular with software developers, the only audience he cared about. Developers flocked to Brumme's blog because he had no competition. There are few people with his technical knowledge, and none who write about the innards of .NET, so he got away with posting infrequently and no one ever doubted either his passion or his authority.

Authority is the other essential element of a successful blog. Blog what you know. If you're a plumber, an auto maker, an NBA team owner, or maybe a French t-shirt maker, showcase your knowledge to audiences who care.

That advice isn't as easy as it sounds, but a good way to start is to talk about what it entails to do whatever it is you do. Look at how Thomas Mahon did it in his English Cut blog,[29] discussed in Chapter 5. Mahon demonstrated what he knew about—cloth, fit, measuring, and so on—everything about making fine suits. He posted pictures of suits in the making. He demonstrated he knew what he was doing.

---

[20] http://www.whatsnextblog.com

[21] http://blakeross.com

[22] http://www.ernietheattorney.net

[23] http://www.loiclemeur.com/english

[24] http://www.mcgeesmusings.net

[25] http://sethgodin.typepad.com

[26] http://www.newmediamusings.com/blog

[27] http://www.hyperorg.com/blogger

[28] http://blogs.msdn.com/cbrumme

[29] http://www.englishcut.com

Enticing influential people to link to you is extremely beneficial. You get exposure to large audiences, and the implied confirmation of your authority brings all sorts of benefits. For instance, one of the guys we trust entirely is Doc Searls. We've been reading him for years, and we both tend to think if he says something, we can assume it to be true. So, when he links to something and says it's great, we trust him, and we confer that trust and authority on the site to which he pointed.

Get five popular and widely trusted bloggers to link to a new site, and you've hit a home run. You might be able to fool one guy, but it's very hard to fool five.

Tip #6: Add comments.

A good blog is a conversation, not a one-way PR channel. Get over the fact that you won't have full control. Instead, embrace the extension. If you don't allow Comments, your corporate blog is likely to be seen as a PR channel and will be far less likely to be either trusted or followed. This does not mean you need to tolerate excessive rudeness. After Scoble and Israel were hit with some truly ugly comments, Israel imposed his "living room rule," which states: "If you are a guest in my home and you are rude to me or my guests, I will ask you to be more polite. If you do not comply I will make you leave, and you will not be allowed back in. The same goes for anonymous commenters. If you will not let me know who you are, then you are evicted." The "living room" policy has made life easier and more pleasant. We advise you to post it once and enforce it ever after.

Tip #7: Be accessible.

If you want something nice to unexpectedly happen to you, make it easy for people to contact you through your blog. We know of more than a few cases of people trying and failing to contact bloggers through their sites, and the bloggers subsequently losing out on invitations, networking, and job opportunities. It's surprising how many people start conversations with blogs but foolishly choose to make themselves unreachable through e-mail or phone.

Scoble publishes his cell phone number and his e-mail address on his blog. One Saturday afternoon, he was playing miniature golf with his family when his cell phone rang.

"Hello, is this Robert Scoble?"

"Yes."

"Hi, I'm the design producer for ABC's *Extreme Home Makeover* show."

It turns out that ABC didn't want to make over the Scoble family home to Robert's disappointment; the producer just wanted to ask if Scoble could help land some computers and equipment for another Seattle-area resident. ABC had first tried to reach Microsoft's PR agency, but could find no one around on a Saturday. But through Scoble's blog, the producer found him, and Scoble jumped into action. By Monday, the family had received donated equipment that met their needs.

You never know who wants to get hold of you, or how they'll make over your business or career. You'll never know if you don't have at least an e-mail address on your blog. And, as ABC's producer demonstrated, some people just don't have time to wait for e-mail. In those cases, phone contact information matters. Our experience tells us the risks of publishing your contact information are exaggerated. Scoble's phone number has been posted for years, and so far, he's received only two crank calls. But because he's made himself accessible, he's enjoyed friendships and taken advantage of opportunities that might otherwise have been missed.

Tip #8: Tell a story.

Corporate blogging is all about telling a story. *Your* story.

Seth Godin has written a book called *All Marketers Are Liars*.[30] The title may be sensational, but it sells books. When you dig into the book, what he's really saying is that marketers need to tell compelling stories.

Think about the elements of a good story. Conflict is a powerful tool to use, and business writers use it a lot. But be careful. Use it, and you will increase the chances that you'll get a lot of attention.

How about love and romance? Dave Winer tells us he regularly "teases" his readers. But be prudent with sexual metaphors; they can be overdone, and they can cheapen what you're trying to say.

---

[30] http://www.allmarketersareliars.com/

What about name dropping? "Did you hear what Adam Curry said about Jones at Gnomedex?" Yeah, that works. Watch out for turning off your audience, though, because that can create jealousy, and if overdone, it can turn off your readers.

David vs. Goliath? Absolutely! If you are an underdog, point it out.

Case studies also work well. Facts, objectively presented, are strong in business blogs. Mass audiences appreciate balanced analysis, particularly if the narrator is a trusted authority.

Tip #9: Be linky.

Before Scoble was at Microsoft, a former boss directed him not to link to sites outside his own organization. This is part of a concept called "stickiness" that emerged during the dot-com era. The idea is to entice people to your site, where they would get "stuck" like flies to paper, and never leave. This is a contemptuous way to treat customers. It's why we named the Google corporate blog as an example in the preceding chapter of doing it wrong. The Google blog links only to other Google sites—the opposite of how Scoble treated customers in the camera store where he worked in his youth. When customers could get a better deal elsewhere, he directed them to other stores. He lost one deal, but he gained customer trust and loyalty.

Let's take three imaginary groups:

- Group A links only to group A's sites.
- Group B links only to group B's sites.
- Group C links to everyone's sites, including Groups A and B; Groups D, E, and F; and so on.

Group C becomes the authority by telling readers what's good anywhere. A good blog will link to everyone, not just those who are friendly to the parent company. And, oh, by the way, Group C will rank higher than the other two groups on Google, meaning it'll get to head off visitors before they even see the links to Group A or B.

Link to your enemies. Link to your competitors. Link to everyone. Instead of being sticky, be *linky*. Be the absolute best resource you can be for your readers, and they will reward you with lots of inbound links.

Tip # 10: Get out into the real world.

Blogging has lots of advantages. Lots of people can get to know you with a minimal amount of effort on either side. But, when push comes to shove, it's no way to build a deep relationship. If the only way people know you is through your blog, you become one-dimensional. There's a reason why industry conferences and trade shows are still well attended. Nothing beats face-to-face meetings. They are certainly more intimate and memorable than meeting through a grid of pixels on a computer screen.

If you become a popular blogger, go out and speak when you can. Get yourself on panels. Attend meet-up events anywhere that people can see that you are a real person. If you don't get out much, technology can help. Start a podcast or video blog. Both show people more about you than just your text blog. Even a photo blog is a good add-on. You can drop in everything from family and pet shots to the products you are working to support. These techniques are all very humanizing, and all of this gives you more to talk about on your blog.

These are all subjects that other bloggers will help you learn about. The tools are simple and usually free.

Tip #11: Use your referrer log.

If someone near you at a cocktail party starts talking about you, don't your ears perk up? Don't you feel impelled to get involved in the conversation? Well, there's a simple tool to listen in on what people are saying about you: your referrer log. The referrer log is the technology that keeps track of who's linking to your site and how much traffic those sites are sending to you.

We read our referrer logs every day to see if someone new has linked to us. One trick is to read the log from the bottom up. Radio UserLand shows who has linked to you from the highest traffic sites to the lowest. TypePad shows you the referrers from most recent to oldest—not as useful perhaps, but TypePad has Trackback, which shows who is linking to each post.

Most referrer logs let you click on the web address of the site that is linking to yours. That way, you can read what people are saying about you. Even better is the Bloglines Citation feature.[31] It is a referrer's log, but it also lets

---

[31] http://bloglines.com/citations

you look at who is linking to any site on the Web. Just put in a URL, and you'll get a list of people who are linking to it.

Here's one for our *Naked Conversations* site:

> *http://www.bloglines.com/citations?url=http%3A%2F%2Fwww*
> *.nakedconversations.com*

and another for redcouch.typepad.com:

> *http://www.bloglines.com/citations?url=*
> *http%3A%2F%2Fredcouch.typepad.com&submit=Search*

This all relates to how conversations work in the blogosphere. Once you follow a link and see what someone has written about you, you can post something on your own blog responding to that person and perhaps linking back to him or her again. That demonstrates you're listening and willing to link beyond your own company turf. All these links, of course, help you with Google and the other search engines, and that always helps.

Understanding the blogosphere is fundamental obviously, but so is understanding the culture and rules of where you work. Nearly 100 incidents of people claiming they were fired because of their blogs contribute to fear, uncertainty, and doubt. The next chapter is designed to ease your concerns and to ensure you keep your job as long as you wish.

12 How to Not Get Dooced

*"Good marketing is partly a matter of following the rules.
Great marketing often happens by breaking the
rules."*

—*Philip Kotler*

Mark Jen lasted just two weeks as a Google employee. We can only guess at why he was fired because Google won't talk about it. We think Jen pushed Google's corporate culture too hard, and they sacked him for it. His co-workers told us they didn't like the skepticism he was expressing about Google. In your first two weeks at a new job, you should be more positive, they contended. Jen lost co-worker respect and internal support. There was no one sitting in power at Google who was willing to defend him. When he made the additional mistake of sharing previously published financial information and questioning analysts' rosy forecasts just before a quarterly financial report, when co-workers were about to become vested, he got axed.

In the blogging world, this is called getting "dooced." Web designer Heather B. Armstrong coined the phrase in 2002 after she was fired for blogging on Dooce.com, her blog about her work and colleagues at Yahoo!. There have been other highly public examples of employees getting fired. A Delta flight attendant was dismissed for posting a provocative picture of herself in her uniform on her blog "Diary of a Fired Flight Attendant."[1] A Microsoft

---
[1] http://queenofsky.journalspace.com

contractor was terminated after posting a picture on his blog of the company loading dock piled high with Macintosh computer equipment. A Friendster developer got sacked after sharing technical product details in the blogosphere. According to the Blogger's Rights Blog,[2] nearly 50 companies have disciplined or fired people for something they did on their blogs.

It may seem to some people that working in the public eye is dangerous to their employment tenure, so they call for rules or guidelines. There are reasons why guidelines may be necessary, but don't overrate them. They don't necessarily prevent destructive behavior. "I can drive 65 mph on an icy road," you might say, "because it says here that the speed limit is 65."

In this chapter, we'll look at some danger zones. For example, the Delta flight attendant, Ellen Simonetti, appears to have been fired for putting an image out there that the PR team was trying to change. We say "appears" because, in all of the cases discussed here, we know only the fired employee's side of the story. Companies don't talk to aspiring authors about terminated employees. Their lawyers won't let them. We do know Delta was particularly sensitive to the issue because the company had previously been attacked for sexism in advertising. We assume Simonetti was extending an image that the company wanted to ditch—that airlines hired only sexy flight attendants and that passengers wanted that. By posing in a company uniform, Simonetti pushed Delta's corporate culture in a direction it wasn't willing to go, and she got fired.

To avoid Jen's or Simonetti's blog-based mistakes, you need to know your corporate culture and what it is and isn't willing to accept. Here are some of the danger zones we've heard about from bosses, PR execs, and legal professionals at Boeing, General Motors, Target, Microsoft, and Sun Microsystems and have gathered through our own experiences:

- Not matching up with the PR image
- Leaking financial or other confidential information
- Disrupting the workplace by pissing off co-workers and bosses
- Breaking news in advance and generating unexpected work for the PR team
- Exposing dirty laundry
- Creating legal liabilities
- Damaging a company's relationships with partners, competitors, or other entities that affect its standing

---

[2] http://rights.journalspace.com

These all make obvious sense. Good bloggers have to be good employees if companies are going to not only tolerate but encourage blogging. While we argue that employers should trust employees to blog, employees must obviously behave in a trustworthy manner. But company decision-makers also need to cut a little slack. They need to keep in mind that blogosphere sentiment is decidedly opposed to the broadcast marketing and corpspeak that, in the eyes of most bloggers, have corrupted other communication channels. Employee cheerleading works credibly only when their employers at other times tolerate their dissent and criticism.

Stretching the Corporate Membrane

On his Scobleizer blog, co-author Scoble has at times been among the most critical voices of Microsoft, and many people have been surprised that Microsoft did not respond by firing, or at least disciplining, him. Instead, Microsoft has continued to encourage his blogging, and his superiors watch his back to protect him from command-and-control hatchets. Perhaps one day Scoble will go too far, or perhaps one day Microsoft management will change its attitude. But the benefits seem clear. The freedom that Scoble and the other Microsoft bloggers enjoy makes a statement about corporate tolerance and culture, and that has turned out to be good for Microsoft.

Like many prolific bloggers, Scoble seems to accomplish much of his blogging at around 4 a.m., when we assume Microsoft's PR team and bosses are asleep. How does he know what he can and cannot get away with?

We often think of corporate rules as lines in the sand, something that employees know not to cross unless they want to get fired. But our experience tells us there is no straight line of dos and don'ts. It's more like a membrane, something you can push and stretch, something more flexible at some companies than others. The membrane might be very flexible at your company, but pulled taut like a snare drum at ours. At four in the morning, a blogging employee needs to understand the membrane of his corporate culture.

At large companies, the membrane's texture even varies from team to team. One might not allow any blogging, while another might be actually comfortable with a blogger constructively criticizing the CEO. Understanding how tightly—or loosely—stretched your corporate membrane is may be your best blogging guideline. It would be impossible to write a universal blog guideline that works for every company and every team. You need to understand the flexibility in your own company membrane, and you need to "blog smart" accordingly.

Here are a few questions you might ask yourself in determining what you can or cannot do in a blog where you work:

- **Is the company averse to letting employees put their face in front of the brand?** For instance, Target, the #2 discount retailer in the United States, has a strict culture. Even its CEO doesn't often talk much to the press. The company's culture would make it hard for them to blog, employees told us. The company told us it will watch the blogosphere, to see what is said relevant to it, but the company will be slow to have employee bloggers.
- **Do you have a "one-voice culture"?** Apple Computer tells its employees that only the PR team and its CEO and CFO are allowed to communicate with the external world. While a handful of Apple employees are blogging, they play it very safe, making for blogs that are unremarkable. Whereas Sun's 1,000 bloggers, whom we discussed earlier, reveal an open culture that is improving perceptions of the company, Apple's blogger paucity is not.
- **Does your culture understand that "markets are conversations"?** If your boss hasn't read *The Cluetrain Manifesto*, would it be well received if you presented him with a copy?
- **What will your boss tolerate?** Show him or her some blogs and get an opinion. It's best to know before you start.
- **How legally cautious is your company?** Talk with your lawyers. Find out what scares them.

The Safety Knob

Every blogger should keep a hand on a virtual "safety knob." Turn it one way, and you'll have a safe, boring blog. Turn it in the other direction, and you might post something remarkable. Write about conflict, death, destruction, greed, corruption, lust, or lascivious living, and you will probably generate high traffic. They're the building blocks of novelists and Hollywood script writers. If you apply them to a corporate blog, however, they morph into internal conflict, dirty laundry, cross-company conflict, chaos, mess, and questionable behavior. You can discuss defects in products or people. However, along with traffic, your postings could be salacious, make people mad, earn you a pink slip, or all of the above.

The trick is to find the highest "safe" setting on your safety knob. If you don't play it a little close to the edge now and then, your blog can end up boring. It won't get you fired, but it won't get you much else either.

The stories you tell will decide your personal brand identity, and they become embedded in the corporate brand. Your company may not want these stories told, if you ask, but if you're a good narrator, in a company with a flexible membrane, you might be able to not only get away with it, but you may actually help your company in the process.

Why discuss these matters at all? Command-and-controllers regularly suppress these dissenting stories in favor of messages that imply a unified voice of unanimous company thinkers, implying monolithic precision and uniform happiness. This is the kind of "one-voice" policy that got Microsoft likened to the Borg to begin with. A great many people just don't trust one-voice companies. Blogging is part of a proactive many-voice strategy.

Sometimes it makes sense for a good blogger to stretch the rules, to see whether the corporate membrane can handle it, and in so doing, help the company become more transparent. For example, when Scoble posted that CEO Ballmer had announced a change in Microsoft's support of Washington state legislation to ban employment discrimination against gays, Scoble posted with righteous indignity, singling out Ballmer as a betrayer of the reasons Scoble was proud to work for Microsoft and stating flatly that the action made him less prone to stay there. While some people speculated that Scoble would be soon asked to leave, the amazing result was that, in less than a week, Ballmer returned the company to its original position.

If you want to be a top-level blogger, you need to get over your fear of breaking rules. At the end of the day, you need to tell an interesting story. You need to be artful in the way you conduct tours of your sausage factory. Do it one way, and it's fun. Do it another, and an unemployment form may be in your future.

Let's examine how to safely turn the knob.

Do Nothing Stupid

Of course, people don't need to blog to get themselves fired. Employees have been getting fired since shortly after the first one was hired. An NEC executive did it by posting racist remarks in a public newsgroup. Scoble's wife, Maryam, saw an employee get fired for inappropriately hitting on women. Still, blogging does provide a prime opportunity to create embarrassment and conflict when undertaken by the careless or clueless. In most states, there are no protections for employees against "at will" dismissals. An employer can show you the door because he or she doesn't like the smell of your breath or your taste in clothes. Whatever you say in public—on a blog or at a social gathering—you risk making someone mad enough to ask your boss to fire you.

Perhaps our simplest advice if you are considering a blog is this: "Do nothing stupid." Practice the same rules on your blog as on the rest of your job. Do nothing to embarrass or hurt your company. Blog smart.

Here are some general rules for how to adhere to the advice; you can refine them to address your personal experience.

- **Read your terms of employment—the ones HR made you sign on your start date.** At big companies there are rules to help employees deal with working in the public eye. Pay attention to them if your company offers them.
- **Avoid litigious issues.** If your company is public, be very careful about making statements on financials, or on other forward-looking issues that could impact stock price. Know the company's policy on intellectual property and the restrictions on discussing details of unannounced products. This latter issue may vary greatly between companies even in the same marketplace. Find out whether your legal department requires you to put a disclaimer on your blogsite.
- **Talk to your boss.** Know what he or she wants—and doesn't want—you to do in public. More important, know what will be done to back you up if you step into a bucket.
- **Know who owns what.** Find out who will own your blog's content and any ideas shared on it. What happens if a customer leaves a comment containing a new product idea and then your company ends up building something similar? For that matter, is it okay to blog on company time and equipment?

- **Find out about blog policies.** As we write this, companies have begun scrambling to write blog policies. Find out whether your company has one or whether one is planned. If the latter, consider getting involved in its development so you can help shape the policies.

Following this advice may sound like an awful lot of work, but for better or worse, it has become increasingly necessary to anticipate issues involving blogging, and the trend is not likely to reverse itself. Mark Jen told us that part of his problem was that there were no Google guidelines for him to review. He was out of work for only a couple of weeks before Plaxo, a social networking company, hired him. His first assignment—we should have guessed—was to write a company blogging policy.

It might be a good idea to read a few other company policies as a starting point. Here are some to review:

- **Groove Networks:** http://www.ozzie.net/blog/2002/08/24.html#a50
- **Plaxo, Inc.:** http://blog.plaxoed.com/?p=41
- **Nelson Publishers:** http://michaelhyatt.blogs.com/workingsmart/2005/03/corporate_blogg_1.html
- **Sun Microsystems:** http://www.tbray.org/ongoing/When/200x/2004/05/02/Policy
- **IBM:** http://www-128.ibm.com/developerworks/blogs/dw_blog_comments.jspa?blog=351&entry=81328
- **Harvard Law School:** http://blogs.law.harvard.edu/terms
- **Feedster:** http://feedster.blogs.com/corporate/2005/03/corporate_blogg.html
- **Fellowship Church:** http://www.leaveitbehind.com/home/2005/04/fellowship_chur.html

Official Company Blogs

Most blogs discussed in *Naked Conversations* are by individuals in business who blog. However, in increasing numbers, true "company" blogs have been forming. In them, multiple employees share a common space on a company-hosted site. Bloggers do it as part of their jobs, on company time. Such collaboration is likely to generate more traffic than a blogger might muster on his or her own. Company blogs also clarify ownership issues: If you are posting to a company space, then your company owns the content. If a comment gets posted that inspires you, it probably would be unwise to go across the street and form a startup based on it without permission.

Group blogs require different guidelines than standalone blogs and have a different tone to them. While they will test the membrane less, they also discourage the personal journal aspects of blogging. Company blogs are usually bad places to post pet pictures, unless maybe you work for a pet-food company. Multiple bloggers need to comply with a uniform style on a company blog. While our personal preferences may remain with the edginess of personal blogs, we think many companies will be more comfortable with corporate blogs, where there is some conformity. Our caution is for companies to not cleanse and refine what employees post, but to let them remain interesting, provocative, transparent, and human.

The Dangers of Doocing

So far in this chapter we've talked mostly about blogging as an employee, but what if you are the boss? On one hand, allowing employees to blog is a form of empowerment. It boosts morale and demonstrates that their management trusts them. On the other hand, some employees will persist in posting content worthy of getting themselves terminated.

If you do have to fire an employee, remember that doocing one is a public action and can backfire. Whether it's justified or not, the blogosphere tends to hold its own as martyrs when they get sacked. The former employee gets to tell his side of the story, while the employer needs to remain silent for legal reasons. Friendster,[3] another social networking company, fired an employee because of a blog incident and suffered customer boycotts. The company's only public recourse was to awkwardly state that the boycott was "small and ineffectual," which we consider an unwise way to describe angry customers.

The best course to take as an employer is to give employees guidelines under which they will have the freedom and incentive to become world-class bloggers. Make it clear that you trust your employees to blog smart. Define the taboos in your company membrane. Then step back and let them say what they want. From time to time, some will be critical of company products or

---

[3] http://www.friendster.com

policies—and they'll do it right out there in the open where your customers, competitors, and the media can see it. And all of those people will see the openness and tolerance of your company culture.

Negative postings, employers and managers told us, were their biggest fear of blogging. However, by maintaining a policy that tolerates unflattering posting and comments, many companies gain more than they lose. Blogging creates a general perception of an enlightened employer, one who wants to hear constituent opinions and is willing to adjust course accordingly. The blogosphere champions these companies, and so will your customers. The PR benefits are significant and long-lasting. Prospects see the kind of company they'd like to do business with. Recruits see the kind of company they'd like to join, and employees feel they are being heard with greater strength than the company suggestion box implies.

In your guidelines, make clear your desire to keep your employees well informed. Have your PR department, R&D team, sales and marketing staff, and other executives feed information to your bloggers. Treat them as insiders and influencers. Fill them in on confidential background information that lets them see the company's intended direction, and they will be able to help steer you there without inappropriate leaks. Your bloggers will be able to remain true to strategy and vision without spilling the beans. Instead of trying to speak in a single, contrived voice, your company will sing with many voices, and they will all sing in harmony.

That, of course, is a best-case scenario. Not all employees will always be wise and judicious in their criticism of bosses and places of work. Not all bosses will exude magnanimous objectivity when an employee several ranks below them on the org chart mouths off. Some employee bloggers have been downright bone-headed. For example, an employee at Waterstone's, the prestigious British retailer, was shocked . . . *shocked* . . . when he was sacked for likening his boss to the pointy-haired manager in the Dilbert comic strip.

Will this backfire? From time to time, yes. Occasional gaffes are a reality of business, with or without blogs. But so far, the numbers indicate low risk factors and lower actual incidence of businesses damaged by employee bloggers. Out of several million people in business blogging tens of millions of posts daily, we found fewer than 50 incidents in which employers felt compelled to take action, and some of the actions taken were quite mild. For example, Technorati CEO Sifry asked employee-blogger Nial Kennedy not to post something, and the employee complied.

In Chapter 3, we discussed Intel CEO Paul S. Otellini, who had his request to keep his blog private violated when one of his 86,000 employees leaked a few of his postings to the *San Jose Mercury News*. He did not follow up with a witch hunt, or so we were told. Instead, he asked employees not to do it again in a tone that was described to us as "assertive but calm." Nearly a year later, additional breaches had not occurred. Bloggers generally don't want to spoil it for other bloggers, and they also don't want to violate the trust of enlightened employers.

Another wise course for employers is to set up an intranet page or, better yet, an internal blog. Use it to post blog policy. Then let bloggers loose to post tips to each other on smart blogging. With the right guidance, your company bloggers can transform themselves into a new form of interdepartmental, interactive power. Your employees become the preachers, as Church of the Customer describes them, and your customers become the congregation inspired to evangelize your company gospel.

But for the most part, these will be stretches of the membrane where both sides learn that in some places flexibility is limited. The strongest business cultures tolerate test stretches to their corporate membrane. Scoble has generally been recognized as a poster child for this sort of risk taking. He has publicly taken on his CEO, saying that Ballmer's action on a social issue made Scoble want to leave the company. Strong words coming from someone six levels down on the org chart. Another time, he declared a Microsoft department to be lame from a blogger's perspective. "Anyone who develops a web page today that is not RSS-enabled should be fired," he shouted in another posting, leading of course to the head of that department demanding that Scoble be fired.

Scoble blogs with zeal. It may appear that he gets carried away, but that is rarely the case. He believes in strategic risk. When he strolls out on the plank, he has informed his wife, his boss, and Microsoft's PR agency what he's intending to do. He doesn't really know whether what he will do will get him dooced or not—but he assesses the risk before he takes it. By contrast, Mark Jen told us he had no idea he had placed himself at risk at Google with his blog, and said he would not have written it had he known.

The Corporate Weblog Manifesto

In 2003, Scoble published his Corporate Weblog Manifesto on Scobleizer, for two reasons. First, he used it to remind himself of his principles. Second, he published it to get reader feedback because he noticed an increasing number of people identifying themselves as company employees who were blogging. He has updated it for the first time for *Naked Conversations*.

1. Tell the truth, the whole truth, and nothing but the truth. If your competitor has a product that's better than yours, link to it. You might as well. We'll find it anyway.

2. Post fast on both good news and bad. If someone says something bad about your product, link to it—before the second or third site does—and answer its claims as best you can. The same if something good comes out about you. It's all about building long-term trust. The trick to building trust is to show up. If you don't answer what people say, if you don't show up, then you build distrust.

3. Use a human voice. Don't get corporate lawyers and PR professionals to modify your speech. We can tell, believe us. Plus, you'll be too slow. If you're the last one to post, the joke is on you. Don't worry about having a messy blog from time to time. If we don't see an occasional typo, we'll start to wonder if you're really human.

4. Make sure you support the latest software/web/human standards. If you don't know what they are, find out. If you don't know what RSS feeds are, find out. If you don't know what tagging is, find out. If you don't know how Google, Technorati, Feedster, and Flickr work, find out.

5. Have a thick skin. Even if you are behind the world's favorite product, people will say bad things about it. That's part of the process. Don't try to write a corporate weblog unless you can answer all questions—good and bad—professionally, quickly, and nicely.

6. Seek out as many grassroots news resources as possible so that you know what's being discussed in areas of interest to you. In the technology world, that's Slashdot. In politics, it might be Wonkette or InstaPundit.

7. Talk to the grassroots first. Why? Because the mainstream press cruises weblogs looking for stories and looking for people to quote. If a mainstream reporter can't find anyone who knows about a story, that reporter's organization cannot publish something trustworthy. People trust stories that have quotes from multiple sources. They don't trust press releases.

8. If you screw up, acknowledge it. Fast. And give us a plan for how you'll unscrew it. Then deliver.

9. Under-promise. Over-deliver. If you expect to ship on March 1, say you won't ship until March 15. Folks will start to trust you if you behave this way. Look at Disney theme parks. When you're standing in line, you trust the signs. Why? Because the line usually goes faster than the sign says it will. (The signs are engineered to say that a line will take about 15 percent longer than it really will.)

10. Know your influencers. Know the mavens, salesmen, and connectors of your marketplace. If you can't connect to them during a crisis, you shouldn't try to keep a corporate weblog. (And the influencers had better know how to get hold of you because they often know when you're under attack before you do.)

11. Never change your weblog's URL. We did it once and lost much of our readership. It took several months to build up the same reader patterns and trust.

12. If your life is in turmoil and/or you're unhappy, don't write. It affects the writing quality in subtle ways, and your readers will notice.

13. If you don't have the answers, say so. Not having the answers is human. But get them and exceed expectations. If you say you'll know by tomorrow afternoon, make sure you know in the morning.

14. Never lie. You'll get caught, and you'll lose credibility that you won't get back.

15. Never hide information. Just like the space shuttle engineers, your information will get out and you'll lose credibility.

16. If you have information that might get you in a lawsuit, consult a lawyer before posting, but do it fast. Speed is key. If it takes you two weeks to answer what's going on in the marketplace because you're scared of what your legal hit will be, then you're screwed anyway. Your competitors will figure it out and outmaneuver you.

17. Link to your competitors and say nice things about them. Remember, you're part of an industry, and if the entire industry gets bigger, you'll probably win more than your fair share of business and you'll get bigger too. Be better than your competitors—people remember.

18. Be nice to everyone. When a big fish comes along, most people do whatever they have to do to keep him happy. Personally, we believe in being nice to *everyone*, not just the big fish. You never know when

a janitor will go to school, get an MBA, and start a company. We've seen it happen. You never know who'll get promoted. We've learned this lesson the hard way.

19. Be the authority on your product/company. You should know more about your product than anyone if you're writing a weblog about it. If there are others who know more, you damned well better link to them (and you should send some goodies to them to thank them for being such great advocates).

20. Know who is talking about you. Use services such as Technorati, Feedster, and PubSub to see who they are.

21. Be transparent. Show you have nothing to hide. Blogging is a great way to build strong relationships with other people, and nothing builds trust and confidence like people who demonstrate they aren't hiding anything.

22. Build relationships offline, too. Online relationships are loosely coupled. Put strain on them and they disappear. But if people get to know you face to face, they'll stick by your side more often than not. It's why we spend so much time at blogger meetups and conferences.

23. Disclose all conflicts and biases. Is someone paying you? Tell your readers, even if you don't think it affects your writing. Being transparent with your readers about your conflicts and/or your biases will help you remain credible. Own stock in a company you write about? Disclose that! Got a free product to try out? Tell us! Get taken to dinner by a company or a person because of your blog? Write about it.

24. Don't blog on demand. Is your marketing department demanding that you write about something? Push back. Your blog is your own. Tell the guys in marketing to get their own blog if they think they have something people should know. Always make sure it's *you* saying something, not someone else. You are responsible for the content that goes on your blog.

25. Keep confidences. If someone says, "this is not for your blog" before telling you something, don't write about it. Word gets around if you aren't trustworthy. On the other hand, set the ground rules upfront for any conversation. It's not fair for people to give you a demo and afterward say, "You're not going to put this on your blog, are you?"

26. Be clear when you're speaking for your company. If you're writing a personal blog, sometimes the company might want you to write

something on it. If that happens, be very clear about when roles change. Also, when you're writing about company stuff but you're writing your own opinion of it, it's a good idea to say "This is my opinion" or some other similar qualifier to make sure your readers understand the information isn't vetted or approved.

27. Be careful with legal issues. Commenting on legal issues is very risky. Things like discrimination, ongoing lawsuits, employee actions, and patents are potentially career-threatening issues. Be equally careful with culturally sensitive issues and politics. We're not saying don't write about them, but be very careful. Remember that blogs are read worldwide by people who might not see things the way you see them.

28. Demonstrate passion. Post frequently.

29. Respond to your readers. Read your comments, check your referrer log frequently, and link back to those who are talking to you. Link to others, and they will return the gesture.

30. Be ethical. Read and follow Charlene Li's[4] and Allan Jenkins's[5] ethics policies. They are quite good and will help you avoid ethical dilemmas.

31. Realize that you don't have free speech. If you are identified as a member of a corporation, what you write reflects on the entire corporation. Your writing probably will be judged under the legal standards for corporate speech, especially if you're an executive of the company, so you must take care to be accurate in product claims.

32. Have a conversation with your manager about blogging before you start and find out what kinds of blogging he or she will defend.

33. It is always risky to attack the boss. Do it sparingly. I'm not saying don't do it, but do it with your eyes open and expect backlash.

34. If you want to change something about the world, ask yourself "How will I best get the change I want?" Realize that it's easier to change your company from inside than outside.

---

[4] http://blogs.forrester.com/charleneli/2004/11/blogging_policy.html
[5] http://allanjenkins.typepad.com/my_weblog/2004/12/code_of_bloggin.html

Playing with Dynamite

You can follow all the rules and guidelines that exist and still find yourself in trouble. It's really easy to damage relationships with partners, customers, bosses, and co-workers. So what do you do if you get into trouble?

First, removing your post won't help. When you publish, your words are redistributed through syndication networks. Even if you remove your original content, your words are still out there somewhere. If a reader notices that you removed or changed content, he or she might link to you and say, "So-and-so just removed this post; here it is again. I wonder why they removed this?"

Instead of removing a post, we recommend putting up a correction. Say you're sorry, and perhaps strike-through the original content, and note that you have learned that you were incorrect. If you posted something really damaging (like the source code to your company's product), then delete that but leave a note up saying something like "Some content here was removed because we discovered it was in error for us to post this." It probably is too late to save your career in such an instance, but at least you might be able to avoid a lawsuit.

Whenever you're accused of doing something wrong, don't fight back—at least not at first. Listen, listen, listen. Try to get into the other person's shoes. Try to understand why he or she is angry with you before reacting. Always learn something from the interchange, even if you get fired. Don't go dark, either. Over-communicate with everyone around you during a crisis. Say you're sorry if it turns out you were wrong. Mean it. If you are right, be respectful and as humble as absolutely possible. Give the other person a way to win, even if he or she is wrong. It's always best to live to see another day.

Employee blogging is a lot like mining for gold. Gold is often hidden inside granite. Miners often use dynamite to blast ore into manageable chunks. Mishandle dynamite, though, and you can easily blow off your arm.

Like the gold miner who carefully plies his trade, a corporate employee can do a lot of great things with a blog—make the company more approachable, build relationships and partnerships, scale out evangelism or PR efforts, or even just arrange a dinner for fellow geeks. But if you mishandle your responsibilities, you can find yourself dooced or worse (yes, there are worse things than getting fired—for example, sued).

So, blog, and blog often, but be careful out there!

13 Blogging in a Crisis

"When written in Chinese, the word 'crisis' is composed of two characters—one represents danger, and the other represents opportunity."

—*John F. Kennedy, 35th U.S. president*

For better or worse, the true power of blogging is clearest during times of crisis.

In the past several years, blogging has played an increasing role in providing fast, valuable, striking, and comforting information in times of crisis. During dramatic national and international disasters, "citizen-journalists" have reported from ground zero with personal, often poignant perspectives on events that mainstream media could not possibly catch via satellite observations, official spokespeople, or news teams deployed after the fact. People on the scene have transmitted information through camera phones and handheld devices, or have rushed home and uploaded cam recordings and posted text about what they saw and experienced firsthand. Bloggers sent out breathtaking and horrifying footage of tsunamis engulfing vacationers in Thailand in the last days of 2004. In 2005 bloggers were on the scene with camera phones as stunned London commuters staggered out of transit tubes where terrorists had detonated bombs and, again, to show as-it-happened videos of Katrina devastating New Orleans. The odds of a mainstream journalist being on the spot of such occurrences are incalculably remote.

Citizen journalism can also force media attention on smaller crises. When Wisconsin-based technology journalist David Koch disappeared from Vancouver's Grouse Mountain in May 2005, we converted our *Naked Conversations* blogsite into a space where Koch's family and friends could share information with the public. The family hoped that bloggers could generate sufficient attention to get the media to report on Koch's disappearance, and the media coverage would encourage search and rescue teams to continue looking.

During the next week, more than 100 people posted comments on our site, demonstrating expertise on the mountain's terrain, in search-and-rescue operations, and in ways to get media attention. Despite the fact that our blog was set up for people wanting to collaborate on a book project, our two Koch-related postings generated many more comments than any other *Naked Conversations* posting. The family started its own weblog, and numerous other bloggers joined in to spread the word. Media attention shot up, and not just in Vancouver.

The *Wall Street Journal* picked up the story, as did CBS news. Gary A. Bolles, a partner in Microcast Communications,[1] a custom interactive media company, played a connector's role between family and bloggers. He said, "There's no question that the activity in the blogosphere helped increase the visibility of the search efforts to the traditional media, and I believe that in turn encouraged press coverage at a time when interest by local and national print and broadcast outlets had started to wane."

Bloggers also supported the family with computer equipment and space in the Vancouver area. Unfortunately, the story culminated sadly, with Koch being discovered dead in a ravine more than a week after he had disappeared. It's small consolation, but the extended effort gave the family a final answer to their ultimate question.

These, of course, are not business-related examples of blogging in a crisis. Nor would we be so callous as to argue that what a business considers a crisis equates in any way to acts of terrorism, natural disaster, or a loved one lost on a mountain. However, these examples do contain applicable points of similarity. In a crisis, blogs play a fundamental role in the sharing and spreading of information, and they do it with unprecedented speed. Blogs enable businesses to jump in quickly, and effectively control, reduce, or eliminate damage. We previously discussed the unfortunate cases of Electronic Arts, Kryptonite, and Kensington. It is perhaps an over-simplification that an

---

[1] http://microcast.biz

Engadget video cost Kryptonite an estimated $10 million, because the company might have always had the best interest of its customers in mind. It is less debatable that not blogging cost Kryptonite a significant chunk of a reputation built over 30 years.

At the Speed of *Blink*

As we have discussed, most companies have traditionally used well-trained spokespeople, press releases, conferences, and web sites to communicate with the public. Most of these tools, however, are slow to reach audiences that matter, and nearly all of them are one-directional. A press release shows you are speaking, but not listening. In a crisis, listening and responding can prove infinitely more effective than any attempts to command and control the discussion about the situation.

Most companies have standard operating procedures for "managing crises," a term we find oxymoronic. The process usually begins with an executive and managerial meeting, followed by fact-finding processes. Once the facts are gathered, key decision-makers hold more meetings to determine the appropriate course of action. They call in lawyers to discuss risks, and they consult PR people to present the situation in the best possible light. Eventually, the company issues a single, unified public statement. This process takes time—perhaps about 10 days for a large company moving aggressively.

But, as we keep saying, the world has become a faster, smaller place, and these same old techniques are no longer sufficient in many cases. In this new Information Age, words flow and opinions form rapidly. Rumors and facts muddle together, and people get agitated, perhaps even hysterical. Ten days may have once been lightning speed, but it's enough time for a company's reputation to be made or lost in the blogosphere. Kryptonite spent 30 years building a superior reputation. For a mere 10 days, the company ignored a conversation on an unfamiliar new medium, and doing so cost it dearly—in dollars and reputation. Further, quickly formed impressions of a company can persist long after the crisis has been resolved. We doubt that everyone who heard about the problem with Kryptonite's locks has yet heard that the company eventually made good for its customers. In fact, when we posted information about the situation on our blogsite nine months after the crisis, one of the first comments was from a Kryptonite customer who wanted to know if the exchange program was still in effect.

Companies wait because they want to have the complete story before they act. This sounds logical enough, but it is often the wrong strategy.

As Malcolm Gladwell points out in his fascinating book, we live in an age of *Blink*. The author talks about how people often make the right decision in a microsecond. Unconsciously, they are using the wisdom of their experience. Gladwell says we do this by "thin-slicing," taking the fewest facts that are most important for making the right decision. Too many facts, he argues, can confuse a situation, bog down response—or worse, lead you to the wrong decision. One example he uses involves an emergency coronary treatment unit that found triaging patients with chest pains based on just three facts proved more accurate in identifying heart attacks and saved more lives than waiting for the full picture by gathering all the facts. Responding quickly saves lives. Compiling a boatload of data does not. Responding quickly can also save millions of dollars and preserve a company's reputation. Sometimes, like it or not, you have to respond in a blink.

Registering Disbelief

As we wrote this chapter, Scoble became involved in a situation that demonstrated how blogs can put a lid on a crisis if you react at blink speed. Writing in *The Register*, an RSS-enabled news site, reporter Andrew Orlowski[2] charged that the beta version of Microsoft's new Internet Explorer 7 browser blocked users from Google or Yahoo! toolbars, requiring them instead to use Microsoft's own MSN toolbar. Such charges would be serious for any company, but for Microsoft it was potentially a crisis of major proportion because it implied that the company was defying its well-publicized antitrust settlements with U.S., European, and several state governments.

Less than three hours later, Scoble posted evidence on his Scobleizer[3] site that the charge was patently false. Throughout the night, other bloggers tried the beta software, which had been released that morning, and confirmed Scoble's side of the story. They concluded that although there might be some anomalies with old versions of Google and Yahoo! toolbars, the early beta worked seamlessly with any current version. Further, the general consensus

[2] http://www.theregister.co.uk/2005/07/28/ie7_nukes_rival_search
[3] http://radio.weblogs.com/0001011/2005/07/28.html#a10776

in the blogosphere was that isolated compatibility problems that might occur during a beta test—when presumably some features are still being developed and perfected—do not constitute evidence of intended predatory practices.

For the next 24 hours, fires raged on Scoble's blog. Accusations and insults were often injected into the conversation, which turned more than a little ugly at times. Technorati found over 1,300 links[4] to the Scoble postings by 4 p.m. the following day.

What happened next is relevant: *Nothing* happened. *The Register's* unfounded charges did not spread to other media. Although other bloggers enthusiastically pointed to the brouhaha, they did not amplify Orlowski's charges. When Microsoft executives woke up the next morning, they did not see a damaging article prominently displayed in the *New York Times* or *Wall Street Journal*. Microsoft's stock did not falter the next day, and as far as we know, no watchdog at the U.S. Department of Justice went running down the hallway to report an infraction to his superior. By Friday night, interest in the controversy appeared to be on the wane, and the blogosphere's tech sector went back to commenting on the beta product rather than the charges.

Scoble and the Internet Explorer team had moved quickly. They got their facts into the word-of-mouth food chain, and by aggressively blogging and answering comments almost in real time, they averted a crisis. Compare that with Kryptonite's story, and you have to conclude it is a safer and wiser course to respond by blogging than to go through "official channels."

Why would companies choose to move slowly and methodically when the world is talking about them, perhaps unfairly and inaccurately? Ignoring, dismissing, or challenging accusatory voices seems all too often to be part of enterprise crisis management procedures. Companies also tend to deny the potential repercussions of incidents that start small—such as Electronic Arts did when a disgruntled spouse spoke out against working conditions. It seems to us that often the prudent course can prove fatal. Instead, companies need to respond to criticism in ways that show they want to get at the truth and they want to protect their customers' interests and well-being. You don't achieve that by discrediting accusers. Stalling can easily give customers and observers the impression that you are more on the side of corporate profits than customer well-being. Credibility is very much like virginity. Once you lose it, it is impossible to regain.

---

[4] http://www.technorati.com/search/ie7%20beta

Delays and Credibility

Just look at what slow response has done to NASA, the American space agency. For more than 40 years NASA has had the best manned success record of any space exploration organization. However, tragedy has marred its image three times. In January 1986, the space shuttle *Challenger* exploded 73 seconds after takeoff, killing seven astronauts. Seventeen years later, the aging spacecraft *Columbia* overheated during re-entry over Texas, killing seven astronauts. In 1967, Gus Grissom was among three astronauts killed in an *Apollo* launchpad fire.

After all three tragedies, criticism was immediate and widespread. To its credit, NASA did not completely clam up. It expressed sorrow for the loss of human life and sympathy for the families. It gave the details of what had happened. But it took several months to publish the Rogers Commission Report on what happened to *Challenger*, and it took seven months to publish the *Columbia* Accident Investigation Board (CAIB) report. Further, the CAIB report asserted that culture—as much as loose tiles—was responsible for the tragedy.

The CAIB report reinvigorated and amplified criticism of NASA. After remaining stoically silent for many months, saying it was waiting for the report, NASA elected to stay silent again after the report's publication—this time to study it. NASA officials eventually found their way onto the talk circuit, discussing what they were doing to improve culture and safety. To those still following the story, it appeared they had indeed taken some significant steps.

But in the court of public opinion, it was too late. Most people had made up their minds about NASA long before space agency officials finally got around to speaking. When there were glitches seconds after a launch in July 2005, the public criticism was swift and harsh, and some would say the agency was forced to delay the next manned flight unnecessarily. NASA had lost a great deal of public and political support, and might not be able to regain it for a long time to come. How NASA's public perception impacts future budgets and programs remains to be seen.

Would blogging have helped NASA? We don't know the inside information, nor did we even attempt to contact NASA to discuss it. But we are certain that organizations will almost always fare better by talking to the public, listening to critics, and responding politely and constructively—the earlier, the better. Telling the public what you know and don't know always helps. Demonstrating that your company is represented by real people who actually care about safety, quality, service, integrity, and satisfaction can only help.

Despite what a lawyer tells you, saying that you regret that something bad happened doesn't make you culpable in the all-important court of public opinion. And further, *not* expressing concerns very often makes people suspicious of you. Organizations are unwise when they shut down communications, get defensive, or react to hard-nosed but justifiable questions as if they were insulting assaults.

Registered

Intel was another company that learned the hard way. In the summer of 2000, the world's leading microprocessor company launched its Pentium III 1.113 GHz processor, promising breakthrough speed for the time. The company's PR machine wrapped the introduction into much hoopla, and the computer industry and mainstream press received the new computer chip with enthusiasm. However, two electronic newsletter editors—Tom Pabst[5] and Kyle Bennett[6]—working independently of each other, both found and reported[7] compilation problems in the new chip. The precise problem applied only to a technically arcane Linux application, one unlikely to confront a typical computer user. But that is not what Intel said. Official company spokespeople flatly dismissed the reports, denying the problem and saying the company had fully tested and benchmarked the processor. Intel had spent millions on the launch, and it wasn't about to renege on its claims of the new CPU's accuracy because of two niche publications. Intel had its story, and it was adamantly sticking to it.

But *The Register* was there[8] back in 2000, and this particular time the publication accurately reported on a controversy. From there, the discussion moved quickly into the more trusted business and technology press. A day or two later, Dell Computer quietly stopped offering its new computer based on the processor—and *The Register* reported that as well. The *Wall Street Journal* cited *The Register* when it reported on Intel's surprise problems the next day, and Intel's stock started sagging. Less than three weeks after Tom Pabst's initial report, Intel announced it had replicated the problem after all. A PR

[5] http://www.tomshardware.com
[6] http://www.hardocp.com
[7] http://www.tomshardware.com/cpu/20000801/index.html
[8] http://www.theregister.co.uk/2000/08/28/intel_recalls_1_13ghz_pentium

spokesperson described it as a "marginality" impacting too few computer users to require a recall. By then the whole world seemed to know that Intel had launched a new chip and it was faulty. There was a perception problem, and Intel's testing processes came under question. Intel seemed to have taken a "customer be damned" attitude, and public fear, uncertainty, and doubt rose quickly.

Several weeks after the incident broke, Intel recalled the processor, at great expense. More costly still was the ding in Intel's reputation. Its processors, of course, remain inside most of the world's personal computers, but at that time, many computer makers started talking about not putting all their eggs into one basket, and archrival AMD started making inroads that are now well paved.

You would think a company like Intel would learn from such a caustic lesson. But it apparently had not. Back in 1994, it was revealed that a Pentium error caused an error in spreadsheets. Intel reacted dismissively, saying the glitch would happen only once every 27,000 years. It backfired and the company backtracked, offering to replace the processor. Those who ignore history are indeed doomed to repeat it.

But what can a company say before all the facts are in, before a solution is available, before it is ready to financially commit to make amends, if such amends are in order? How should it deal with the public when lawyers are telling company officers that to reduce risk they should fess up to nothing?

A company can (and should) say this much: "We're listening. We're sorry this happened, and we don't yet know why it did. We're working on the problem. Our hearts go out to those who have suffered. We'll tell you more as soon as we know more." Most important, the company should read what is being said about it in the blogosphere, because increasingly it is being said there first. One person should be assigned to monitor the blogosphere at least once an hour and report to higher-ups when something breaks.

Blogging buys a company what it needs most during a crisis—time. When a company shows that it is listening and responding, people stop yelling at it, just as the folks at Vichy learned. By buying time, a company can then use whatever systems it has traditionally used to figure out a solution that will minimize costs to the company, and retain customer loyalty and confidence.

First Couple's Trouble

Back in 2001, Ben and Mena Trott were the blogosphere's "First Couple." Like so many talented technologists, the two unexpectedly found themselves laid off. Retreating from Silicon Valley to their hometown of Petaluma, California, they rented an apartment and tried to figure out whether to look for jobs or start a family. Mena increased her blogging posts on her personal blog dollarshort[9] in part to kill time and "in part to become famous." But the glitchy tools of the time frustrated her. So she asked Ben, an accomplished Perl software program coder, to build something she would find easier. He did, and as developers often do, he wanted to share it with other people who thought it was cool. But the Trotts also realized that Ben had created something important, and they proceeded under that assumption. Ben's program became Movable Type, the most popular authoring toolset for business blogs worldwide.

At first, it seemed that nothing could go wrong. "When we first released our software there was no blogging industry so expectations weren't what they are today," Mena told us. "We had to set our own. Ben and I decided that once we started, we'd need to commit to go all the way. Other [software] companies had started and then disappeared, leaving users unsupported. We knew that we might have our lives tethered to Movable Type and had to decide whether we were committed to do so. We had no business plan, but we did have a vision to make a tool that everyone could use and it would give them power."

While much of this company's incredible growth has been smooth sailing, a single wrong maneuver would almost sink the boat.

Their first day, back in 2001, Ben and Mena received over 100 downloads, many from blogging's most influential people. These people wrote glowing early reviews, inciting an avalanche of downloads. A bit later, the Trotts started TypePad, which was still easier to use and became rapidly adopted by end users, many of whom were less sophisticated computer users. The number of downloads doubled about every six months for the next four years. Ben and Mena eventually became Six Apart, and they moved into San Francisco offices. When Pyra, publisher of Blogger, was acquired by Google, Six Apart became the only company focused exclusively on blog authoring tools. By facing the formidable troika of competition from Google, Yahoo!, and Microsoft, Ben and Mena became underdog heroes—and the world loves an underdog.

Just about then, the crisis hit the fan. Since they had started, the Trotts had made clear that to continue to upgrade the software and to support increasingly less technologically sophisticated customers, they would eventually

---

[9] http://mena.TypePad.com

have to charge users. Movable Type had a license system that had been built ad hoc, and over time, it became as complex as a Rube Goldberg machine drawing.[10] There were corporate customers paying $150 for licenses and supporting 2,000 users with it.

When Movable Type v3.0 was ready, the company surprised its customers with a new license policy, one that would be expensive to group blogs, often shared by consumers rather than corporations. Response was immediate, negative, and nearly violent. More than 1,000 hostile comments were posted in the first 48 hours. By blind-siding its users, Six Apart had infuriated them, and they were threatening to defect en masse. "We knew people were going to complain," Trott told us, "but we didn't know there would be a thousand people who personally wanted my head on a platter." Six Apart appeared to be in a tailspin, and observers predicted a crash landing.

The Trotts didn't panic, nor did they behave defensively, and they were anything but dismissive of their critics. They listened very closely, and they did it out in the blogosphere where people could see them doing it. Mena's official blog, Mena's Corner,[11] kept comments open, and through Trackback, a visitor could see everything being said about them on the blogosphere, even the unkindest swipes.

"The responses were really hard for us to take. It was like the first dent in your new car. Until then, everyone seemed to think we were perfect, and now we weren't." But the Trotts listened closely to what was being said and tried to keep their emotions out of it. And what they learned was that people really wanted unlimited blogs more than free use.

Six Apart had directed its new strategy at corporate abuse. According to Trott, she and Ben had never intended to penalize the individual users. The irony was that the company saw few ripples from business customers, who expressed relief that the company finally had coherent licensing. Corporate customers have long understood that in enterprise environments freeware is often expensive to use because of the problems it can cause.

Second, the Trotts learned an absolute business truth. People hate unpleasant financial surprises. "We should have explained our issues in advance. We should have talked with our customers before acting," she reflected.

Finally, Six Apart had to figure out what to do next. "We couldn't just say, 'Oh, never mind' and change back to the old model. We had to figure out what

[10] http://www.rube-goldberg.com/html/gallery.htm
[11] http://www.sixapart.com/about/corner

wasn't going to work, and we needed to start charging for Movable Type." The Trotts spent about a month getting the licensing straightened out and spent a good part of it in continuing conversations with customers. Mena kept users current by blogging often, usually more than once daily.

"We had to take our time. We had to get it right," she told us.

Once it became clear the company was listening, the negative comments steadily subsided. Just as Vichy would experience in another country a full year later, comments became constructive and collaborative in tone. End users showed they were sensitive to the costs of developing and supporting software. Finally, Mena announced the revisions via Mena's Corner, using a straightforward collaborative style. There was little response. The crisis was resolved, and Six Apart managed to avoid a fatal stampede of defecting customers. Today it's hard to detect even a trace of bitterness among customers and observers. The company's rapid growth rate has not suffered.

What's Good for Six Apart . . .

We think Six Apart's handling of a potential disaster should be an MBA case study for how blogging can deflect or diffuse a crisis. The company's crisis actually occurred, and blogging averted a devastation of its corporate image. It's more difficult to pinpoint crises that were averted altogether.

Let's face it, crises happen. Most companies have standard procedures for what to do when they face one. But that procedure probably predates the new social media. In a crisis, you should have the best possible tools for handling them at the ready, and you should already be experienced in using them. Being as prepared as possible to handle a crisis is among the most compelling reasons to start a blog well in advance. When Bob Lutz used his blog to explain GM's side of an advertising boycott of the *Los Angeles Times*, people knew his blog and had already decided whether or not they trusted him. If he had just started to blog at the issue, it is likely that audiences would have been suspicious. Further, his past blogging experience made him adept at how to use the communications channel.

Steve Rubel,[12] at CooperKatz PR, has been a vocal advocate of being prepared for a crisis. He has devised a crisis management blogging lockbox, along the lines of "In case of emergency, break this glass." The agency works

---

[12] http://www.micropersuasion.com

with its clients to anticipate the crises that could possibly occur. Together they then plan and design a "failsafe" blog—a blog to be used only in case of emergency. Clients know who will speak for their organization, what issues will be addressed, and what some of the toughest questions will be. So far, no such lockbox has been used, Rubel told us in August 2005.

We think the day will come when such blog lockboxes are simply part of corporate management toolkits. And the tools in those kits are rapidly improving and becoming more diverse. As we will see in the next chapter, companies are starting to have more choices in what they can use, not just in emergencies, but in every situation.

The Big Picture

"*All the guys who can paint great big pictures can paint great small ones.*"

—Ernest Hemingway

14 Emerging Technology

"The future ain't what it used to be."

—Yogi Berra

Twenty years from now, people will look back at the blogging tools we use today and smile at how quaint they were. What will have replaced them? We haven't a clue. Technology will always continue to surprise us, and when we look back at yesterday's promises, some seem inane.

Twenty years back we saw prototypes of telephone headsets that looked like band-aids we would someday attach beneath our ears, letting us speak and hear through vibrations. We also remember VRML technology, created by developers who believed they could extend it to enable holographic versions of the people we were talking with to climb out of our computer screens and chat with us in our living rooms. These visions never materialized, of course. What did materialize instead were technologies that most people could not have dreamed of two decades ago, including home Internet access, WiFi, camera cell phones, and the iPod.

During just the six months of 2005 when we were writing *Naked Conversations*, related technologies such as RSS and podcasting exploded into mass adoption. Innovations kept changing our story as we wrote it and will change it even more before you get the chance to read this. Many show great promise but are still awaiting mainstream acceptance. We'll get to them in a moment, but first let's take a look at what has happened so far along the Internet continuum.

From Surf to Search to Syndication

In a little over 10 years, the Internet has blown through its first two phases of mass use and is well into a third. In late 1994, the Age of Surf began. Graphical web browsers let average people visit multiple Internet content sites, and they were fascinated as they bopped around from one place to another. The more people surfed, the more businesses built sites for them to visit. Like Godin's Purple Cows, the first site of nearly every category seemed remarkable at first, but in a few short years, most of them became pretty much alike. The Internet had promised interactivity, but it turned out that it was difficult and expensive to keep updating a site. Once built, most sites were updated infrequently or not at all. Some served as nothing more than static online brochures and were as remarkable to read as an outdated train schedule.

During the Age of Surf, search engines were generally useless. You would request a needle and receive a haystack of information back, perhaps with your needle buried inside.

Then, in 1998, a couple of Stanford kids came up with Google, which dramatically improved search results by employing intelligent algorithms rather than simple keywords, and the Age of Search arrived. Modern search engines are indeed remarkable, usually delivering the information that people want at the top of the results pile. Still, inefficiencies remain, particularly when you are trying to find the most current information. In addition, the current-generation engines are good at finding what companies have to say about themselves, but not what people have to say about the companies. Looking for updated information has been tedious, requiring a page-by-page scan to see if each page has been updated since the last visit. The average person can visit and examine about a dozen sites in this way in an hour, and it is not joyful labor.

RSS: Diamonds from Coal Mines

Blogs and social media are now fueling a new Age of Subscription. Instead of your going to the information, it comes to you. Instead of having access only to what the company has to say about itself, you can see what people have to say about the company. When they occur, updates are fed to you as news breaks. Blogging has fueled this change, but the enabler is the syndication technology Really Simple Syndication (RSS), and its full implications are just being realized.

RSS is a data distribution protocol that lets you subscribe to almost any blog. If you have the appropriate RSS support in your web browser, you can simply click a Subscribe button when visiting an RSS-enabled web page that interests you, and that page is added to your subscription list. You then start receiving all updates to that page as they occur.

You can read the feeds to which you have subscribed in a variety of ways. You can have them sent to your e-mail inbox, you can use a standalone RSS reader application, or you can use a web interface that aggregates and displays your feeds. But the most efficient way is to receive updates into your e-mail client. When something new is posted to one of the blogs being tracked, the label on your subscription folder turns bold, so it's obvious that there's an update. Within a folder, headlines appear for each post, with the new ones also in bold. You can skip or delete any that don't interest you—without even reading them. You never leave your e-mail client during this process, another time-saver.

All these time-saving snippets add up. Manually visiting each site to check for updates, you might be able to scan perhaps a dozen web sites a day. RSS lets you power-scan perhaps 100–200 in an hour. Scoble, who has been called "blogging obsessed," tracks more than 1,300 RSS feeds regularly, aggregating an enormous amount of information.

To subscribe to RSS-enabled sites, you need a plug-in "aggregator" such as NewsGator or Feed Burner. However, the three most popular browsers—Firefox, Apple Safari, and Internet Explorer—either already have aggregators built in, or will at next release, adding to the efficiency. On the day before we wrote this section, Google jumped into the fray with its Google Sidebar,[1] which contains an aggregator called "Web clips"—a term considerably less intimidating to end users than "RSS feed aggregator."

The full promise of RSS becomes clearest when you see what the new RSS search engines such as Google Blog Search,[2] IceRocket,[3] Bloglines Citations,[4] Technorati, PubSub, and Feedster can do. If web search engines of today extract needles from hay-stacks, then the new RSS search engines deliver diamonds from coal mines—whole clusters of them.

---

[1] http://news.zdnet.co.uk/software/applications/0,39020384,39214432,00.htm

[2] http://blogsearch.google.com

[3] http://www.icerocket.com

[4] http://www.bloglines.com/citations

Let's suppose you are edging your way into the market for a new car. Twenty years ago, you would start reading ads and asking friends what they drove and where they found good prices and service. You would read a few magazine reviews and maybe a consumer report.

In the Age of Search, web search engines increased your options. You could find more research than ever before. You could buy vehicles direct from online sites and even find the Kelley Blue Book value of your trade-in vehicle. But the only customer comments you could find easily were the ones the automaker selected to show you. The rest you had to search for on web sites, one at a time.

It's different these days. Let's suppose, what with environmental considerations and the price of gas, you want to get a new hybrid car, but you don't know anyone who owns one. RSS search engines, often called "blog search engines," enable you to see what people all over the world have to say about the cars you're considering. You might also be able to find a few comments about dealers near you. And you no longer have to treat the information you harvest from the Internet as a frame frozen in history. You get updates delivered every time someone has something new to say on any topic that you've told the search engine to watch on your behalf.

There is much competition among RSS search services. In addition to the five we mentioned earlier, numerous new ones are emerging. Yahoo! and Google have joined the fray, and Microsoft is expected to soon follow.

When you have that level of competition, innovation abounds. New features are being added from one search provider to the next almost daily, with each trying to tempt customers with new capabilities and conveniences. While these companies continue to duke it out, end users keep on winning.

Spilling Out of the Blogosphere

RSS capability is not limited to the blogosphere, however. Almost any content page on the Web can be RSS-enabled, and more of them are doing so every day. The BBC and the *New York Times* have RSS on their web pages, enabling you to subscribe to them through RSS feeds. The next generation of web browsers, including Firefox, Internet Explorer, and Apple Safari, will sense where RSS feeds are enabled on web pages and enable you to subscribe with a single click, providing you all updates of that page from that point forward. Evidence is gathering that a great portion of the Web is heading toward being

RSS-enabled. This means that end users will soon be able to receive home delivery of information that covers a vastly wider circle than just the blogosphere.

There are also numerous handy little applications incorporating RSS becoming available all the time, each of which makes the Internet a faster, easier place to get what you need. RSS Auction,[5] for example, notifies you when a particular product is being auctioned at a particular price on eBay. At Yaywastaken.com,[6] Sean Nolan offers RSS feeds to notify you about books that interest you when Amazon.com offers either new or used copies. The site performs similar services for Overstock.com[7] bargain hunters as well. And at Ben Hammersley's Dangerous Precedent,[8] you can use his free RSS code string[9] to track a FedEx parcel as it winds its way toward its destination. Such new efficiencies are emerging quickly, and we assume a great deal more are on their way.

RSS Ads on Demand

Where there is innovation, you will usually find direct marketers circling, looking for a vulnerable spot where they can bite into that 2 percent of the public who seem so consistently susceptible to their "amazing offers." RSS may be the first way for direct marketers to serve the people who want them without annoying the rest.

Let's suppose your refrigerator breaks down and you suddenly need a replacement. RSS technology is starting to provide true ads-on-demand services, so you can subscribe to all the ads for new or used refrigerators, for example, during that one time in 20 years that you want them, and you'll find the deal you like, in your area, along with other information on models and brands and reputations. Once you make your selection, you can unsubscribe to the ad feeds.

When you sign up for an e-mail relationship with online marketers, you're often stuck with that relationship forever. Not only do these marketers persist

---

[5] http://www.rssauction.com

[6] http://www.yaywastaken.com/amazon

[7] http://www.yaywastaken.com/rss/overstock

[8] http://benhammersley.com/weblog/2004/07/04/track_your_packages_in_rss.html

[9] http://www.benhammersley.com/tools/fedex_package_tracking_in_rss.html

in sending you unwanted e-mail for the rest of the time you use that e-mail address, they sell your name to other database marketers. With RSS, however, when you unsubscribe, they go away. They have no choice. RSS empowers the receiver, not the sender, to decide when subscriptions will terminate. There is no way for the sender to know who has subscribed. Because you never register your e-mail address, the sender has no way to assail you with new and unwanted material.

RSS recalibrates the playing field, changing the tilt from the company to the user. The customer chooses whether and when to start a relationship. Through RSS, the customer gets to watch you and decide if he or she trusts you. The customer can make the company go away at any point and for any reason. In our refrigerator search, the customer knows more about how the dealer operates before he or she ever steps foot into the showroom.

This new equation doesn't mean a company loses. If a company elects to trust prospects to make the right decisions, more are likely to become customers. If a company is transparent in how it operates and shows its trust of employees by letting them blog or otherwise directly converse with customers, more people will subscribe to what they write, and the company will build with present strangers who become future customers.

Into the "Podosphere"

After Dave Winer and Netscape compromised to give the world the RSS 2.0 standard, Winer created an additional feature that lets people subscribe to audio blogs, or *podcasts*. This, in part, resulted from a collaboration between Winer and former MTV celebrity VJ Adam Curry, who simultaneously developed a software downloading application called iPodder and produced the *Daily Source Code*[10]—the first podcast—on August 13, 2004. No one knows how many people were listening at the time, but less than a year later, Curry had nearly 100,000 daily listeners, according to Citizen Spin.[11] In the same timeframe, Pew Research said that 6 million Americans have listened to podcasts.[12] This is a considerably faster rate of growth than for text blogs.

---

[10] http://live.curry.com

[11] http://citizenspin.typepad.com/citizenspin/blogwatch

[12] http://www.pewinternet.org/PPF/r/154/report_display.asp

Podcasting received a huge additional boost when Apple Computer's iTunes service introduced iTunes 4.9 on June 28, 2005, enabling iPod users to directly subscribe to RSS feeds. The result was that many podcasters saw their traffic quadruple overnight. By mid-summer 2005, iTunes was offering over 3,000 programs and had become "podcast central." The medium's growth has been spawned also by integration with text blogs that tell you when a new podcast is available and where you can find specific audio content.

Curry is among several producers who are proving you can make a business of podcasting. His Adam Curry Podcast Show Network produces 35 programs, reaching a collective audience of several hundred thousand listeners daily. He said the company has been profitable from the start using a traditional media network advertising model, but has taken in $8.5 million in venture capital anyway to finance rapid growth.

Curry is working on ways to use advertising less intrusively. Why? "Because ads suck. The stuff is boring and people are tuning out," he told us. He said commercial and radio ads work on two factors: human emotions and redundancy. For example, when you're watching TV and the program reaches its climax, you can be certain that the program will segue into a commercial before you get to see its exciting conclusion. Ad redundancy is even worse. "I hate this fact, but the guy who gets elected president is the one whose campaign broadcasts the most ads and repeats them the most often," he told us.

When we talked with Curry, he was preparing to do a "back scenes" podcast on a new Spike Lee movie, in which the film producer would compensate Curry for the promotional benefits while Apple Computer would compensate Curry for making the podcast available exclusively through iTunes downloads. There will be no direct advertising in the podcast itself, and Curry is certain listeners will appreciate the eliminated intrusions.

Curry has first-mover benefits in podcasting, but he is far from alone. There are numerous pioneers attempting to aggregate programs and grow. Along with at least a dozen blogosphere denizens, ABC, CBS, NBC, and NPR are all early players. Why all this early excitement? Because those who make forecasts are outdoing themselves predicting just how big podcasting will soon be. The BBC,[13] which is experimenting with about 20 podcasts of its own, cites Jupiter Research's estimate that 56 million Americans will own digital music playing devices by the end of 2010. Forrester Research[14] estimates

---

[13] http://news.bbc.co.uk/1/hi/technology/4658995.stm
[14] http://www.webrankinfo.com/english/seo-news/topic-3589.htm

there will be 12.3 million U.S. households listening to podcasts in 2010. No matter how it's measured, the consensus is that there will be a whole lot of people listening to podcasts over the next few years.

Just Give It Away

Does advertising have to be the support spine? Not necessarily.

Doug Kaye, a successful serial entrepreneur, argues that businesses may be wiser and ultimately more profitable if they just give their podcast content away. When he was authoring *Loosely Coupled: The Missing Pieces of Web Services* in 2002–2003, Kaye realized the people he was interviewing knew a great deal more about web services than he did, and he would write a better book if he could stay out of the way of what his subjects had to say to his audience. That's hard for a writer to do, and he soon realized it would be easier and more effective to record and somehow transmit the voices of these experts. After Curry made the first podcast, Kaye soon followed by podcasting his *Loosely Coupled* interviews. The experiment gave birth to IT Conversations,[15] which grew into a network of tech-related podcasts. By Labor Day 2005, he was producing about 56 programs, all addressing technology community audiences.

When we interviewed Kaye in early August 2005, IT Conversations was using sponsorships—as well as Kaye's pockets—to survive. But our sense was that his heart and mind were already pumping on his vision for IT Conversations 2.0, a concept in which citizen-podcasters would record what people had to say from the dais of public gatherings everywhere, on all topics. Then IT Conversations would produce the audio record of what people in the front of the room told live audiences on a given day and in a given place. Program moderators would be severely limited, and there would be no interviews—sort of open-source podcasting—not because anyone could add or alter it, but because anyone could participate. And the podcast would be open to anyone who searched by topic, place, speaker conference, or whatever. It would be available tomorrow morning or a hundred—or thousand—years from now.

Why should businesses care about open-source podcasting? Well, many already do, but in a way that Kaye thinks misses the big picture. He told us that most enterprise efforts treat podcasting as just a new iteration of streaming media, the Internet broadcast system that has been in use for years.

---

[15] http://www.itconversations.com

The corporate ROI for traditional Internet broadcasting is found in database marketing. A distinguished speaker is hired to address a company-sponsored gathering. The talk is recorded and distributed over the Internet free—with a catch. You must register—giving your name, e-mail, and perhaps a demographic fact or two—before you are allowed to download the stream. Usually, the registration form also includes an often-unnoticed pre-checked little box, authorizing the company to send you "additional information." This permission is invariably used for direct marketing purposes. A company determines the success of the broadcast in pure ROI terms: You deduct speaker and production costs from subsequent sales to determine ROI.

From Kaye's extensive experience, he estimates that at best an enterprise might entice 10,000 people to register to listen. Using standard direct marketing averages, 200 actual transactions will take place. The company can also make a few extra dollars by selling the names to a database list company. By registering free, all 10,000 people will pay the toll of receiving e-mail they never requested, promoting products they don't want for the remainder of the time they use that e-mail address.

Kaye thinks that this strategy is short sighted, costing companies in both goodwill and sales in the long run. Plus, more and more people are aware of the catch to so-called free registrations and won't do it. But, by replacing registration requirements with free RSS subscriptions, a company could increase the number of listeners by as much as tenfold. If a much smaller percentage of listeners elect to purchase something from the company, the sales are still likely to be greater than the 200 that the previous model generated. If just 1 percent voluntarily purchased something, the result would be as much as 500 percent over the forced registration model.

According to Kaye, a few companies have started to come around to this way of thinking. He didn't have any case studies yet, but he told us he had recently helped BMC Software to start BMCTalk,[16] a hosted RSS-enabled podcast that covers subjects ranging from the finer strokes of golfing to human integration problems that follow a corporate acquisition. More recently, he advised Salesforce.com on how to develop a similar program, which was under development when we talked to him.

---

[16] http://talk.bmc.com/podcasts/simpleblog_view

One example that demonstrates how podcasting might work for an enterprise is IT Conversations' recording of *Blink* author Malcolm Gladwell's talk[17] at PopTech, a popular conference that blends technology and sociological thinking. When he spoke in October 2004, Gladwell was well received by 500 mostly paying attendees. Over the next 10 months, 67,000 people listened to the podcast version of his talk. Gladwell spoke for free at PopTech, even though elsewhere at the time he was receiving as much as $40,000 per speech. By August 2005, his asking price had gone up to $60,000, and he was among the most sought-after speakers on the circuit. His new book is significantly outpacing his earlier book in sales. Meanwhile, even though PopTech raised its registration rates for its 2005 conference, the event sold out for the first time in its nine-year history, and there was a waiting list. Is there a measurable quid pro quo here? It's not provable. But one can assume that both Gladwell and the conference producers have not been hurt by "giving it away."

Large companies often host distinguished speaker series at which luminaries on Gladwell's level are invited to speak. Would free unregistered podcasts help people's perceptions of the company? Might they influence a potential employee, unaware that this quality perk was part of the employment package? We think so. A podcast lasts virtually forever, and the older it gets, the more prominent web search engines are likely to make it.

Another way a company can use a podcast to its benefit is to broadcast the voices and words of its best and brightest employees. Not only is a company-sponsored spotlight a great internal morale booster, but it would reveal to the world the quality of the employees and would demonstrate that top management takes pride in its team. It would make clear that real people work for the enterprise, and they have passion and authority about what they are doing. That might be more valuable than 200 direct marketing sales.

Video Emerging Slowly

Text and audio blogs have enormous implications, but there is nothing quite like actually *seeing* a speaker. And if you cannot be there when a particular event happens, the power of video is indisputable. Video has been slower to emerge than the former two forms of social media, in part because it is more expensive and difficult to produce because there are eighteen conflicting

---

[17] http://www.itconversations.com/shows/detail230.html

standards, and because the large file sizes effectively exclude anyone without broadband from the audience. Video is also less convenient for the person-on-the-go to experience than audio; people can listen to podcasts while driving or jogging, but it would be unwise to view video blogs during these activities.

Undisputedly, Scoble's day job as Microsoft's Channel 9 interviewer puts him in the center of what is currently the world's most popular business video blog, with nearly 3 million unique visitors per month. While Channel 9 incorporates wikis, forums, and considerable text content, Scoble interviewing the company's most accomplished developers is statistically the main attraction. Some of his videos have been downloaded more than 100,000 times.

Other companies have started to inch toward video blogs. A global media company has told Scoble it is planning to launch a video blog that emulates the Channel 9 model. Amanda Congdon produces RocketBoom,[18] an ad-backed, highly creative and unpredictable video blog that is drawing 60,000 daily visitors with no market effort behind it except the word of mouth of exuberant fans.

But to really take off, the high cost of producing vlogs, as they are being called, has to come down, and the issues of bandwidth and storage need to be resolved (or at least eased). But one company promises an inexpensive solution to the former problem, and another claims a free resolution to the latter.

Serious Magic, Inc.,[19] a Folsom, California, software startup, offers a whole suite of low-cost video communications tools. About half of the Fortune 500 companies use its products in some capacity, according to marketing director Michelle Gallina. *USA Today* uses Serious Magic products for training,[20] for example, and Hyatt Regency[21] uses them to produce videos that entice companies to use hotel meeting facilities. We're more excited by the promise of things to come. Serious Magic CEO Mark Randall told us in February 2005 that his company has technology that will "enable everyday people to produce professional quality videos." We met Randall at Demo,[22] a prestigious conference where startups get six minutes to launch their products live on stage. Randall gave a great, fast-talking demonstration of VlogIt!, the company's video blogging software. It was scheduled for release in Fall 2005 at a list price of about $100. Another new organization, OurMedia,[23] is a

---

[18] http://www.rocketboom.com

[19] http://www.seriousmagic.com

[20] http://www.seriousmagic.com/articles/vc/videotraining/usatoday

[21] http://www.seriousmagic.com/vcarticles.cfm?study=hyatt&crntPg=bus_marketing

[22] http://www.demo.com

[23] http://www.ourmedia.org

nonprofit that offers "free forever" online video storage space, apparently eliminating storage and bandwidth barriers for users. We see a new, low-cost business channel of communication getting into position for rapid emergence.

News and Blog Views

There are too many emerging innovations in text blogging to cover fully here, but one that we think has potential watershed implications is Memeorandum.[24] Memeorandum is the first technology to link together old and new media, offering single-screen views of prominent headlines from traditional media merged with commentary from popular bloggers, thus ending the ongoing, often petty feud between the two, to the benefit of the end user.

At this writing, Memeorandum is a small-time operation, running from a server in the bedroom of former Intel developer Gabe Rivera. So far, Rivera has pumped out only versions for mainstream, political, and technology[25] news. His possibilities seem limitless.

Memeorandum may spell the end for "link blogs," or blogs that point to other blogs, adding sparse new content of their own and intending to make the linker influential. Because Memeorandum uses algorithms to provide results, much like Google does, it automates the linking process, delivering topical results infinitely faster than a human could possibly do it and with the convenience of single-page digests. While this may bode badly for currently prominent blogger ratings, it promises great end-user benefits. We see personal Memeorandums somewhere down the line in which you'll be able to hand-select a few thousand of your favorite blogs, stick them in the Memeorandum engine, and get a truly customized news service.

Find It Fast

Mobile blogs are simply blogs posted from handheld devices. Most are no more than a snapshot taken by a camera phone with a few words in the caption, usually incorporating instant messaging shorthand. But location-based data laid over mobile blogs has very significant implications, and mapping has

---

[24] http://www.memeorandum.com
[25] http://tech.memeorandum.com

become an area where giant players such as Amazon.com, MSN, and Google have been racing to outdo each other.

Amazon's A9,[26] for instance, attached cameras to cars and drove down city streets, a technique long in use by desktop cartographers. But Amazon took it a step further by linking the result into A9's Yellow Pages feature to let you see just what the sushi restaurant looks like, outside and inside. You may be thinking of eating there tonight, or you may be passing by it just as you are getting hungry. Several companies are also working on enabling previous diners to post blogged reviews of the place, to encourage or warn off future customers.

In August 2005, Google introduced GoogleEarth, with maps[27] that are incredibly easy to scroll in a web browser and that indicate the location of restaurants, movie theaters, or shops in the area you request. As frosting on the cake, GoogleEarth also provides satellite photo views and has opened up its technology to allow non-Google developers to add in new applications of their own, such as live traffic data feeds. The Google traffic map would show you alternative routes to avoid snarls, fires, crime scenes, or terrorist attacks.

Maps can also be populated with location-based ads and data, which are useful to travelers looking for the local Starbucks or hospital. Larry Larsen, a technologist at Florida-based Poynter Institute, the R&D arm for the American journalism industry, showed us a prototype of how blogs and news might overlay onto maps,[28] providing a new level of real-time information.

MSN's Virtual Earth[29] team's Chandu Thota developed BlogMap,[30] which lets bloggers see where you are blogging from and the location of other bloggers nearby. In the first week the service was available, 100,000 people downloaded BlogMaps, Thota told us, adding that a next step will be to allow bloggers to post directly onto maps.

Tag, You're Found!

Tagging is one of those simple little innovations that has begun to make big improvements in blog searching. It works in the same way as putting a label

---

[26] http://a9.com

[27] http://maps.google.com

[28] http://www.poynter.org/column.asp?id=31&aid=86690

[29] http://channel9.msdn.com/ShowPost.aspx?PostID=71140

[30] http://www.feedmap.net/BlogMap

on a file folder or sewing your kid's name into her clothing before she goes off to summer camp. At the bottom of a blog post, you simply write the words "Technorati Tag" and then keywords covering the subject you wrote about, such as Apple Computer, President Bush, or CES. Over at the Technorati Tag Page,[31] where over three million tags were being tracked as of August 2005, you can usually find a string of code or the word you are tracking and make the link. But just typing the word will let Technorati find you and make you more discoverable.

To understand how it works, let's say you're attending the 2006 Consumer Electronics Show in Las Vegas, and you want to watch other blog reports coming out of the show. If you go to a web search engine and type in "CES," you'll get a haystack back, much of it irrelevant to what you want. But, if everyone who was blogging at the show you were attending tagged their posts with the same label, say "CES 2006," your search result would be much more satisfying.

Tagging has particular relevance for photos and other multimedia posts that are sparse on text, making it difficult for search engines to find them without tags. Search engines can't look at a photo of a lighthouse and know it's a lighthouse—unless it's tagged accordingly.

Technorati collaborates with online photo services Flickr[32] and Buzznet,[33] as well as linking services Delicious[34] and Furl.[35] A Silicon Valley startup whom Israel consults called Riya[36] launched some watershed technology in late October 2005 that lets you automatically tag all your photos. Once you tell it who your Aunt Ida is, Riya will tag all photos of her, in your computer or on the Riya service.

But the implications go further. Tags can be integrated with maps and mobile blogs to fulfill the long-standing promise of "geo-tagging," which would allow companies and people to tag objects on a map and mobile-blog the information. This would eventually make it easy to find people, places, products, hospitals, or gas stations anywhere, and to read reviews written by people who were at the same place at an earlier time. Numerous companies are working on final assembly of the myriad pieces to this puzzle.

---

[31] http://www.technorati.com/help/tags.html

[32] http://www.flickr.com

[33] http://www.buzznet.com

[34] http://del.icio.us

[35] http://www.furl.net/index.jsp

[36] http://www.riya.com

Your Whole Life Before You

Perhaps the most ambitious project that we learned about during our research for this chapter was in Microsoft's San Francisco labs, where Jim Gemmell[37] and Gordon Bell[38] (father of the DEC VAX computer) were working on MyLifeBits,[39] a system that enables you to keep your whole life stored in your personal computer, where you can access what you have seen in your life for the remainder of your life, or share it with friends or family members. Video, photos, blogs, and other digital detritus are deposited and stored into MyLifeBits software. Another Microsoft research team, this one in Cambridge, England, is working on SenseCam, a small, motion-activated digital camera that you hang around your neck and that transmits to MyLifeBits. When something of note happens, you move your hand in front of it, and the built-in motion-detector starts it clicking away, so that entire lives can be photographed, tagged or geo-tagged, and posted or stored on a personal computer. You keep the moments that matter. You share with people who care.

MyLifeBits has more pragmatic potential as well. Research with stroke victims seems to indicate that photos help them reconnect with memories that the stroke seemingly erased. The two teams are also studying to determine if such life-blogging tools actually help the rest of us better understand what we have seen by letting us literally look back on it. But what is most relevant, we think, is that a simple PC can now store a person's entire life in video.

The Big Picture

In the years since the explosion of the legendary dot-com bomb, it has appeared to many observers that not much was happening in technology, but in fact there has been a lot of innovation stirring behind the scenes, and many of these new technologies are related to blogging and social media. The technologies we discussed in this chapter represent only the tip of the iceberg of what is currently emerging and what will shortly emerge. These technologies are shaping how businesses communicate and how people find and share

---

[37] http://research.microsoft.com/~JGemmell
[38] http://research.microsoft.com/users/GBell
[39] http://channel9.msdn.com/ShowPost.aspx?PostID=46702#46702

information. The next technical innovation may surprise us, but the general direction toward social media seems obvious.

The big picture is clearer than it has been in many years. We have entered into a new era of communications.

15 The Conversational Era

"It's natural enough to think of the growth of the blogosphere as a merely technical phenomenon. But it's also a profoundly human phenomenon, a way of expanding and, in some sense, reifying the ephemeral daily conversation that humans engage in. Every day the blogosphere captures a little more of the strange immediacy of the life that is passing before us. Think of it as the global thought bubble of a single voluble species."

—New York Times *editorial, August 5, 2005*

Sometimes a tool is just a tool. During our lifetime, hammers have changed very little. If we wrote a book about them and took years to write it, not much would have changed. Most tools are like that, but not so blogs.

In the space of the nine months it took to write *Naked Conversations*, innovations to blogs and the blogosphere were relentless. The number of bloggers almost tripled from under 7.5 million users to almost 20 million. Someone started a blog once every second today, and about every two seconds someone else abandoned one. We were constantly aware that we were writing about a moving target. We had to delay completing the chapter on blogging in a crisis because a crisis actually occurred for Scoble at Microsoft. A few weeks later, we had to delay completing our emerging technology chapter because we learned of some new social media innovations as we were completing an early draft.

Throughout the book, we have tried to stay focused on how blogging and social media are changing the relationships between companies and their constituencies. We have offered a great number of tips and case studies that we hope will remain relevant despite the constant technological changes.

Since we began this project until the present moment, we have sensed ongoing changes in the business community's attitude toward blogging. Back when we began Chapter 1, most businesspeople were still dismissing blogging as a passing fad. This was the denial phase. Then we detected a certain level of anger about blogs as a distraction, about them interrupting systems in place that were allegedly best practices. We even had an enraged CEO tell us that blogs were a scam used to cheat on search engine results. And as we went to press, *Forbes* magazine came out with a cover story likening the blogosphere to a lynch mob.[1] But *Forbes* appears late to the party for a demonstration of its anger phase.

Today, more and more businesspeople understand that blogs are here to stay and that companies need to figure out how to incorporate them into the way they communicate. We hope *Naked Conversations* will help people make the right decisions for their companies.

We argued in our Introduction that blogs are part of a revolution— something bigger than the blogosphere—and a great many people disagreed, positioning the phenomenon as no more than a new enhancement to a company's marketing mix. Blogging was evolutionary, not revolutionary, we were repeatedly told. After nine months of research and talking to more than 100 people in business, we are now convinced that blogging is a tool of a very significant revolution, one that has become virtually unstoppable, something that shifts the balance of relationships between companies and the communities in which they operate.

As was the case in the dot-com area, a few companies will emerge from the blogosphere to become giants, while many others will fade. Because of this revolution, businesses will shift where they invest resources—both financial and human—as a matter of cost effectiveness. Marketing budgets will be cut, and perhaps more money will be redirected to both product development and customer support. We have already witnessed the meteoric shifts in who

---

[1] http://forbes.com/home/free_forbes/2005/1114/128.html

influences markets and why they do it. We have continued to struggle with what to call this thing that is "bigger than blogging."

Naked Conversations has not been an objective report. We began the project as blog champions—evangelists convinced that all businesses should blog and warning that many businesses that don't blog might perish. This, we learned along our way, was slightly overstated. We had underestimated the influence of culture, both in businesses and countries. Quite simply, some cultures are open and others are closed. Some leaders trust those under their watch, and others don't. And that difference becomes increasingly important as more people realize that corporate blog policy—written or implied—tells outsiders a great deal about how a company sees its employees as well as its customers.

Culture cannot be overestimated when discussing social media. And as technologies continue to emerge, some companies will be heard in one area and remain silent in another. Adam Curry, who works with Apple Computer, told us that Steve Jobs will soon podcast, even as he continues to discourage his own employees from blogging about their jobs. "Blogging is just not in the company DNA," he shrugged, "but Jobs likes podcasts." Some entities, we are certain, just won't be a part of this revolution. In some instances, the people within the organization who have the power to change the culture will keep their heels dug into the status quo. Not all prominent non-blogging companies will decline or fall. But most will be perceived in the public eye as less interesting or relevant than those that do.

Companies that discourage blogging, such as Google, may start to lose talented people and already are revealing other cracks in their veneers. When we began this project, the foremost search company was undeniably one of the most admired in personal technology. Perhaps it still is, but we sense to a diminished degree. We think a contributing factor is its consistently mediocre corporate blog. Discouraging employees from blogging neither builds internal morale nor attracts talented people. Russell Beattie,[2] a luminary blogger, canceled a Google interview because, he said, the culture felt closed to him and company policies felt duplicitous. He subsequently joined Yahoo!, a company that encourages him and other employees to blog.

More recently, Google announced it would banish CNET[3] for a year, by not answering calls or admitting CNET to events where other press was invited.

---

[2] http://www.russellbeattie.com/notebook/1008565.html

[3] http://news.com.com/Google+balances+privacy,+reach/2100-1032_3-5787483.html

CNET's sin had been to use Google to publish personal information on Google's CEO, Eric Schmidt, to demonstrate the validity of charges that Google made too much of people's personal information all too easily available. This seemed to us a petty matter. Either of the incidents alone would be of no more than passing interest. But add to it the perception that Google's company blog is among the most mundane, and the perception starts building that Google is a less open culture than many people presumed. It will be a long time before this darling of investors and Internet searchers will be in trouble, and before it happens, the company has ample time to wisely change its course, and we have heard rumors that it indeed will reverse its blog policy. It will be interesting to see what happens next.

But if blogging is truly part of a revolution, will it be bloodless? We see a clear and present danger for practitioners of traditional, unidirectional advertising and marketing. We see its champions in a change-or-die situation. Blogging and the social media are steadily pounding a silver spike into the heart of it. In its place is this new phenomenon in which customers and companies settle in on a more even playing field, where they use the casual language of simple, unadorned conversation. Most people trust such voices more than the professional voices incorporated into a 60-second spot. This fundamental change repositions customers from the edge of the corporation to their rightful place in its center. This new customer-centric positioning is in refreshing contrast to companies seeing customers as no more than pairs of sticky eyeballs.

Yes, there is a leap of faith required in buying our argument. The customer, in fact, is *not* always right. Sometimes customer demands are unreasonable. Sometimes they are rude in tone, and most companies we spoke with voiced concerns about being verbally assaulted in public. Both Israel and Scoble have experienced this behavior in blog comments, and neither of us enjoyed it. But we've learned that even when customers are dead wrong, listening will make a company smarter. And demonstrating that you are listening politely will put the majority of observers on your side.

We are not preaching wide-eyed altruism here. This book is about business, efficiency, and profit. Blogging is smart business. Blogging is cheaper and more effective than most marketing programs in use today. Sun Microsystems President Jonathan Schwartz told us he could reach more people through his blog than with a full-page ad in a trade magazine—and as a bonus, they could reach him as well. Customers loved Firefox so much they chipped in to buy a two-page ad in the *New York Times*, and they consequently learned that blogging was a more effective way to get customers, while costing a whole lot less. British tailor Thomas Mahon used a blog to increase his business by 300 percent in a few months and make him the best-known member of his profession. Andrew Carton has more visitors to his Treo blog than the web sites of the two companies that make the device and its software combined, and he has become more influential to Treo products than executives at either company.

Blogging is unquestionably less expensive than traditional ad and PR campaigns, and keeps proving—as it did to the Firefox team—to be more effective. Will today's practitioners wind up in the restaurant service business? Perhaps some will, if they cling too long and too hard to methods that are clearly in atrophy. Others will adapt and prevail in this new era. Many will figure out how to make their crafts more affordable, credible, and interactive, as Shel Holtz, Neville Hobson, and Steve Rubel have done.

While we see a cultural divide forming, we also see signs of convergence and healing in the often vitriolic culture clash between the media and the blogosphere. Less than a year ago, John Markoff, the leading tech journalist for the *New York Times*, voiced skepticism about bloggers[4] as conveyors of news. Although bloggers and journalists still bump on important issues, they are both being used increasingly as information sources, and technologies such as Memeorandum are physically merging the two to benefit the consumer. Besides, journalism is not really defined by the delivery mechanism, but by the practices of those delivering content, through paper, broadcast, or broadband.

Not all of our pre-suppositions panned out. We never found our blogging plumber. Perhaps it's a cultural matter. Plumbers are a tight-lipped lot for the most part. We thought we'd find a great deal of evidence of blogging to support micro markets—what *Wired* magazine editor Chris Anderson calls "The Long Tail"—composed of millions of markets containing from one to a few hundred customers. We didn't find them, but then it dawned on us that the tail goes on the back end of the creature, and blogging right now remains on the leading edge. The long tail will get there in time.

Small, independent merchants are part of what makes every community unique, and blogging is proving to be an enormously useful tool in the hands of independent shops and artisans. Some of the smaller enterprises we covered gave us the most inspiration. Patrice Cassard, the French T-shirt maker, started a blog-based business that profits and grows by letting customers decide almost

---

[4] http://www.timporter.com/firstdraft/archives/000204.html

everything. The team of friendly practitioners at Yokohama's Isshin Dental Clinic shows what a blog can do for a neighborhood business. Ben Williams, owner of Horsefeathers Restaurant, uses a blog to stave off the branded chains that have encroached upon his turf. Grace Bonney might have remained an underemployed consultant without her blog. Instead, she is a rising influence in the design industry. We are convinced that blogging offers enormous opportunities for small businesses, whether they want to reach the immediate neighborhood or customers around the world.

A blog is an impressive tool, but most people we talked with insisted that it was more than just that. People called blogs "a new communications channel," a "credible marketing conduit," a "disrupter of the status quo," a "mainstream media murderer," and a "miracle," among other terms.

We had thought the most appropriate term for this bigger picture was "Conversational Marketing," but we learned it is more than that. Blogging impacts marketing but also transcends it. Blogging is vital not just to outbound communications, but inbound as well. It is a crisis firefighter, a superior research aggregator, a tool for recruiting, a product builder, and customer service and support enhancement. It provides two-way executive access and facilitates employee relations, customer evangelism, and interaction between companies and their constituencies. We have not yet dreamed of some of the ways it will benefit companies in the future.

We recalled our conversation with Yossi Vardi, the adult supervisor of ICQ's four student founders. He pointed us to research showing that storytelling and conversations are at the essence of human culture. In that light, blogging is a point on a cultural continuum that goes back all the way to when our ancestors sat in caves shivering around fires and doodling on the walls. To paraphrase Vardi, blogging is storytelling and conversation on steroids.

Ultimately, blogging has ended one era and ignited another. In this new era, companies don't win just by talking to people. They win by listening to people as well. We call it the Conversational Era. It doesn't change everything, because as John Naisbitt told us, everything never changes. But something has changed, and blogging is impacting businesses of all sizes in most parts of the developed world. It has made the world a smaller, faster place.

And business is the better for it.

Acknowledgments

We offer special thanks and gratitude to:

- Howard Israel, for teaching Shel to love books and for encouraging him during this project.
- Charlie O'Brien, wherever he is, for enduring wisdom, faith, and friendship.
- Andy Ruff, for having the idea that became *Naked Conversations*.
- Buzz Bruggeman (http://buzzmodo.typepad.com/buzznovation), the Connection King, for bringing Scoble and Israel together.
- Dave Winer (http://www.scripting.com) and Dori Smith (http://www.backupbrain.com), for getting Scoble interested in blogging to begin with.
- Vic Gundotra (http://www.vicgundotra.com), for taking a risk and hiring Scoble into Microsoft.
- Loïc LeMeur (http://www.loiclemeur.com/english), for giving us a guided virtual tour of blogging in Europe.
- Six Apart, Inc. (http://feeds.feedburner.com/MenasCorner), for extraordinary cooperation throughout this project.
- *Cluetrain Manifesto*'s authors—Doc Searles (http://doc.weblogs.com), David Weinberger (http://www.hyperorg.com/blogger), Christopher Lock (http://www.chiefbloggingofficer.com), and Rick Levine—for inspiring this book before we even dreamed of writing it.
- The denizens of the blogosphere, for helping us make *Naked Conversations* a better book in so many ways.

- Ernie Svenson (http://www.ernietheattorney.net), for giving us our funniest moment: As he told us how he loved technology, his phone line went dead.
- Jill Fallon (http://www.estatelegacyvaults.com/legacy), for giving us the most interesting story that did not fit into our book.
- Brewster, Shel's loyal companion, and Kinko, who shared his work desk.
- Joe Wikert (http://jwikert.typepad.com/the_average_joe), for buying dinner and proving himself accurate about partnerships between authors and publishers.
- Jim Minatel (http://wroxblog.typepad.com/minatel), for being a friend as well as a superior editor.
- Faithe Wempen (http://www.wempen.com), our development and copy editor, who proved she is well named.
- Steven Streight (http://www.vaspersthegrate.blogspot.com), who posted nearly as many words on our blog as we did and prevented us from selecting a lame book title name.
- Halley Suitt (http://halleyscomment.blogspot.com), for helping us get Tom Peters to write a foreword.

We also thank the hundreds of bloggers who left intelligent, constructive, and useful comments on our blogsite:

- Adam Barr, http://www.proudlyserving.com
- Al Cannistraro, http://www.happinessgym.com
- Alek Komarnitsky, http://www.komar.org
- Alex Bishop, http://www.mozillazine.org
- Allan Jenkins, http://allanjenkins.typepad.com
- Amy Bellinger, http://www.learnandteachonline.com/pmach/weblog.php
- Andrew, http://changingway.net
- Austin White, http://austinwhite.typepad.com
- Bill Lazar, http://www.billsaysthis.com
- Bill Riski, http://radio.weblogs.com/0108035
- BL Ochman, http://whatsnextonline.com
- Blaine Moore, http://www.runtowin.com
- Brian Bailey, http://www.leaveitbehind.com
- Bruce DeBoer, http://www.synthesiscreative.com/blog.php

- Christopher Carfi, http://socialcustomer.typepad.com
- Constantin Basturea, http://blog.basturea.com
- Curt Hopkins, http://morphemetales.blogspot.com
- Darren Rowse, http://www.problogger.net
- Dave Briggs, http://davebriggs.net
- Dave Copithorne, http://www.hearingmojo.com
- David Tebbutt, http://teblog.typepad.com
- Debbie Weil, www.blogwriteforceos.com
- Dennis E. Hamilton, http://orcmid.com/blog
- Dick Kusleika, http://www.dicks-blog.com
- DJ Coffman, http://yirmumah.net
- DL Byron, http://clip-n-seal.com
- Dossy Shiobara, http://dossy.org
- Elisa Camahort, http://workerbeesblog.blogspot.com
- Elizabeth Grigg, http://www.egrigg9000.com/mtpub
- Ephraim Cohen
- Eric Eggertson, http://www.mutually-inclusive.typepad.com/weblog
- Eric Schmenk
- Evan Erwin, http://www.misterorange.com
- Gautam Ghosh, http://gauteg.blogspot.com
- Geoff Jones, http://www.geoffjones.com
- Hugh Macleod, http://www.gapingvoid.com
- Jack Nork, http://www.mason23.com/jack
- James Cherkoff, http://www.collaboratemarketing.com
- James Governor, http://www.redmonk.com/jgovernor
- Jeaneane Sessum, http://allied.blogspot.com
- Jeremy Wright, http://www.ensight.org
- Jim McGee, http://www.mcgeesmusings.net
- Joel Schultz, http://www.joelschultz.com
- Johan van Rooyen, http://www.spanishpodcasting.com
- johnmoore, http://brandautopsy.typepad.com
- Johnnie Moore, http://www.johnniemoore.com/blog
- Josh Bancroft, http://www.tinyscreenfuls.com
- Jory Des Jardins, http://www.jorydesjardins.com
- Josh Hallett, http://hyku.com/blog
- Joshua Allen, http://www.netcrucible.com/blog
- Jozef Imrich, http://amediadragon.blogspot.com

- Justin Gardner, http://www.kozoru.com
- Kathy Sierra, http://headrush.typepad.com/creating_passionate_users
- Ken Dyck, http://www.kendyck.com.
- Larry Borsato, http://larryborsato.com
- Larry Hendrick, http://www.sanleon.net/blog
- Laura aka Blaugra, http://blaugra.typepad.com
- Lisa Williams, http://www.cadence90.com/wp
- Marc Orchant, http://office.weblogsinc.com
- Marc Snyder, http://emm-ess.blogspot.com
- Marcus M. Sommer, http://marcussommer.blogspot.com
- Markus Pirchner, http://www.futurebytes.at
- Michael Kaplan, http://blogs.msdn.com/michkap
- Mike Torres, http://spaces.msn.com/members/mike/ PersonalSpace.aspx
- Nancy White, http://www.fullcirc.com/weblog/onfacblog.htm
- Nick Toop
- Niti Bhan, http://nitibhan.typepad.com/perspective.
- Paul Hanson
- Paul Morriss, http://little-bits.blogspot.com
- Paul Woodhouse, http://butlersheetmetal.com/tinbasherblog
- Pete Dawson, http://peterdawson.typepad.com
- Phil Jones, http://www.nooranch.com/synaesmedia
- Phil Weber, http://www.philweber.com
- Randy Charles Morin, http://www.kbcafe.com
- Randy Halloway, http://www.clrsql.com/weblog
- Rich Westerfield, http://tsmi.blogs.com
- Roy Blumenthal, http://schmucknews.blogspot.com
- Russell Beattie, http://www.russellbeattie.com/notebook
- Sam Katz Sarah, http://theeditroom.blogspot.com
- Shelley Powers, http://weblog.burningbird.net
- Shital Shah, http://www.shitalshah.com/blog
- Simon Harriyott, http://www.harriyott.com
- Sriram Krishnan, http://blogs.msdn.com/sriram
- Steve Garfield, http://stevegarfield.com
- Steve Newson, http://stevenewson.blogspot.com
- Steve Shu, http://www.steveshu.typepad.com
- Tara Hunt, http://www.horsepigcow.com

- Thomas Hawk, http://thomashawk.com
- Tim Aldrich, http://firstdraft.blogs.com/altfunction
- Toby Bloomberg, http://www.bloombergmarketing.blogs.com
- Tom Guarriello, http://truetalk.typepad.com
- Tom Raftery, http://tomrafteryit.net/views
- Trevor Cook, http://trevorcook.typepad.com
- Wilson Ng, http://www.bizdrivenlife.net

Name Index

Subject Index

V

video technology, 220–222
viral blogging, 28

W

Web clips, 213
writing issues, 79
wrong blogging, 149

Y

yogurt company, 63, 75–77
youth factor, 42–43